professional portraiture

Annabel Williams

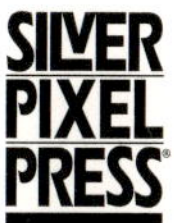

In association with

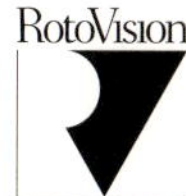

Amy Perry Carter

Professional Portraiture

First North American Edition, 2000

Published by
Silver Pixel Press®
A Tiffen® Company
21 Jet View Drive
Rochester, NY 14624 USA
Fax: (716) 328-5078
www.silverpixelpress.com

ISBN 1-883403-80-4

Written by Annabel Williams

Book design by Kate Stephens

Printed in China

professional portraiture

Annabel Williams

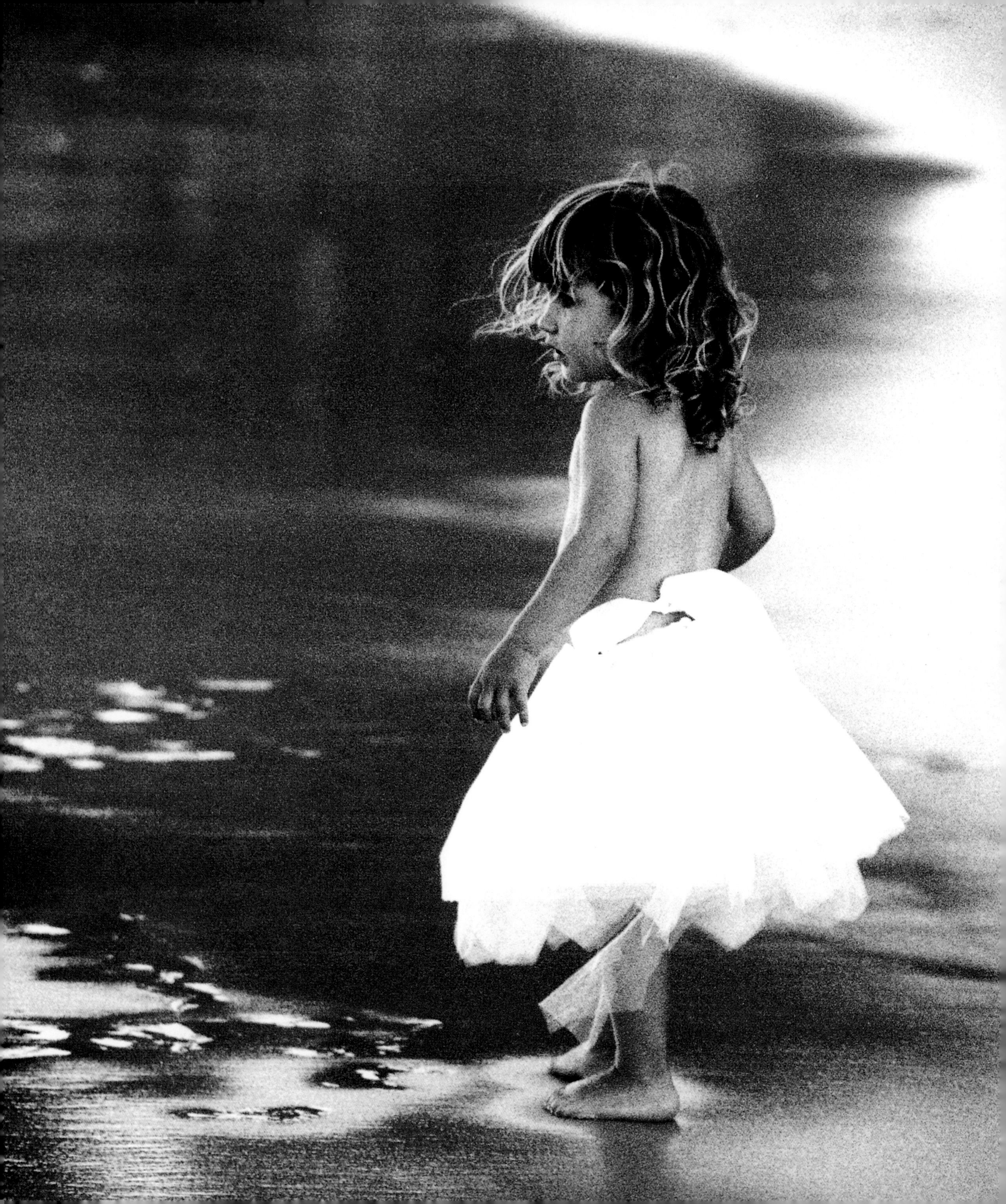

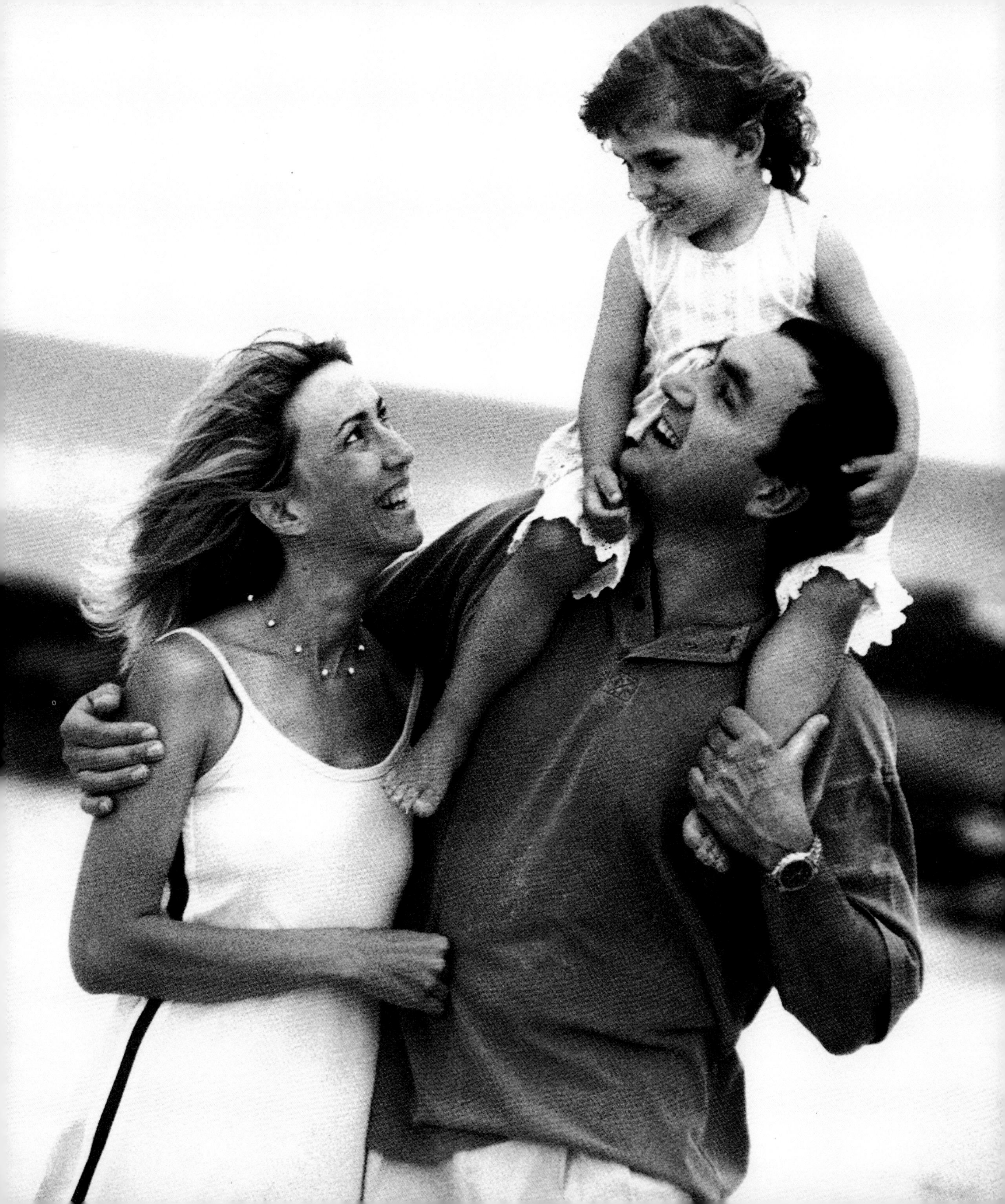

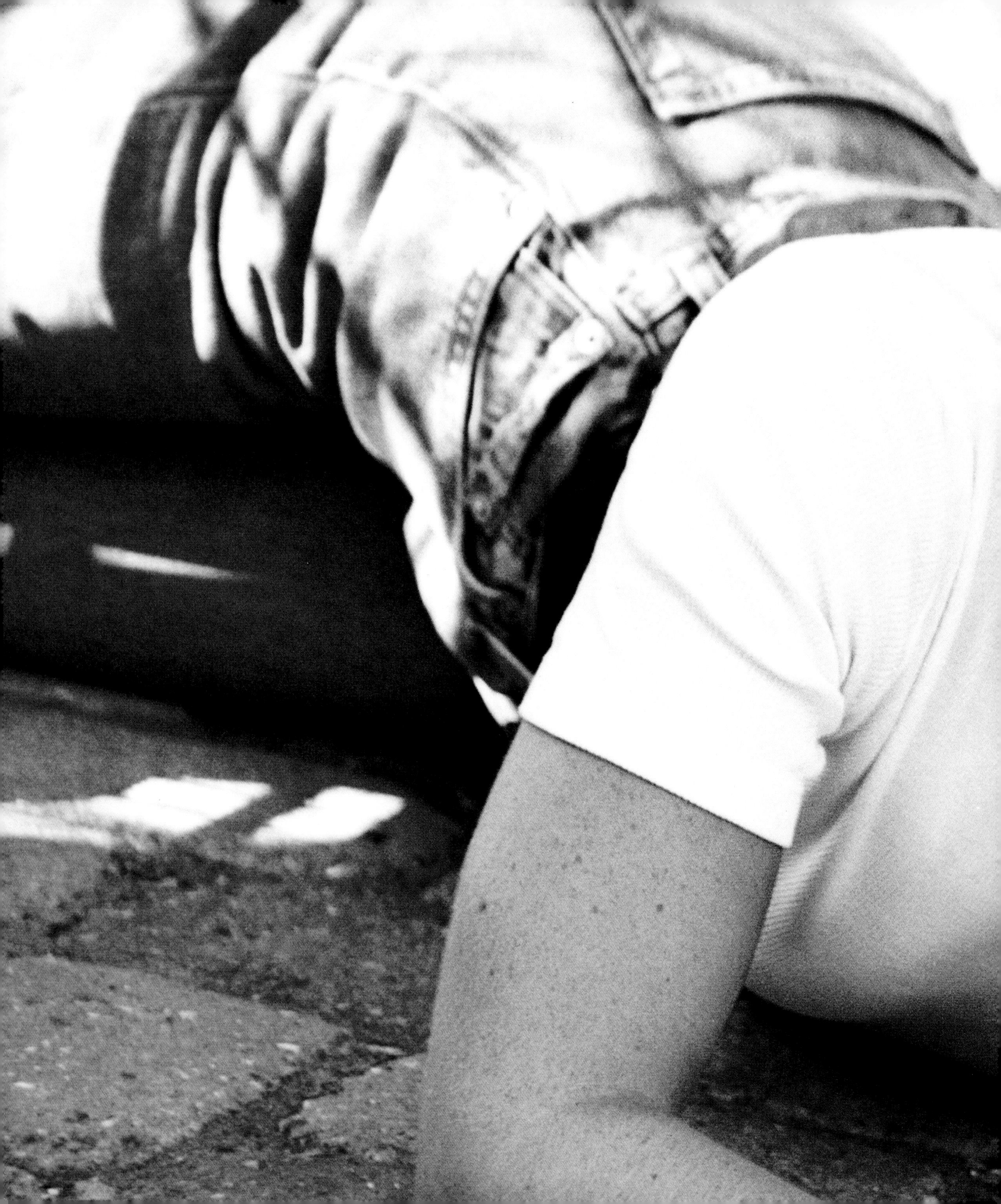

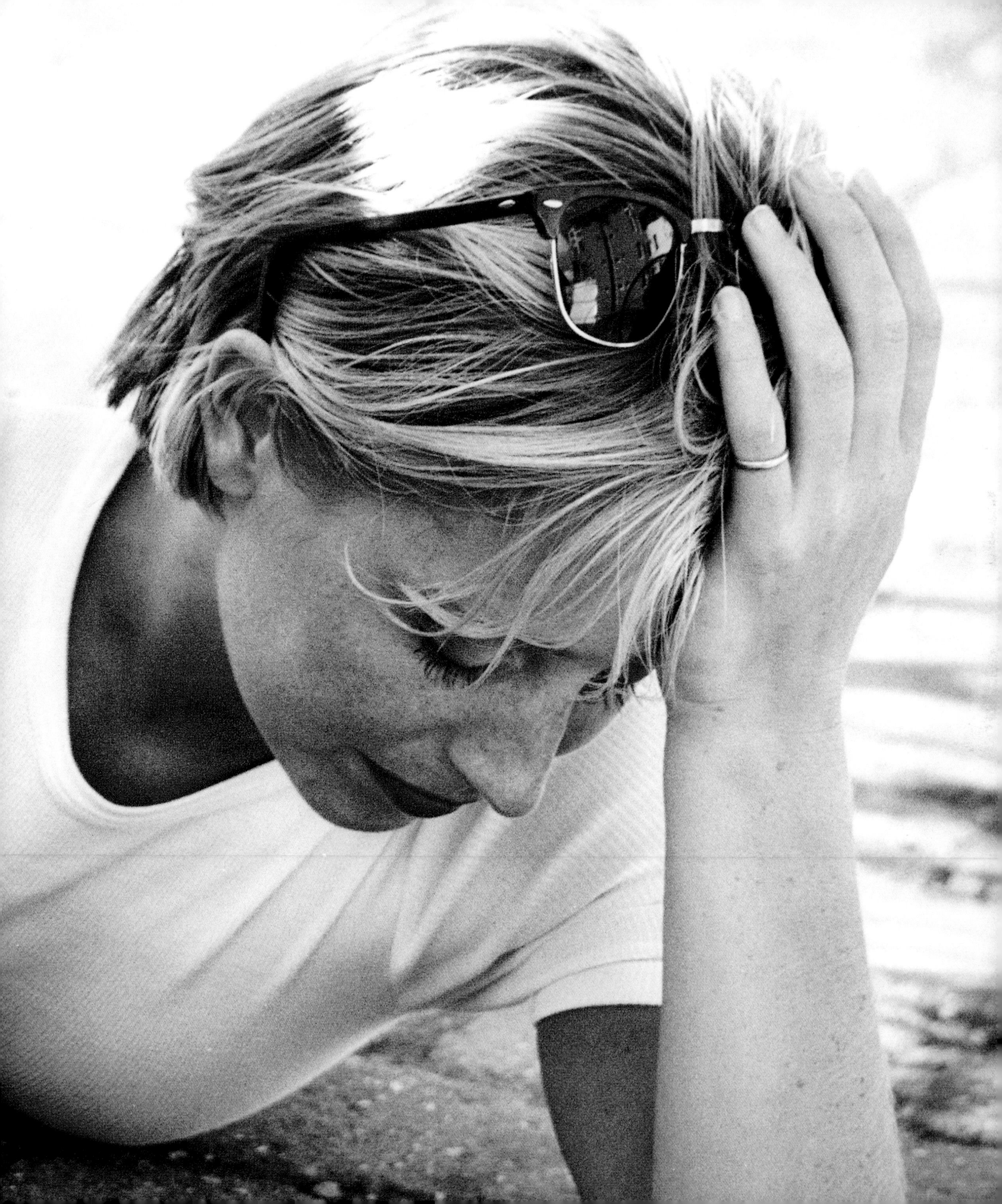

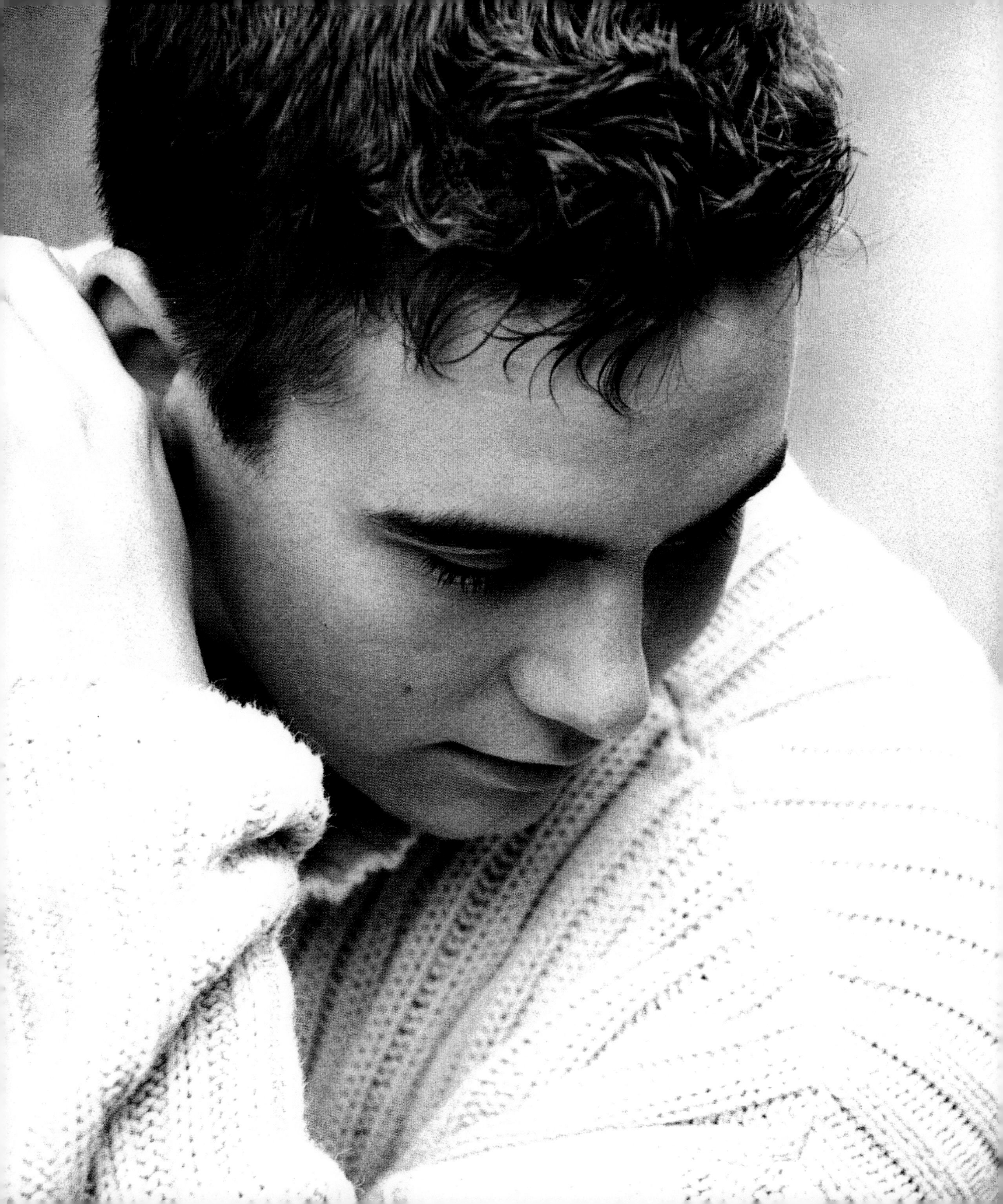

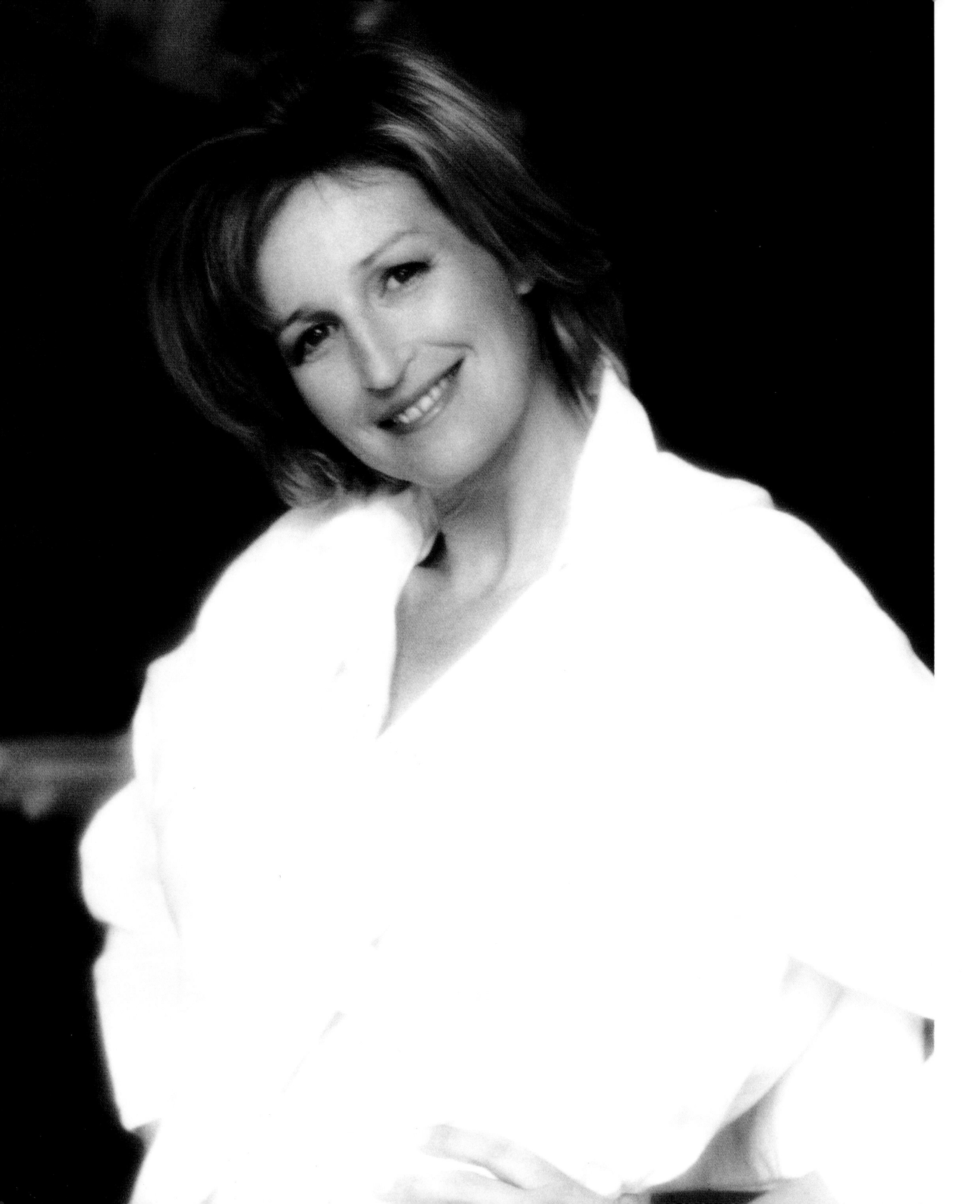

contents

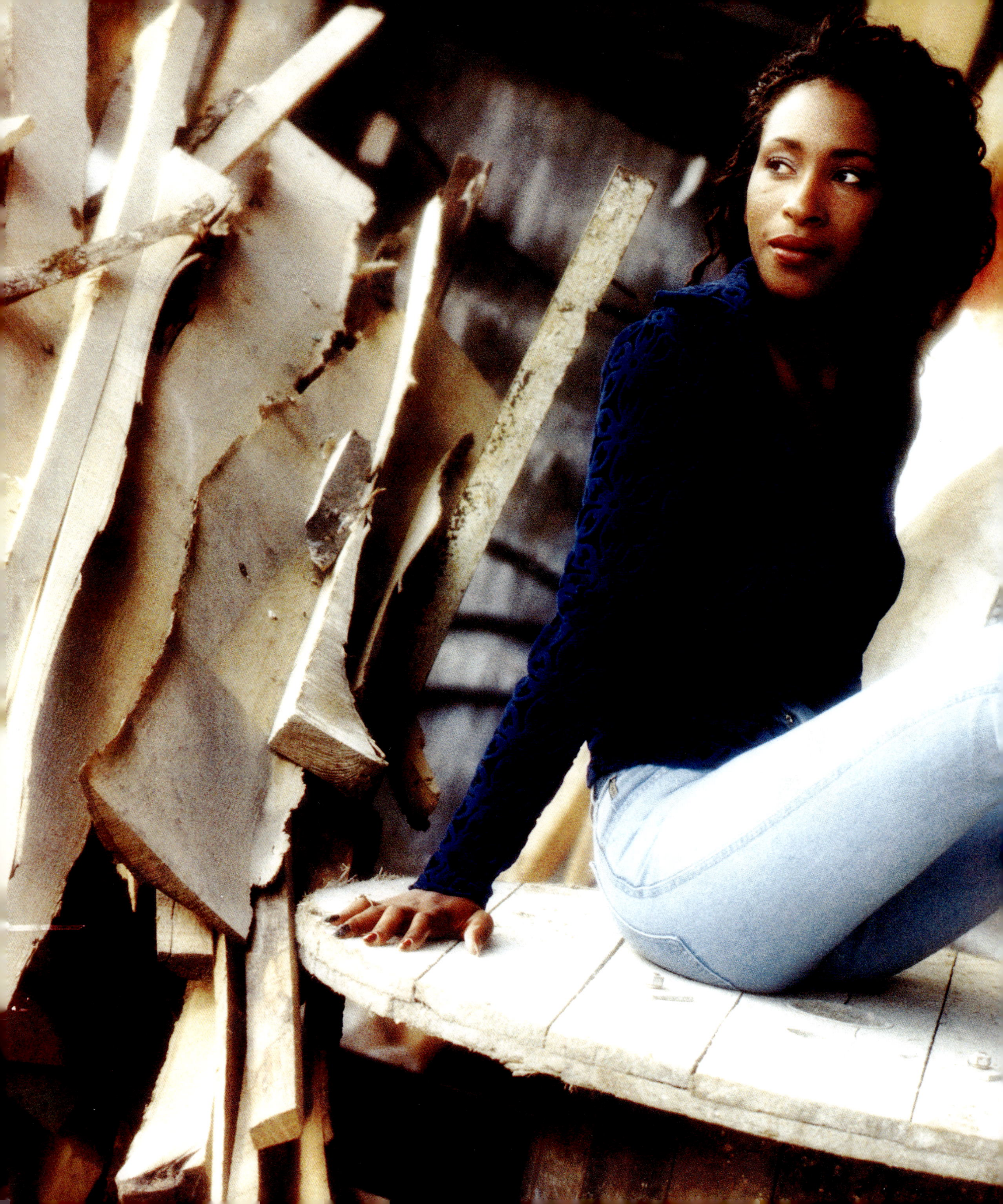

1 contemporary lifestyle photography

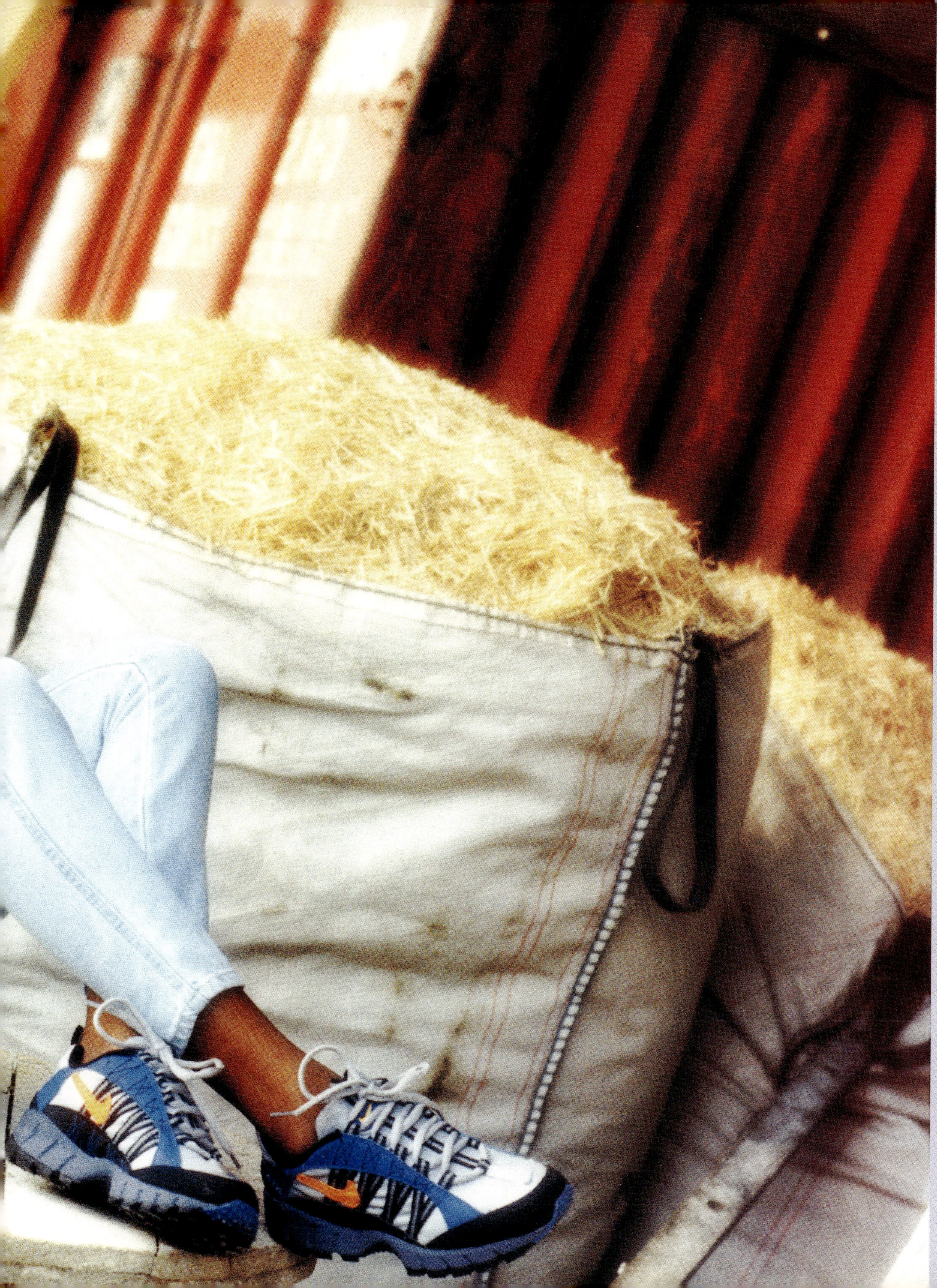

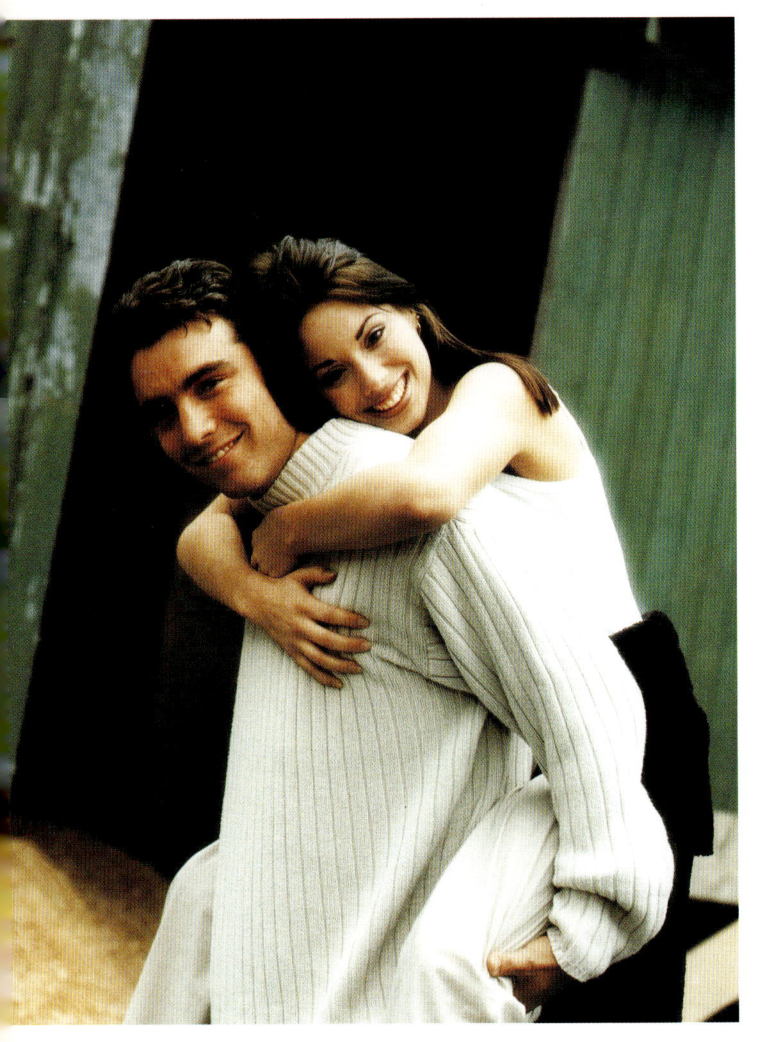

Contemporary lifestyle photography is the art of depicting people as they really are. However, "real life" often needs to be enhanced in order to create the pictures that fulfil the vision we have of ourselves. In truth, we need to take the "snapshot" one stage further to make it a professional picture. Most people see moments they want to capture every day, but are disappointed when the resulting image shows objects which went unnoticed at the time; for example they wanted to capture the child's expression but the finished picture includes the reality of everything that was happening in the background.

To create beautiful images, we need to look closely at the detail and develop a greater understanding of people and the effect of light. Eventually this will become second nature, and then it's possible to work in a truly relaxed style, concentrating on what you should be concentrating on, namely recording your subjects in a way that's still flattering to them, but totally natural. It will be an image of themselves that they're far more likely to recognise, and their reaction to it will be much more positive as a result.

My clients are not professional models, but they usually want to feel and look as if they are. Both these pictures were taken as part of commissioned portfolios, taken on location employing an informal approach.

Left: Mamiya RZ 67, 150mm soft focus lens, Fujifilm Provia 400, cross-processed. Exposure 1/60sec at f/5.6
Right: same details, but exposure 1/500sec at f/8

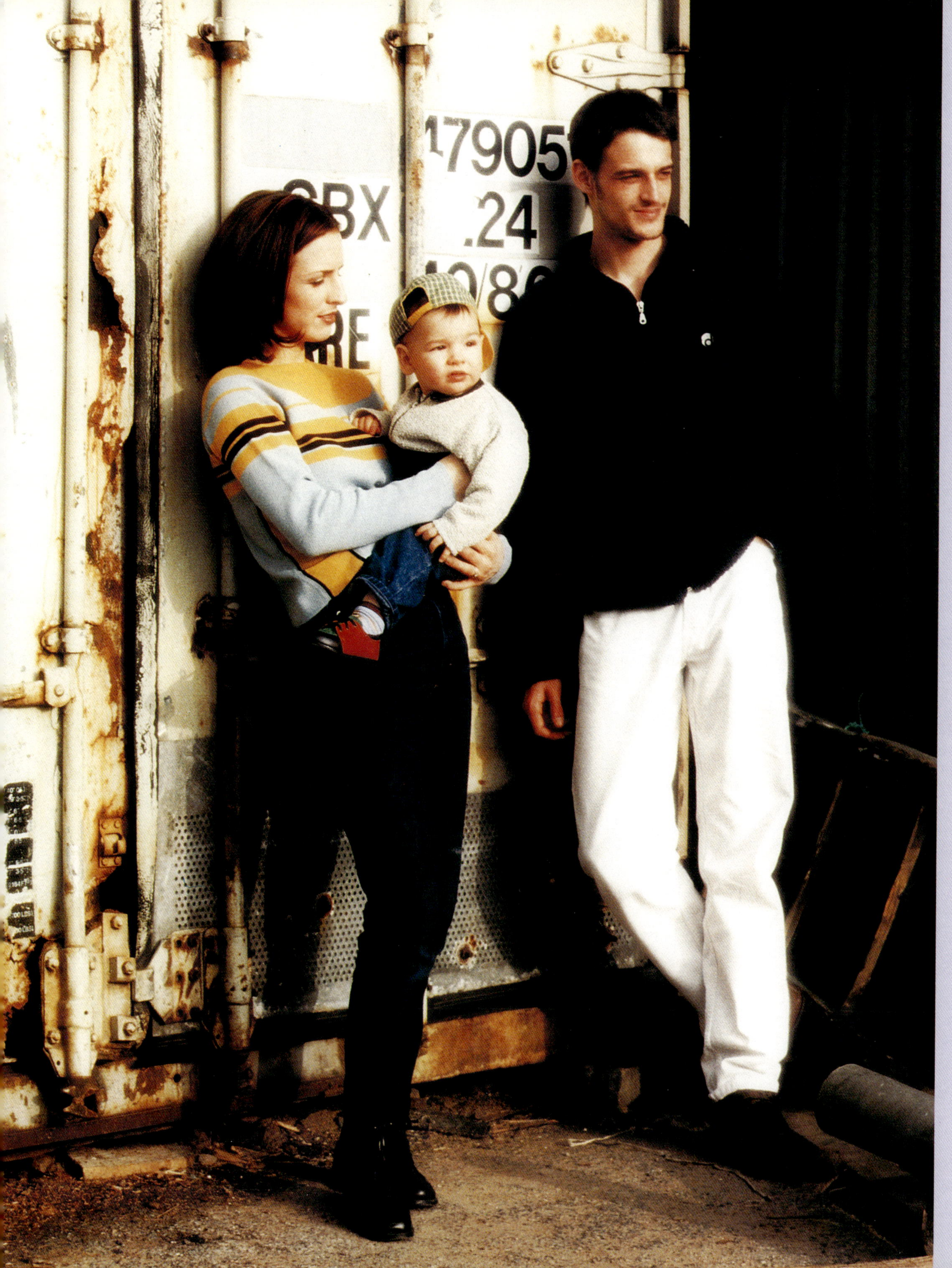

plan ahead to create beautiful images

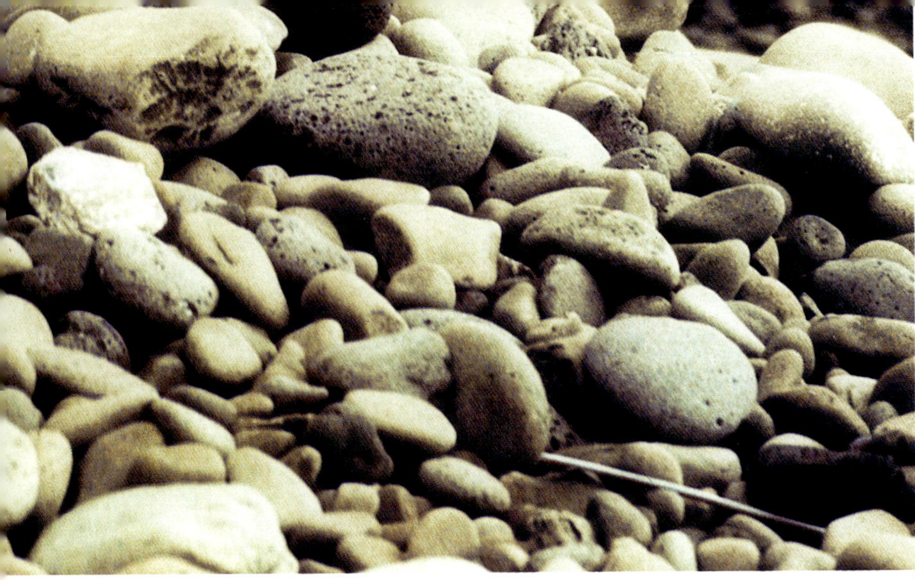

Take time out to look at the detail in a scene. What inspires you? Colour, texture, light? Consider the texture of the flaking paint and worn shapes of the wood. Look at the vivid blue colours blending with the natural tones of the boat and a contemporary image starts to emerge.

This is what you'll need to develop an eye for: in time this approach will almost become second nature, and you'll find yourself intuitively looking for detail wherever you go. As you'll see throughout the book, even some of the most unpromising locations can yield interesting and exciting pictures. It's simply a case of opening your mind and looking for ways that you can use a scene to your advantage.

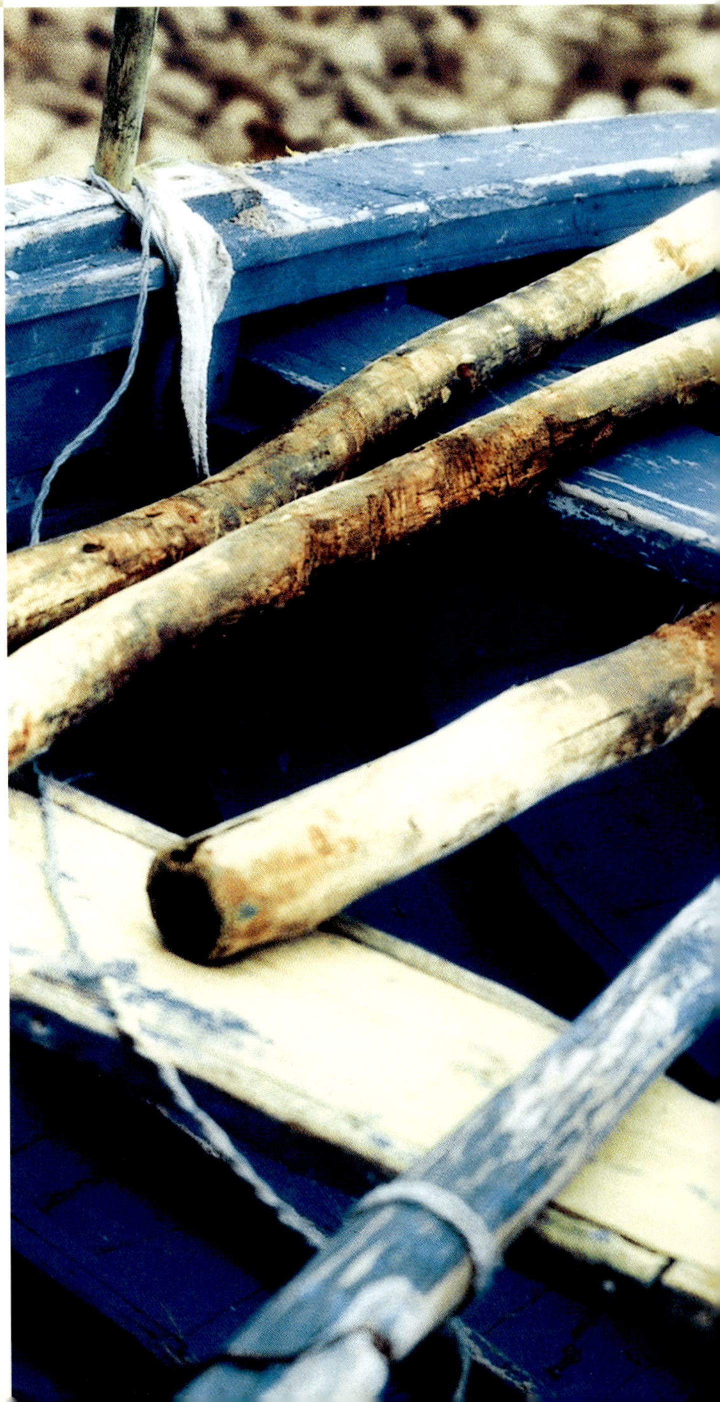

These details on the beach in Madeira intrigued me, and I spent some time walking around to establish the best angle from which to photograph them. Colours and textures are particularly important elements to note in any scene and, once you're sure of how you're going to tackle your shoot, you can introduce your subject.

Cross-processing is a useful technique which can produce amazing results, and it's something that I often use on shoots. I shoot primarily on negative stock because this gives me the greatest flexibility in terms of exposure. However, as I love bright, saturated colours, using transparency film and processing it through chemistry normally used for negative films achieves the desired results. Cross-processing can produce pictures that have weird and wacky colours, however, I ask my lab to print the flesh tones as accurately as possible, and the result is a picture that has lovely strong colours, and yet it still looks very natural. The clients often won't notice the difference, but they'll like the picture more because subconsciously, the colours will be more pleasing to them.

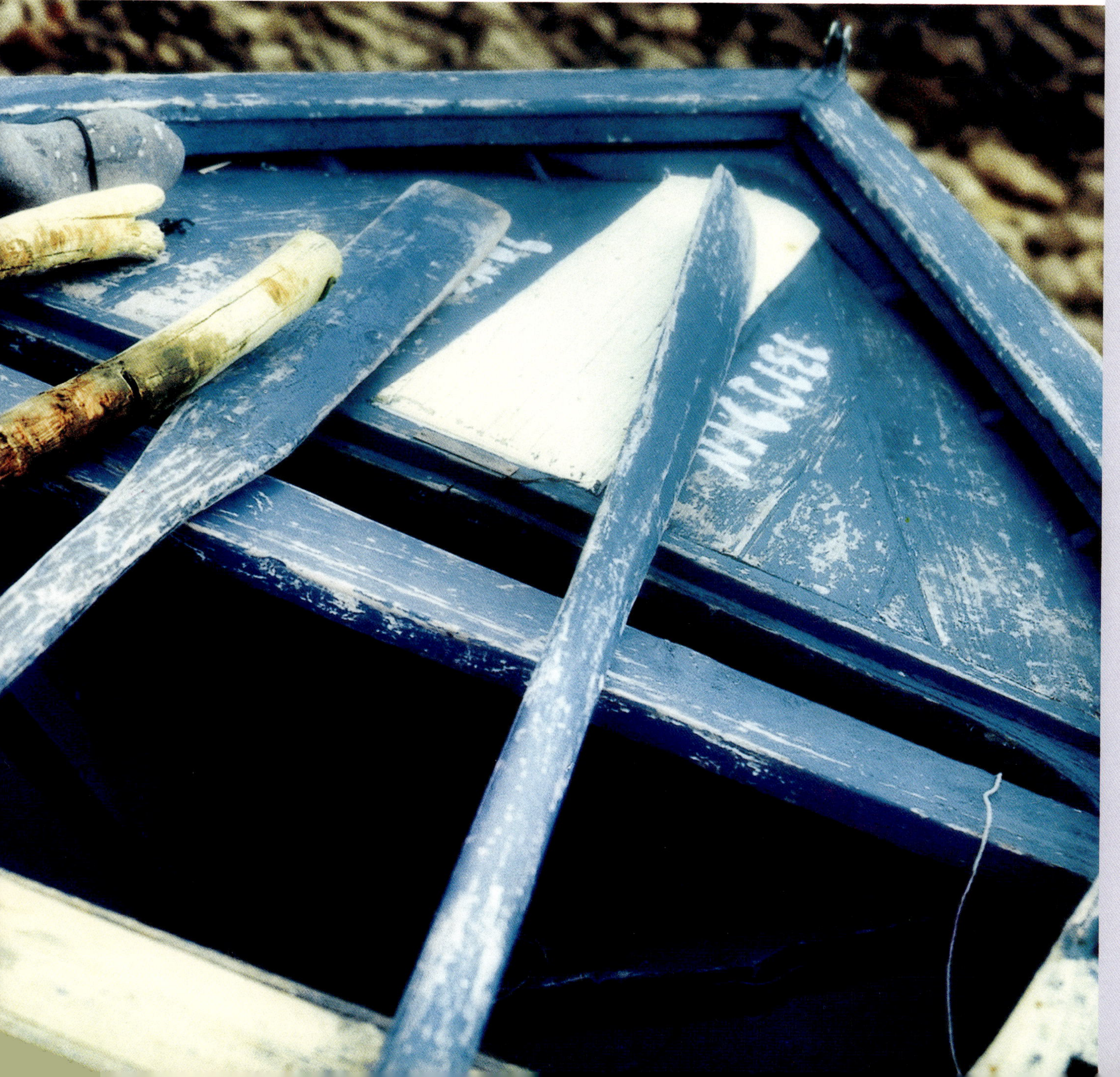

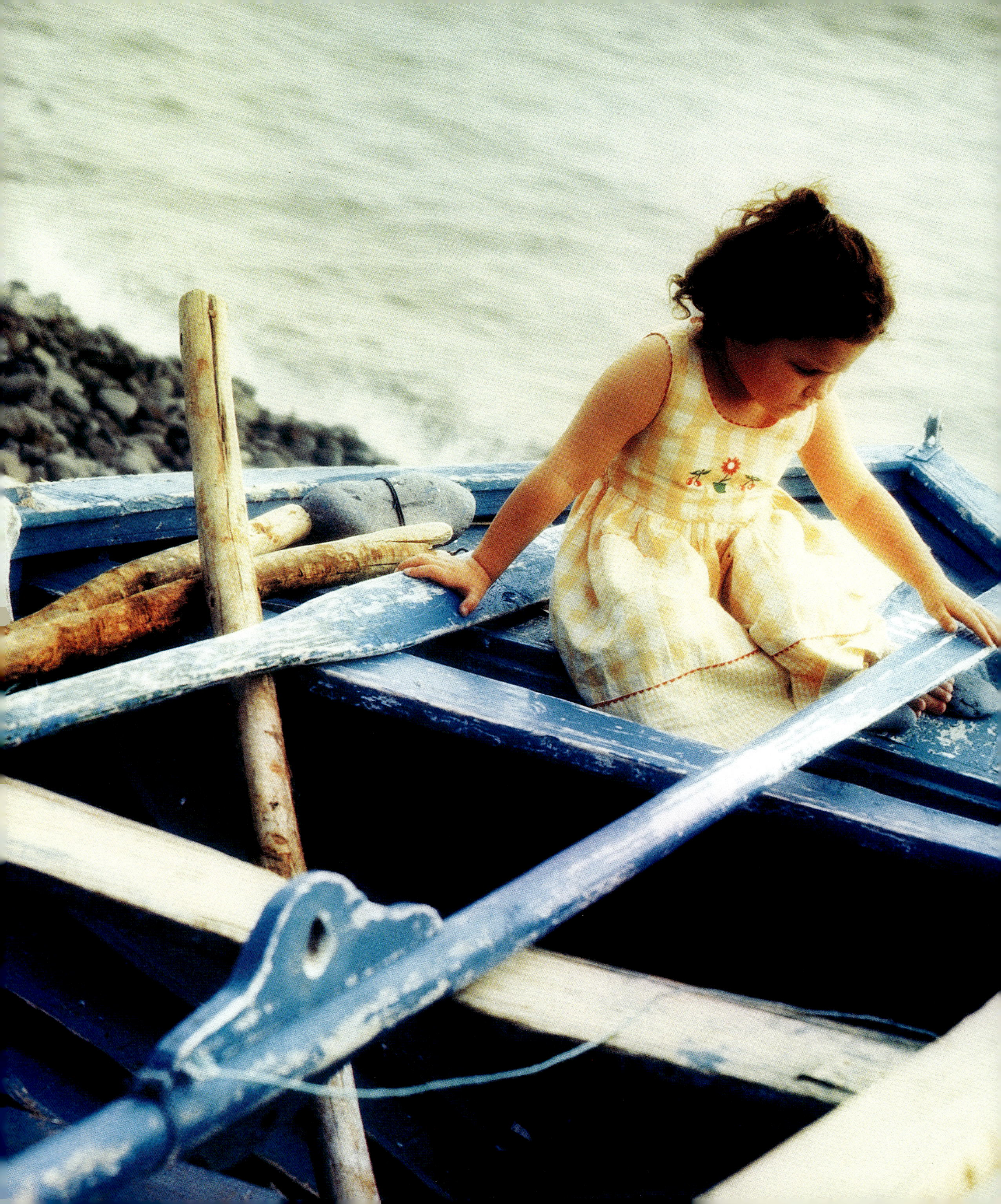

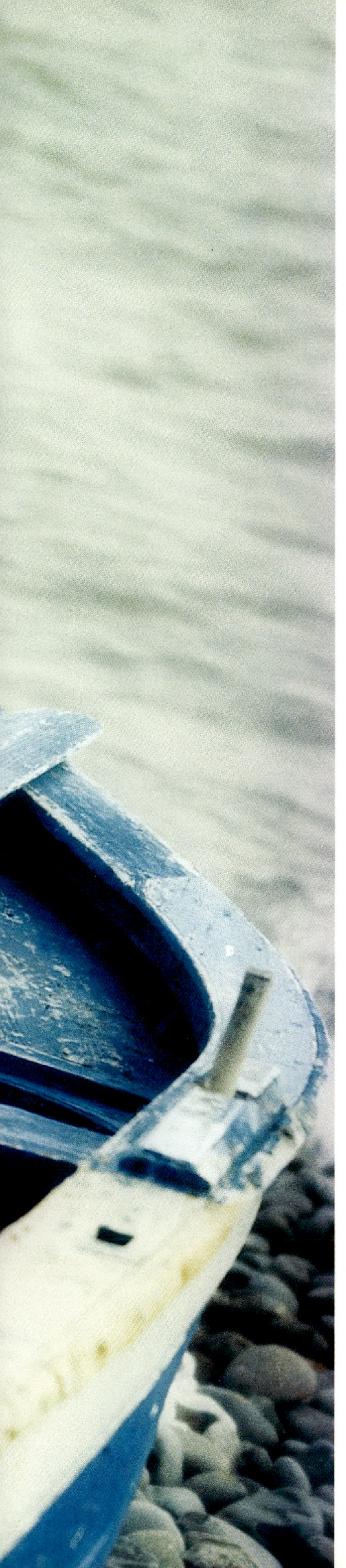

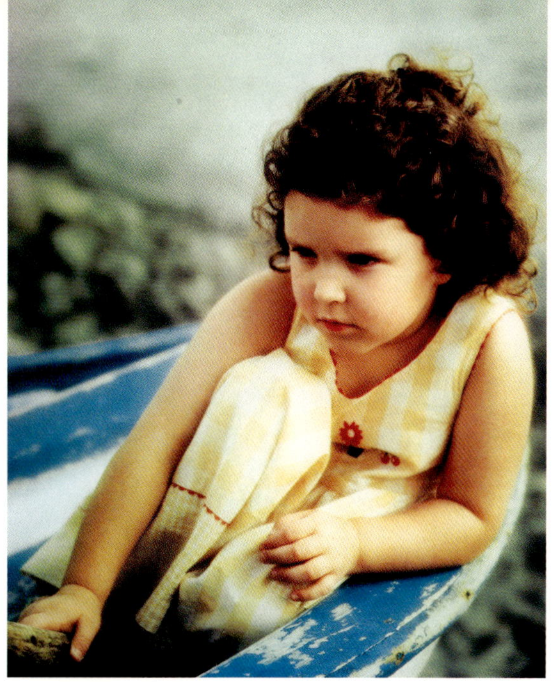

If we do not consider the background details first, we may get carried away by the antics of the child. By making the background an attractive image on its own, we can then introduce the subject and record anything that happens, in the knowledge that the environment will work and result in inspirational pictures. Trying to pose a young child can be very restricting and produce rigid results. Setting up the background first, and allowing the child the freedom to play anywhere within an area, will result in natural, spontaneous and relaxed pictures. The child will also enjoy the experience and develop a relationship with the photographer through play, which allows them to feel comfortable and secure, and be themselves. At this point it is up to the photographer to record what is happening, rather than impose formal restrictions that most young children find threatening and cannot relate to.

Now that I have set the scene using the boat and the beach, I can introduce the subject to the picture. Time spent on getting the basics of the picture right before getting into the photo shoot properly can pay real dividends.

Mamiya RZ 67, 150mm soft focus lens, Fujifilm Provia 400, cross-processed. Exposure 1/60sec at f/5.6

I usually take pictures to serve as establishing shots with a medium-format camera, and for these I'll often use colour film. The majority of my pictures are however, taken on a 35mm camera which I'll use to zoom in closer and take a whole series of more informal black and white pictures throughout the session. It's an extremely flexible format and the Canon EOS 5 I use is easy to hand-hold so that I can move around quickly and shoot a variety of pictures without the need for me to stage manage my subject.

The use of a zoom lens is also designed to give me maximum flexibility. It means I can change my framing very quickly, and can play around with the relationship between the subject and the background, as here. Fast black and white film, usually Fujifilm Neopan 1600, gives me a fine grain which enhances the pictures and allows me to take pictures when the subject is moving, without blurring.

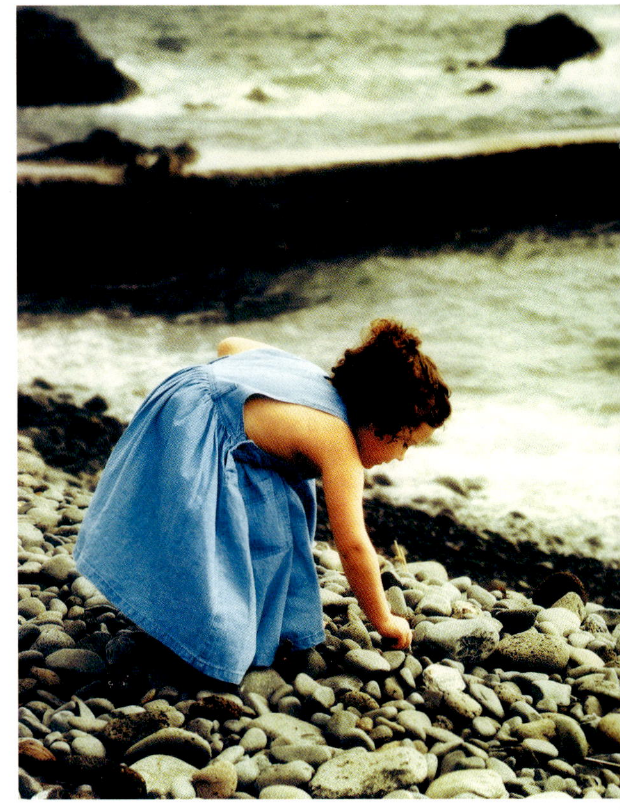

"I'll use a 35mm camera to enable me to move in and to take a whole series of informal pictures throughout the session."

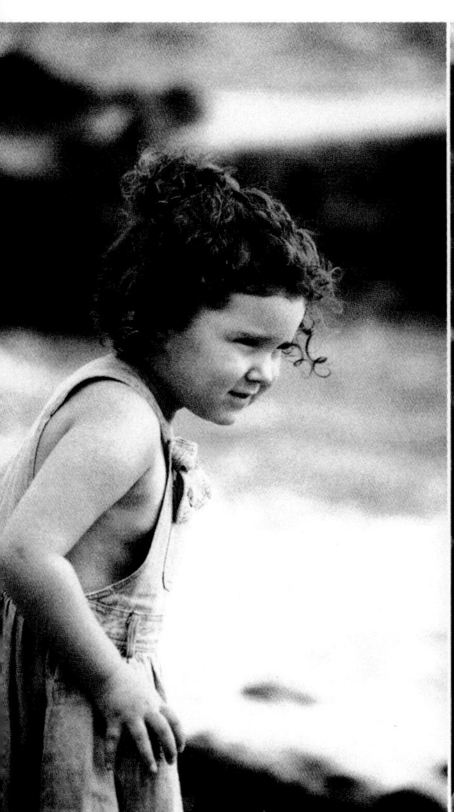
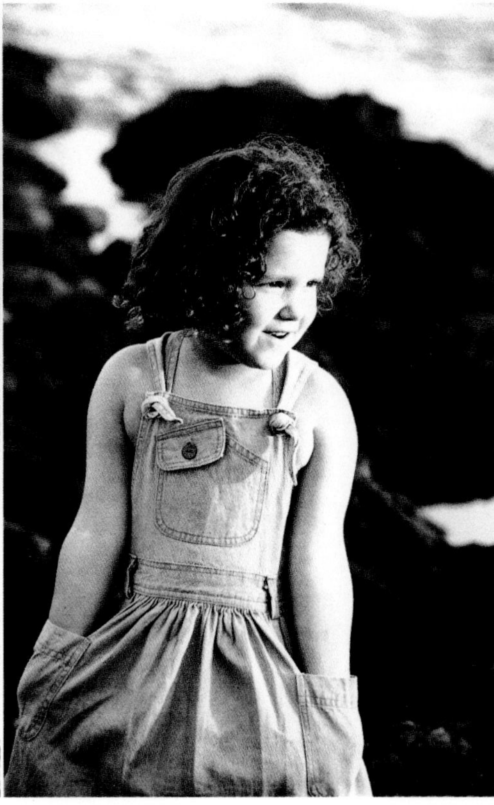
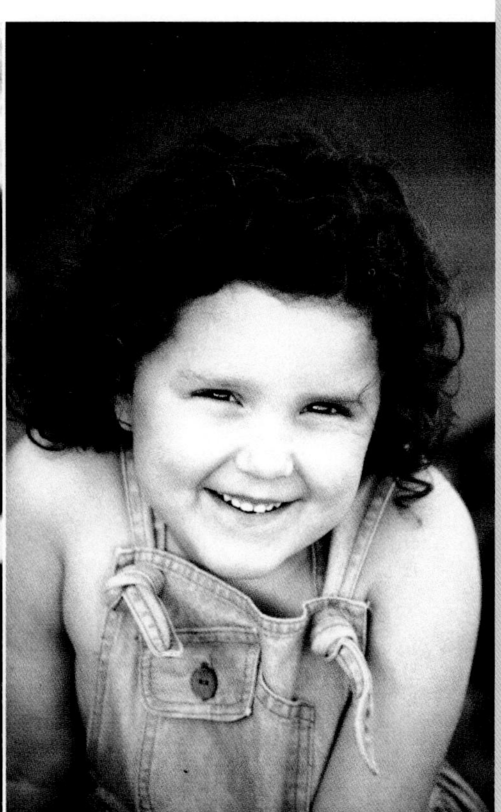

These pictures, to me, are the essence of what portraiture should be about. The little girl is relaxed and natural, and has been allowed to be herself and to enjoy her photograph being taken. It's important to allow children to be themselves, and for them to get a great deal of fun out of the session too.

Colour picture: Mamiya RZ 67, 150mm soft focus lens, Fujifilm Provia 400, cross-processed. Exposure 1/60sec at f/5.6
Black and white pictures: Canon EOS 5, 75–300mm zoom, Fujifilm Neopan 1600, shot on aperture priority

"The world of reality has its limits; the world of imagination is boundless."

Jean-Jacques Rousseau

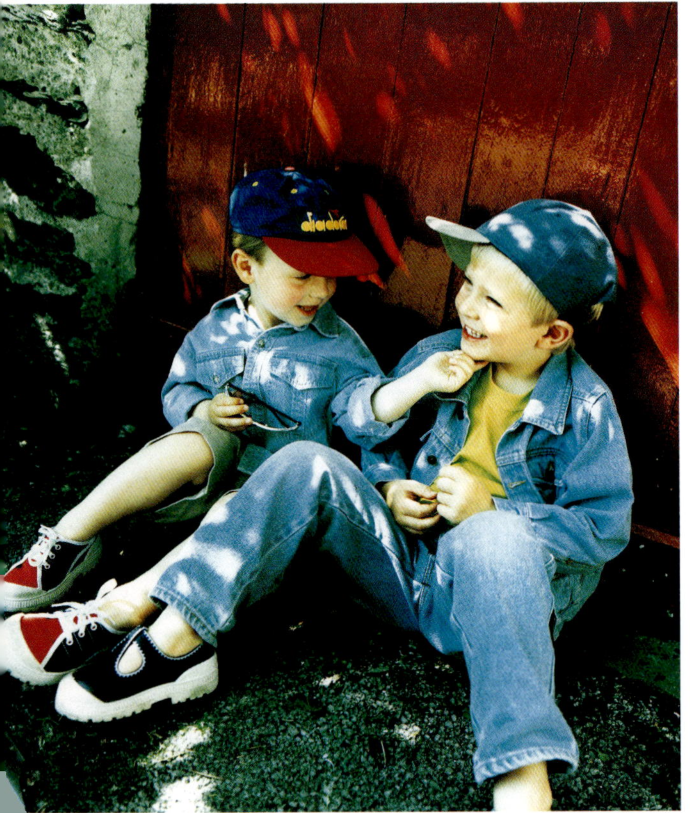

I love this quote, because to me it really says everything about the way that a photographer should approach a session. If you use your imagination, then there really is no limit to the kind of pictures that you can achieve in any situation, however uncompromising it may look initially.

These two pictures, for example, were taken in places that the portrait photographer would traditionally overlook. You don't always have to set pictures of children in pretty places: they're often really happy if you let them sit in the backyard and just play.

The two little boys were photographed against the doors of a garage at the back of a pub, while I arranged the girl by the metal doors of a factory – she's sitting here on a plain concrete floor. Both pictures, I feel, have managed to say something special: the boys, for example, are comfortable and happy, and very much at ease in front of the camera; the girl, meanwhile, is concentrating on what she's doing, and is taking the photo session very much in her stride. She's not intimidated by the camera or me and is relaxed and very natural.

Both these pictures show children being themselves, and this is how the most natural and uncontrived pictures should be taken. I've made things as simple as possible, and given myself every chance to work quickly with my subjects, and with the minimum of interference.

Right: Mamiya RZ 67, 150mm soft focus lens, Fujifilm Provia 400, cross-processed. Exposure 1/500sec at f/5.6
Above: Hasselblad, 120mm lens, Fujifilm Provia 400, cross-processed. Exposure 1/500sec at f/5.6

Allow yourself the freedom to be creative, by thinking ahead.

Set the scene by utilising the elements around you and by looking at the detail.

Use the equipment that is most appropriate for the task, allowing you to be flexible.

Use consistent lighting to enable you to concentrate on the subject.

Don't be afraid to experiment and to take risks.

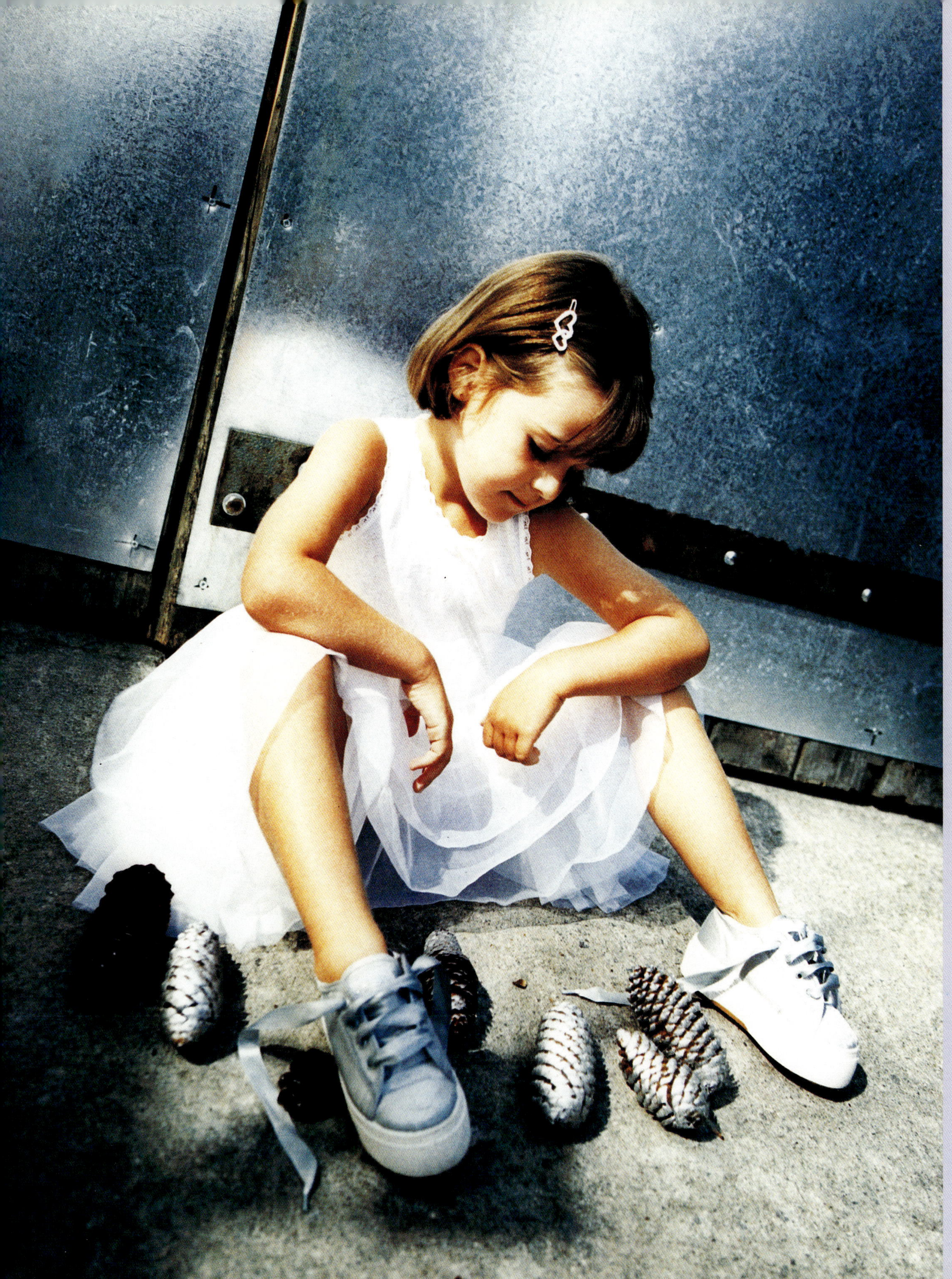

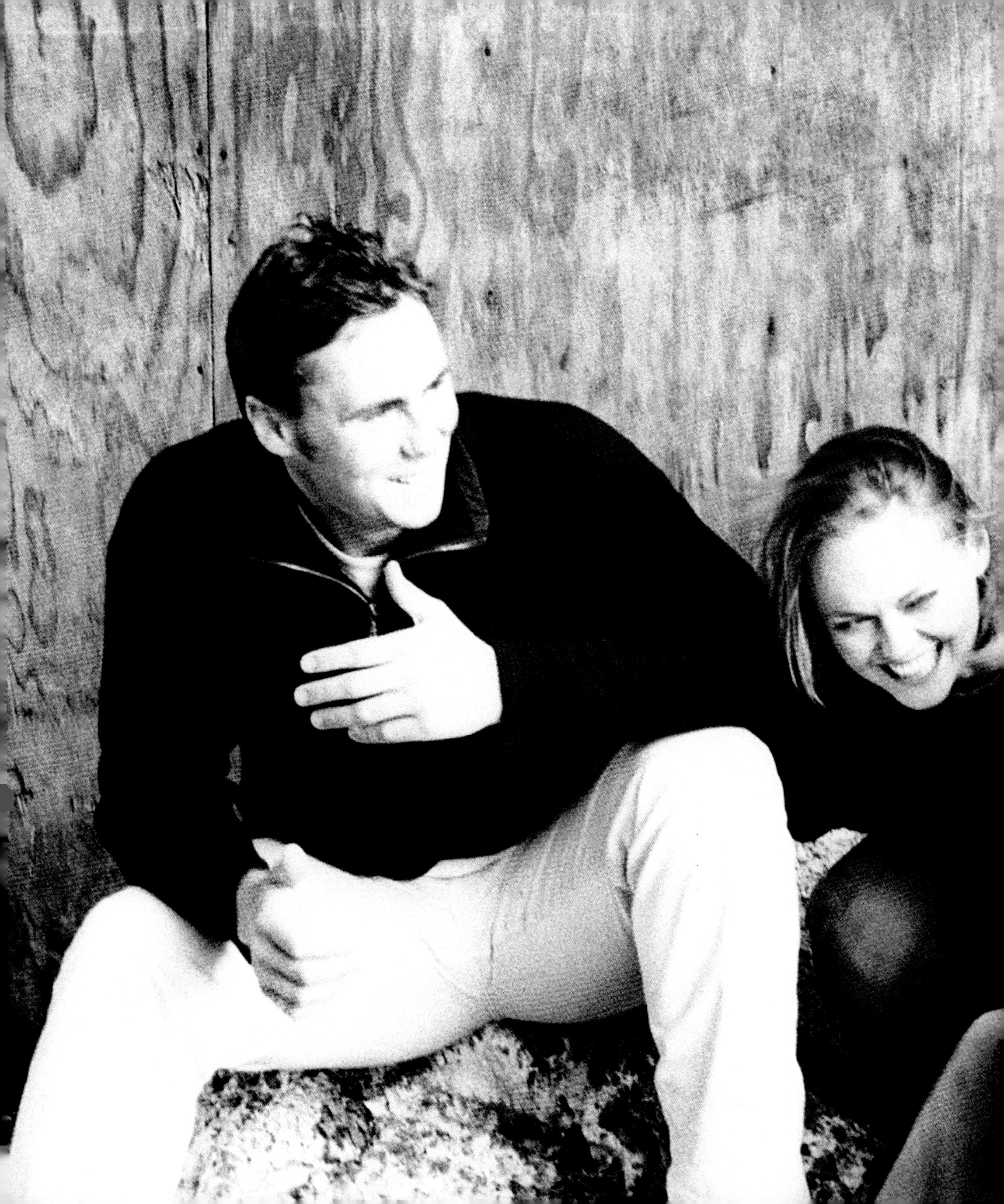

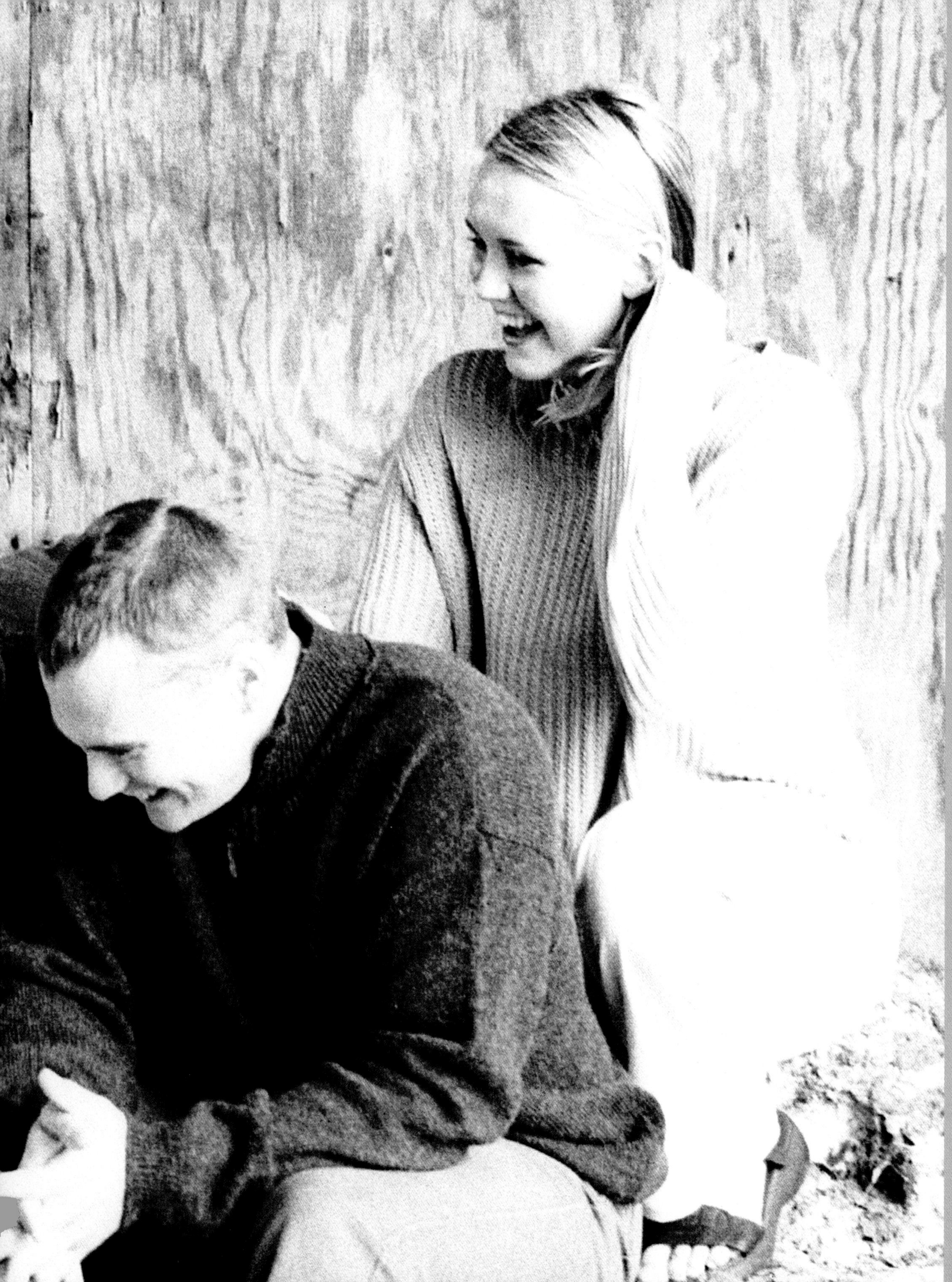

2 developing the client relationship

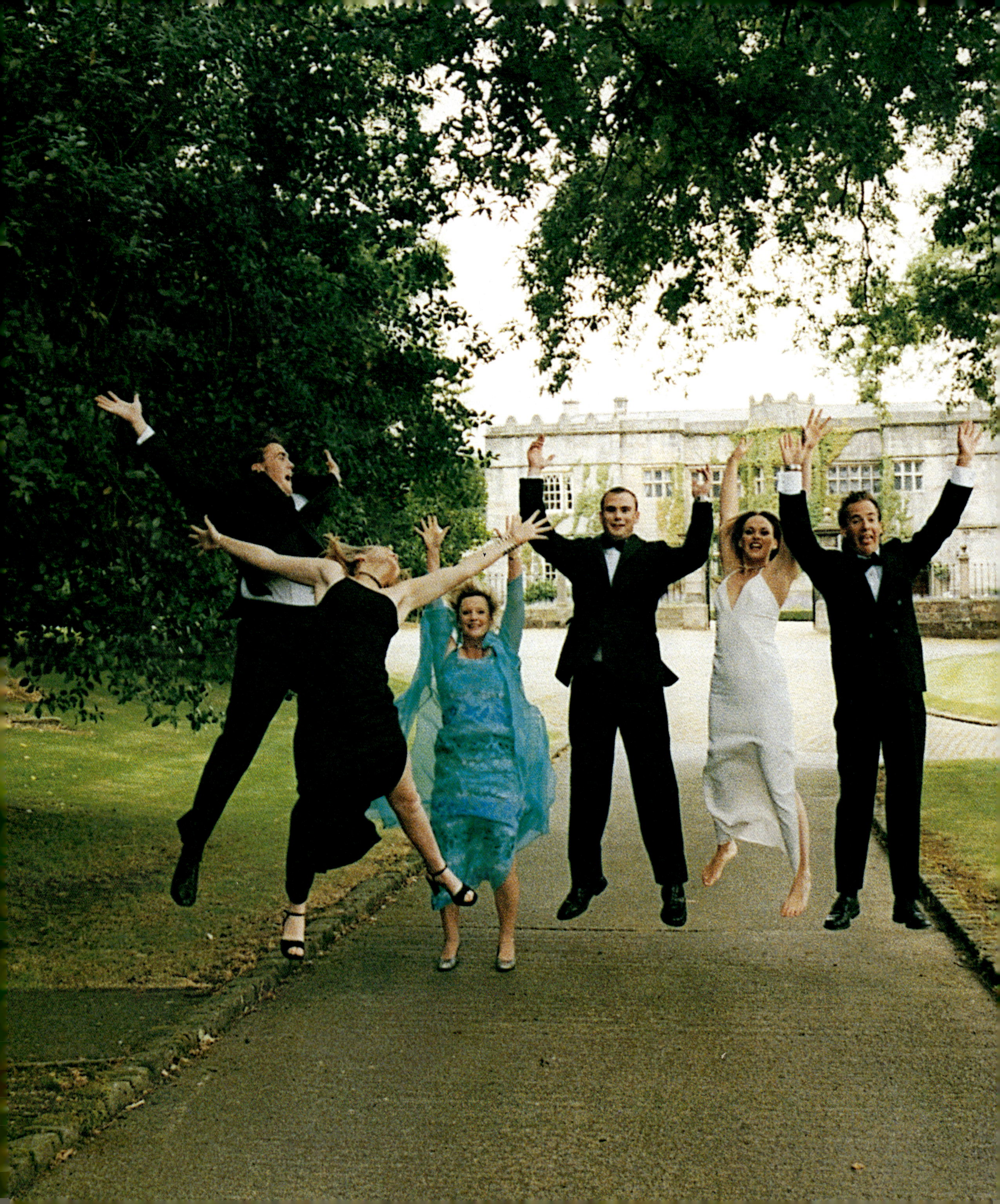

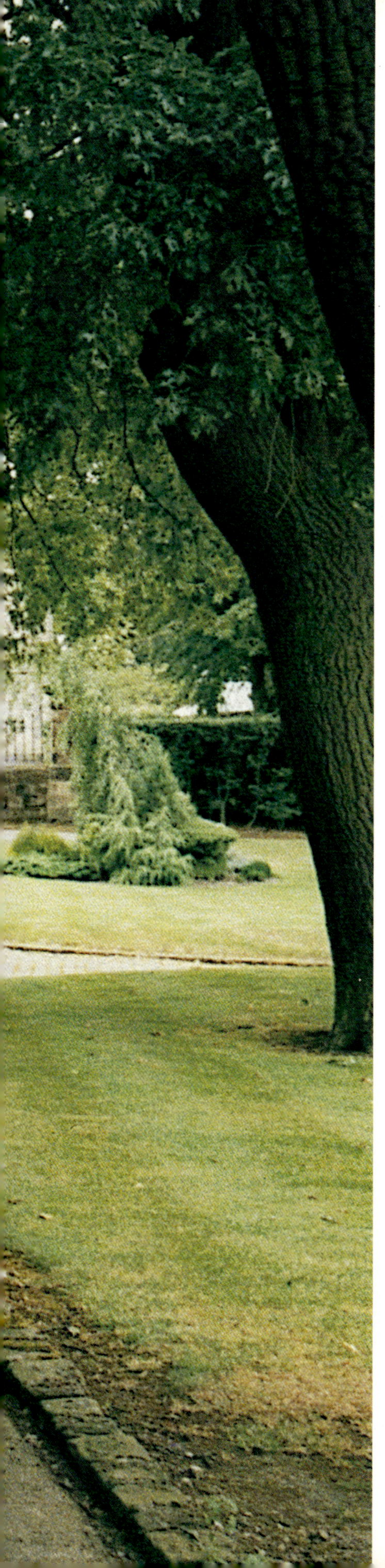

key elements to consider right from the start

Turning an essentially formal shot into an informal and happy picture such as this one doesn't just happen. There is an enormous amount of work that the photographer will need to put in leading up to this point, in terms of putting people at ease, establishing a rapport with them and making sure that they feel completely at ease in front of your camera. Only when you have the trust of your subjects can you expect them to go along with fun ideas such as this one. This chapter tells the story behind this particular shoot, which, in terms of approach, very much outlines the way that I like to work.

These are the elements that you should always consider when you arrive to carry out a shoot such as this:

Assess the environment carefully

Choose a selection of different clothes

Think about the client's personality

Consider the client's feelings

Observe how people interact together and with you

Keep an open mind

Think on your feet

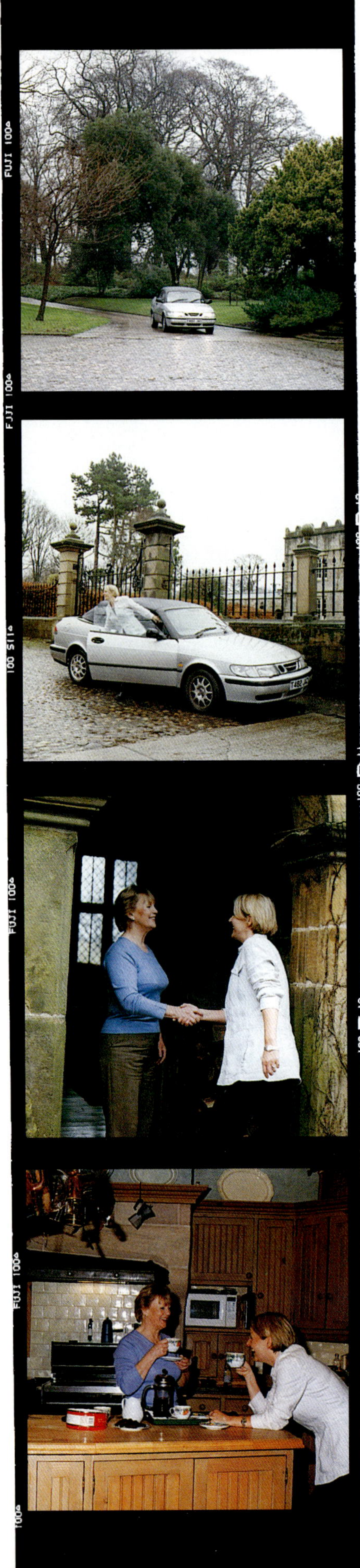

Talking on the telephone: The relationship with the client begins from the very first conversation on the telephone. Chatting on the phone helps me to find out how many people will be involved in the shoot, the names and ages of the children, the kind of location their home is situated in. Is it rural? City? On a housing estate? Is there a park or rural location nearby? Or would they prefer me to choose another location? Do they have a specific reason for having the photographs taken i.e. is it for a special occasion – a birthday, for example?

Arriving on location: Having established on the telephone the kind of environment in which the client lives, I prefer to see the location on the actual day of the shoot. If I check out the location before, I run the risk of losing the buzz I get when I see a place for the first time. I much prefer an element of surprise, and sometimes a challenge!

Meeting the client: Most clients are usually nervous about having their photo taken. Therefore I leave most of my equipment in the car at this stage, because cameras can actually be quite frightening to many people. Besides, there is so much to do, before I even start putting film in the camera!

The family has asked for a formal picture as it is Richard's 21st birthday. The house is selected as a background due to its imposing grandeur and formal gardens, which complement the family's formal attire.

Mamiya RZ 67, 150mm soft focus lens, Fujifilm NHG 800, straight-processed. Exposure 1/125sec at f/5.6

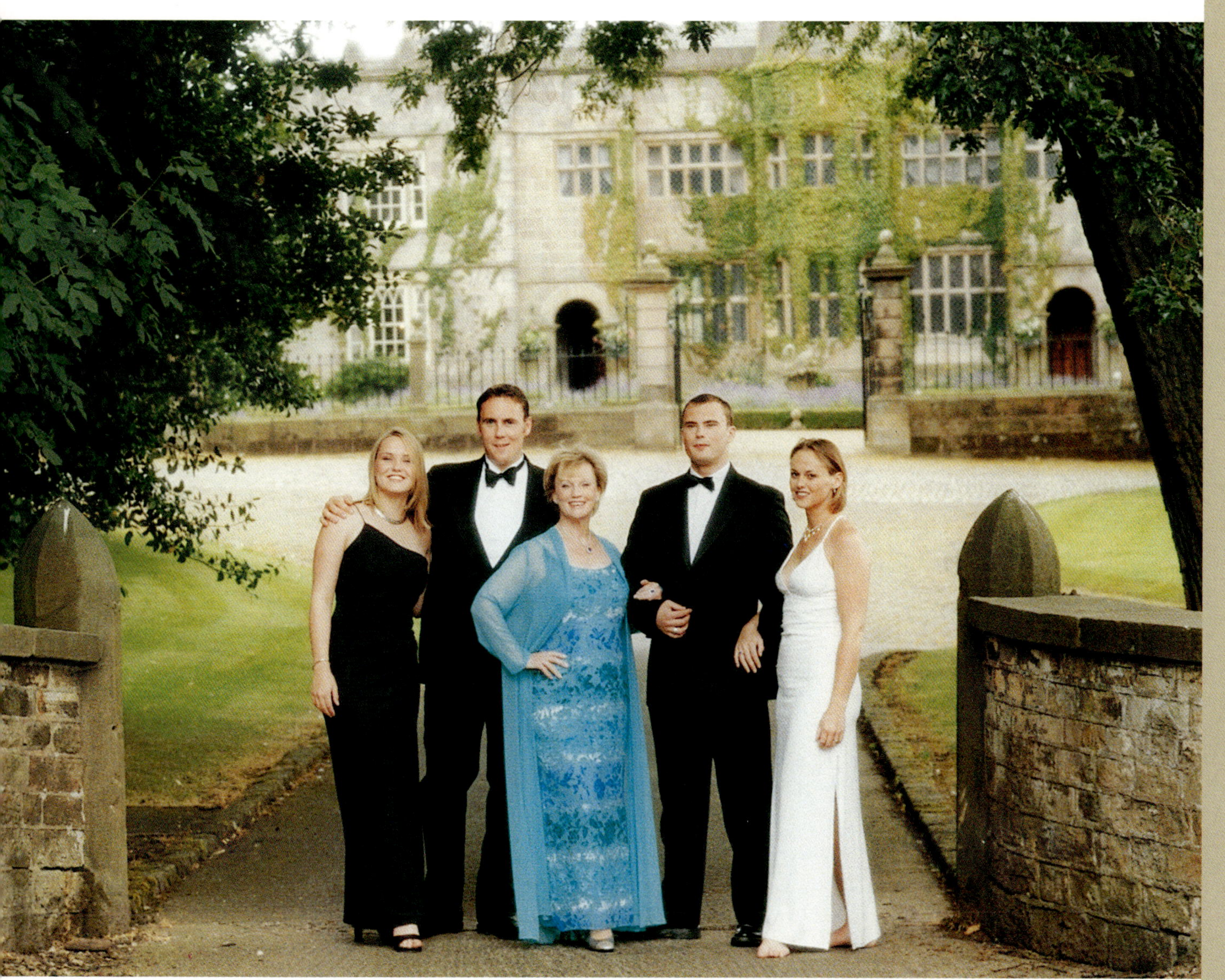

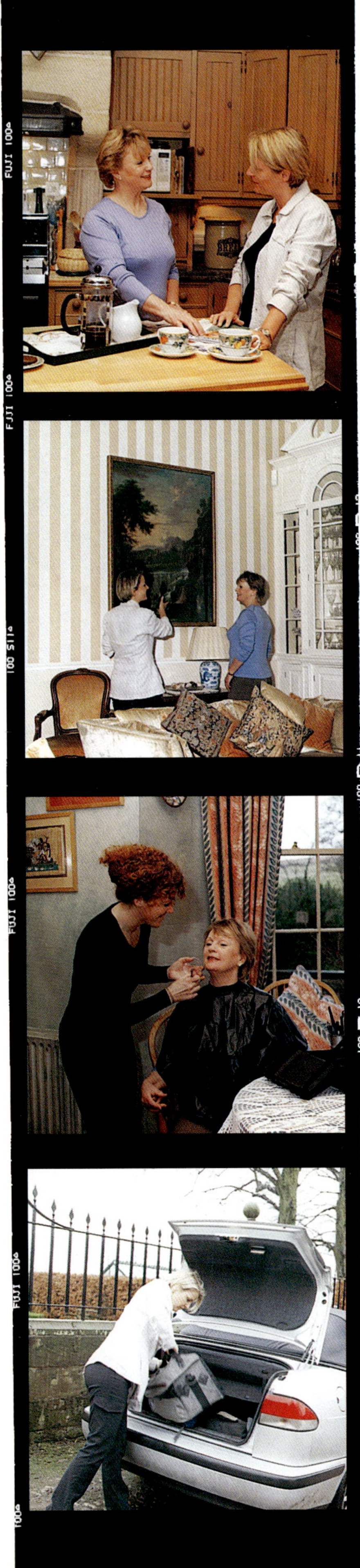

Relaxing the client: It is important that the client starts to relax right from the beginning. Having a coffee gives us the opportunity to chat and get to know each other. I need to find out more about the family so that I can ensure that their personality is reflected in the photographs. How? Over coffee, I ask Eileen all about her job, and chat with her family about what they do. This helps to build up a picture of their lifestyle, and helps us to begin to relate to each other.

Discussing the client's ideas: During coffee, we might look through some magazine pictures to get an idea of the kind of images the client likes. This tells me several things: a) whether they prefer black and white, or colour, or both, b) whether they like formal photos or very relaxed images and c) the kind of feeling they want to see in their photos.

Make-up: Having their hair and make-up done is a very relaxing experience, and makes the clients feel good about themselves, which in turn will ensure they look good in the pictures.

As they start to relax into the shoot we can begin to relax the clothes. It is always better to work from formal to casual, because if the clients are still slightly nervous at the beginning of the shoot, it won't matter when they are wearing formal clothes, and by the time they are really relaxed they will be wearing their casual clothes.

Here, the family are wearing clothes which are still quite smart, but casual enough that they can sit on the doorstep of the front porch and not worry about getting dirty!

Canon EOS 5, 75–300mm zoom, Fujifilm Neopan 1600. Exposure 1/250sec at f/5.6

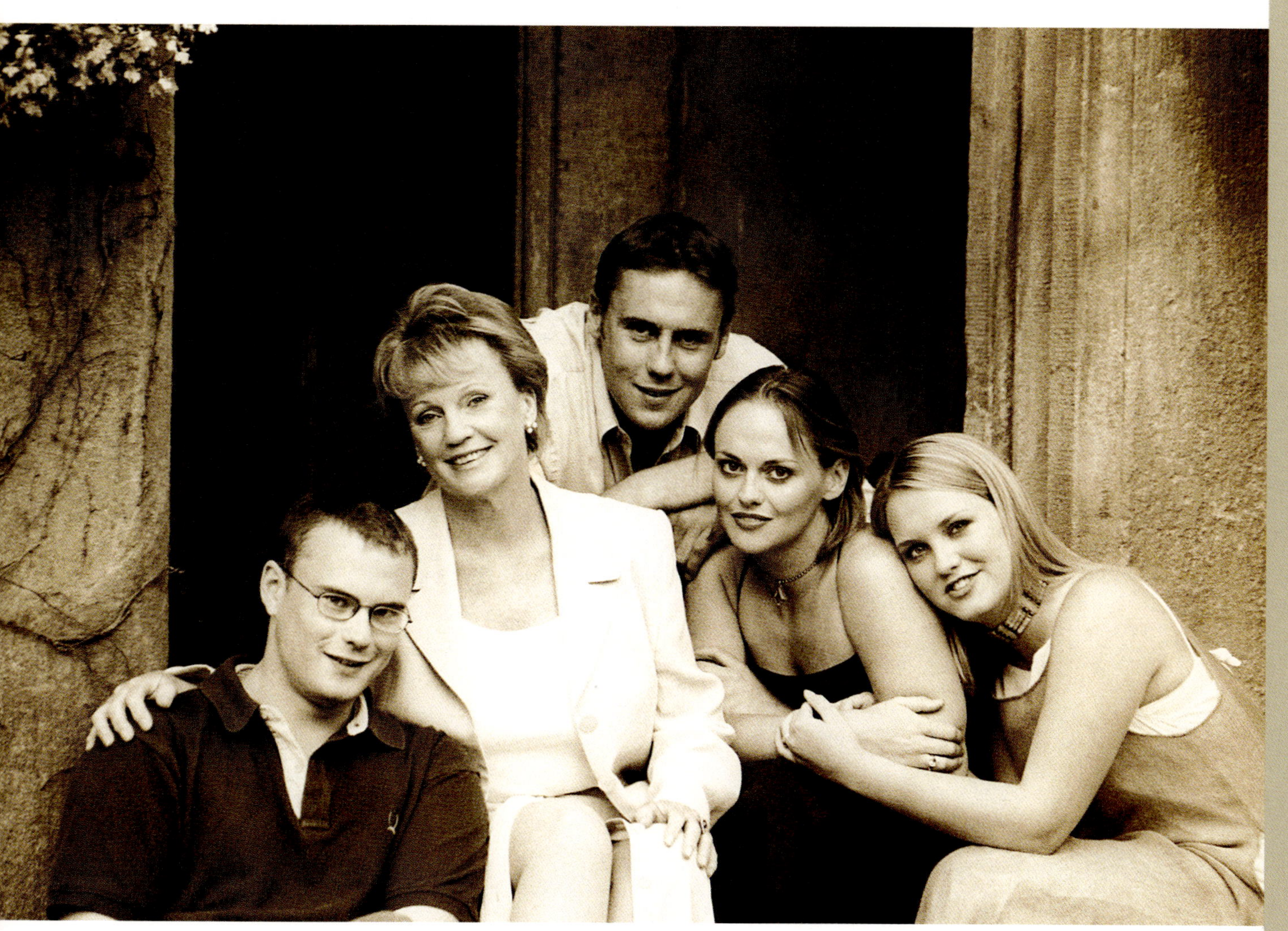

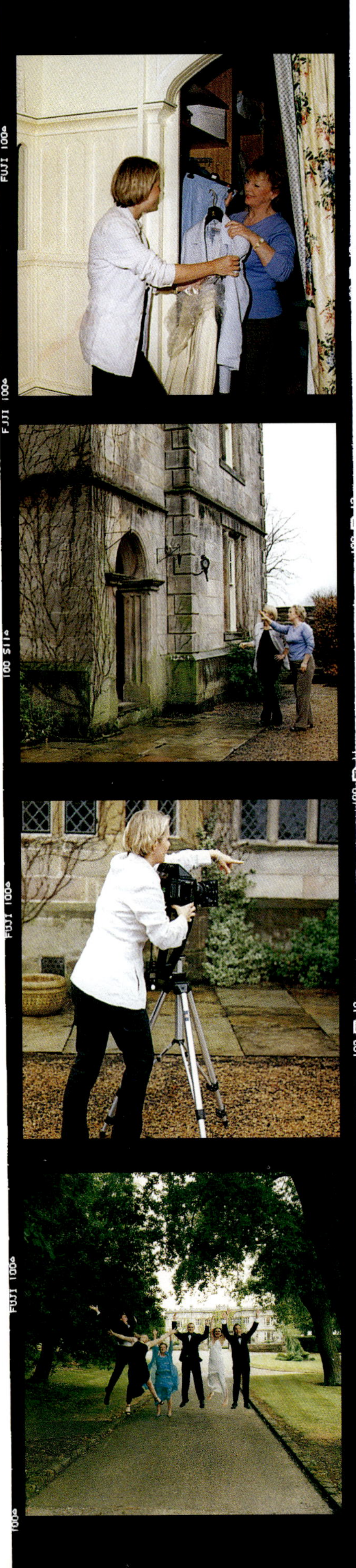

Choosing clothes: It is important that the client feels comfortable and their clothes should reflect the way they feel. Clothes should flatter the client, so choose those that are loose and flowing, rather than tight. Select colours that blend together and work with the background, and change their outfits for each location. In this case we start with formal, move into smart/casual and finally to very casual.

Choosing backgrounds: Deep in conversation, we wander outside to start looking for locations. In this case, there were many choices, and now is the time to narrow them down, so that the clients will not be hanging around or getting confused by all the options later on. It is much better to pick a few places and keep the shoot simple. For this shoot I have selected three different locations.

Interaction: This initial process helps to form the friendly, relaxed relationship with your client that is essential to produce natural and spontaneous pictures. When everyone is enjoying the experience, the interaction between the subjects themselves, and between the subjects and the photographer will be fun and enjoyable. In turn this will create plenty of opportunity for pictures that really reflect individual personalities.

By the end of the shoot the family is very relaxed and can now wear everyday clothes. Many people would not want to wear these at the beginning of the shoot, as they would not feel they had made enough effort to look their best, but in fact it is the casual photos which I know they will prefer.

Canon EOS 5, 75–300mm zoom, Fujifilm Neopan 1600. Exposure 1/60sec at f/5.6

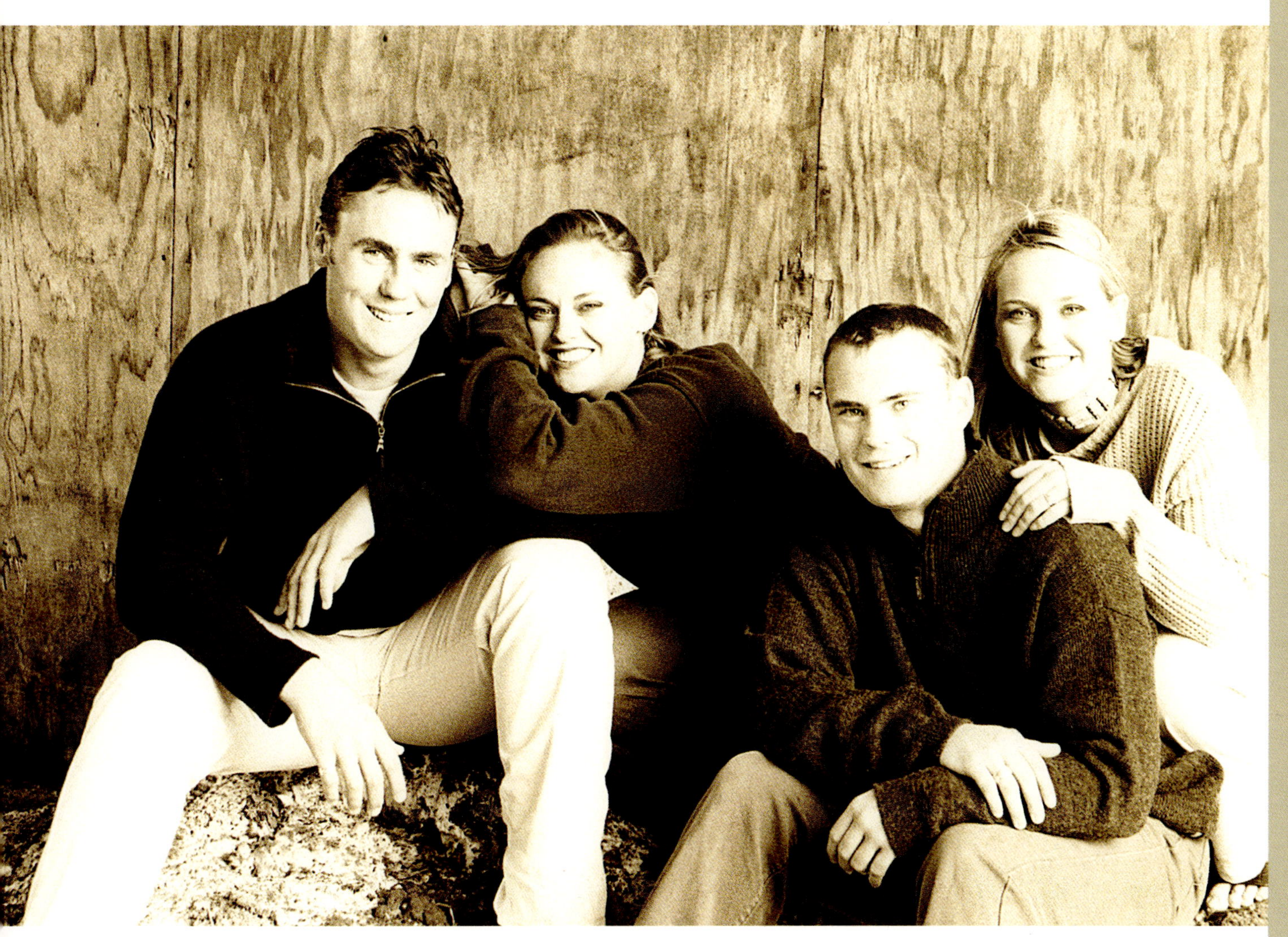

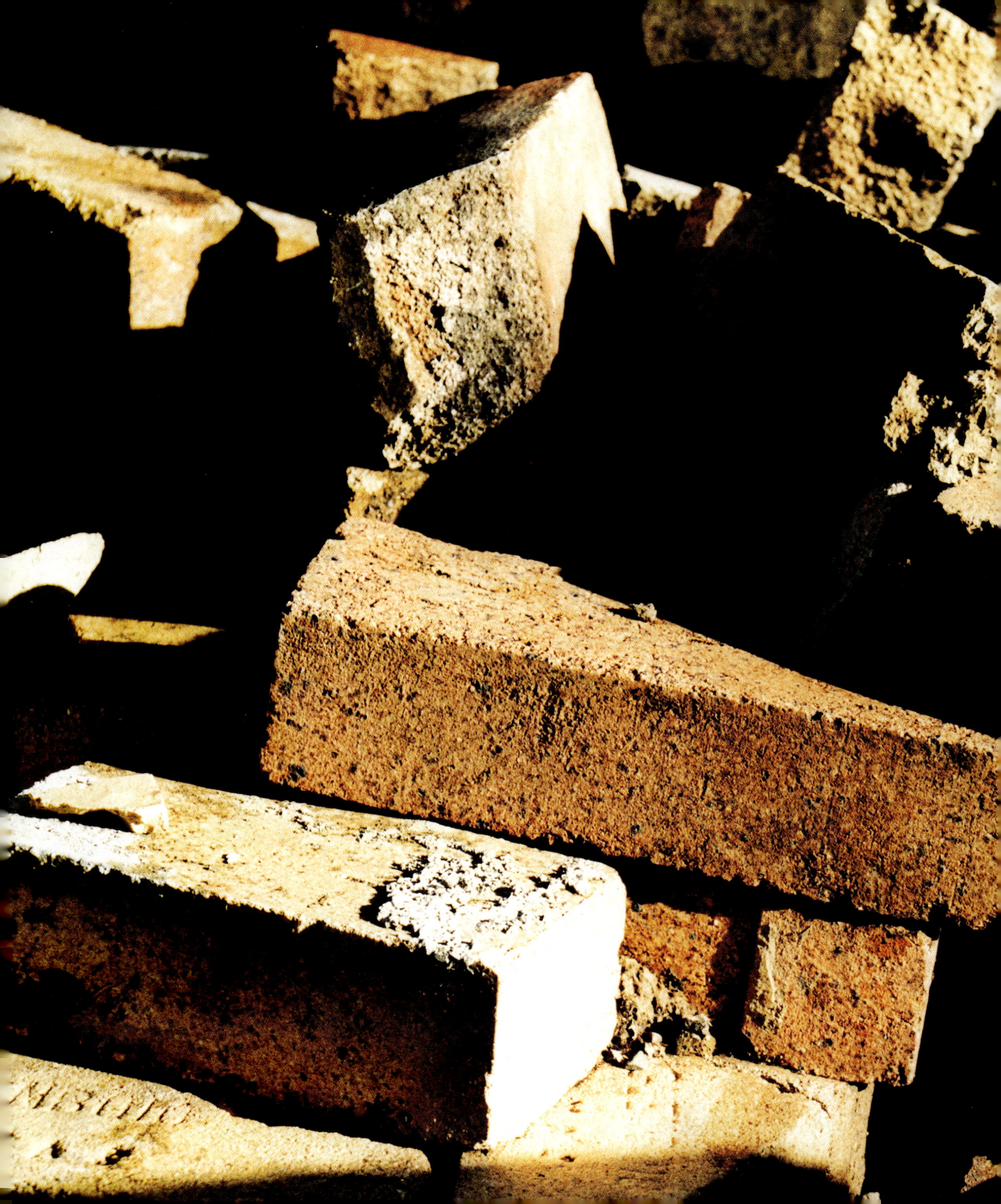

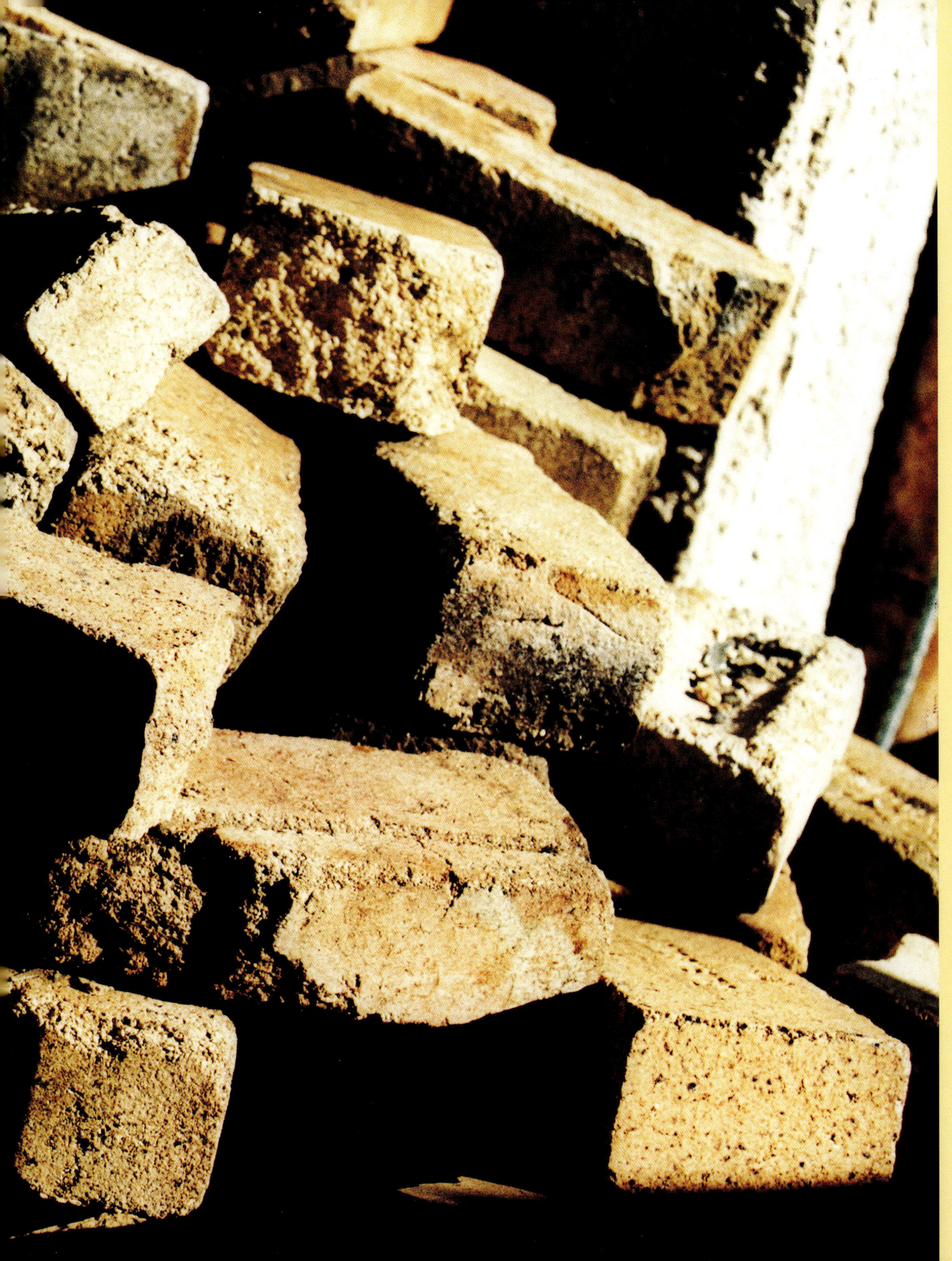

3 location, lighting and technique

I nearly always work with people who have commissioned me to take their picture, and yet those who see my work often assume that I'm using professional models. By shooting in a style that echoes that used by photographers working for the fashion and lifestyle markets, I'm able to give my pictures a vibrancy that is often lacking in social photography.

Canon EOS 5, 75–300mm zoom, Fujifilm Neopan 1600. Exposure 1/1000sec at f/5.6

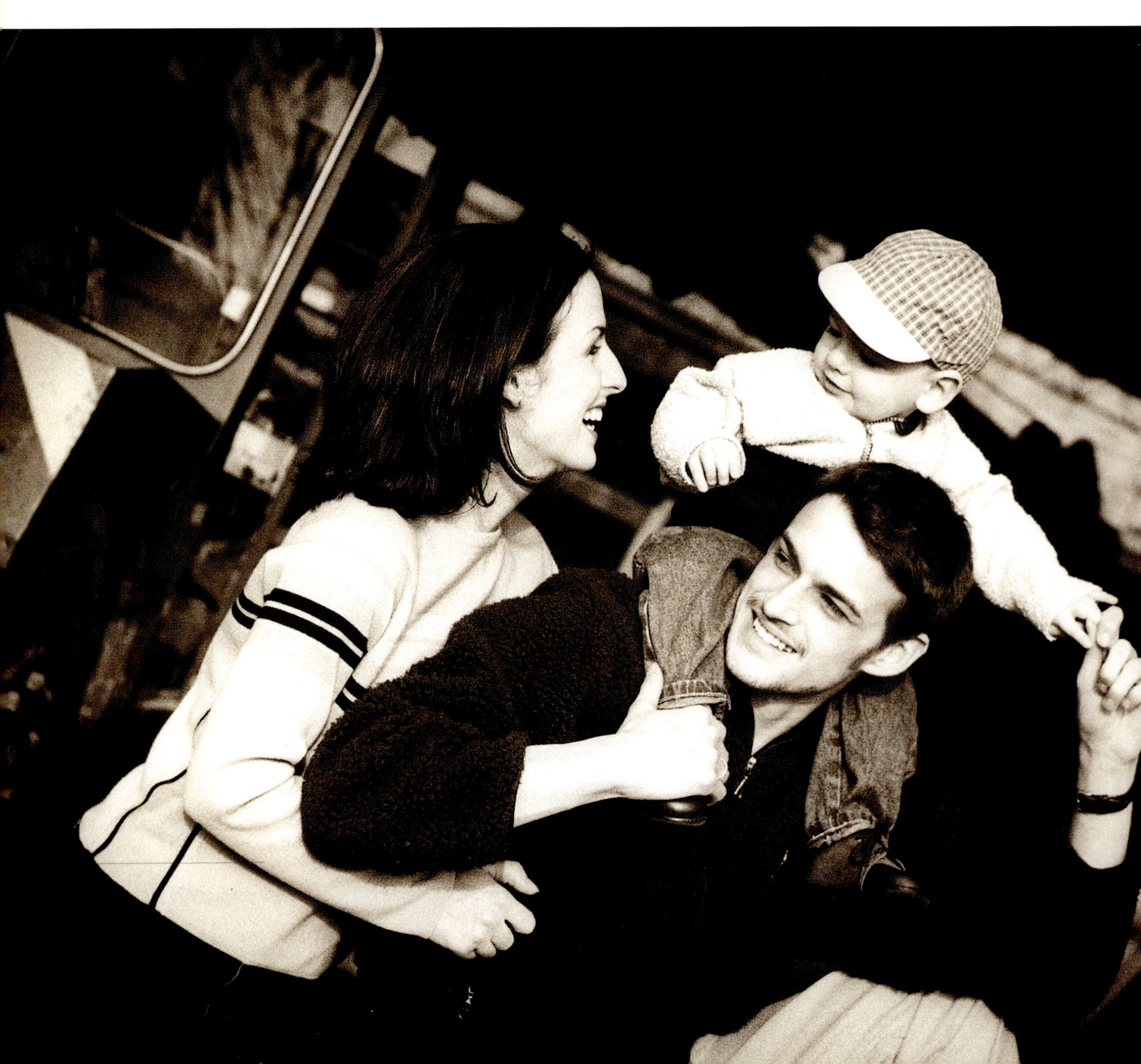

"A painting is never finished, it simply stops in interesting places."

Paul Gardner

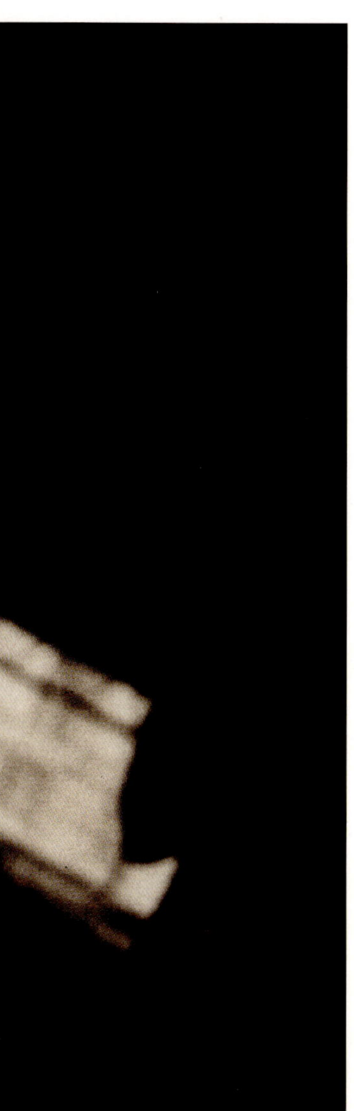

This couple had booked me to photograph their wedding, and when I'm doing this I like to set up a pre-wedding shoot three to four months beforehand so that they understand the concept of being photographed. It builds up their confidence and self-esteem and helps them to relax when the wedding day itself arrives, as they know that I don't work in an intimidating way.

I love to take pictures such as this on location and I look for interesting places, such as this factory that's near to my studio, and is full of shapes and textures which can be used in the background. It's fascinating to see people's reactions when they walk into a place like this: the "what are we doing here?" looks. They can't imagine that they will sit in front of a crane, and yet, with the right viewpoint and a subtle tilt of the lens, such a location will result in a picture like this.

This was a great setting because I was able to use natural light in a really interesting way. We used a building that was shaped a little like an aircraft hangar in that it had doors at each end that were open. By placing this couple and their little boy in the light by the door at the front of the building, I was also able to position myself so that I could feature the light from the door at the other end as an out-of-focus element. This led to an interesting highlight in this area of the picture.

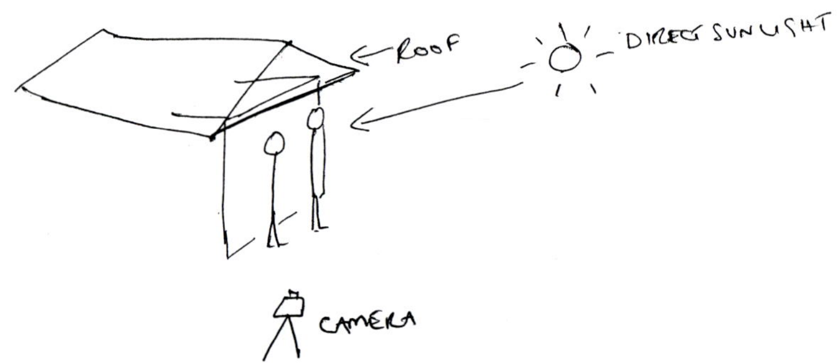

Outdoor lighting is ideal for contemporary lifestyle photography, as today's clients want pictures that are natural and simple. People tend to feel more comfortable and less intimidated outdoors, which adds to the relaxed look of the pictures. However, even daylight has to be very carefully controlled in order to achieve a flattering picture. Lighting from direct sunlight can often be harsh and unflattering, but when used in a controlled way it can create stunning images. When the sun is overhead, as here, if the subject was looking directly at the camera, harsh shadows would be created and this would cause the subject to squint in a very unflattering way. By asking this couple to face away from the camera, however, I was able to achieve this very effective result.

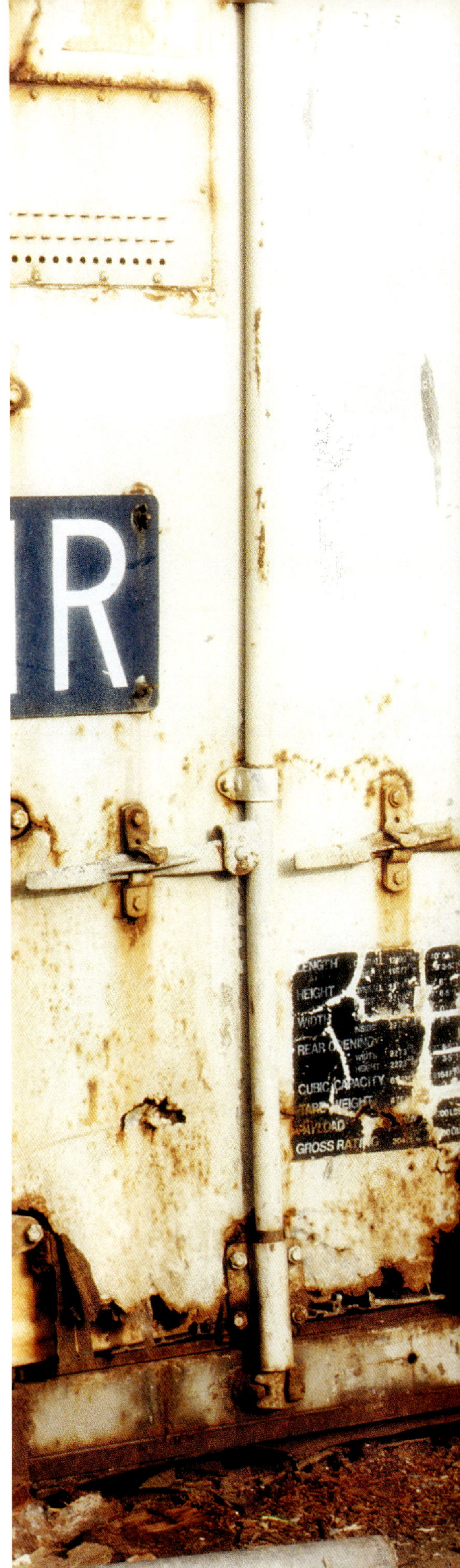

Some photographic rules are made to be broken, such as the one that dictates portraiture outside is best undertaken only at the start and end of the day, when the angle of the sun is low. This picture was taken at midday and yet, positioning the subjects looking away from the camera produces a result that is still flattering and well lit.

Mamiya RZ 67, 150mm soft focus lens, Fujifilm Provia 400, cross-processed. Exposure 1/500sec at f/11

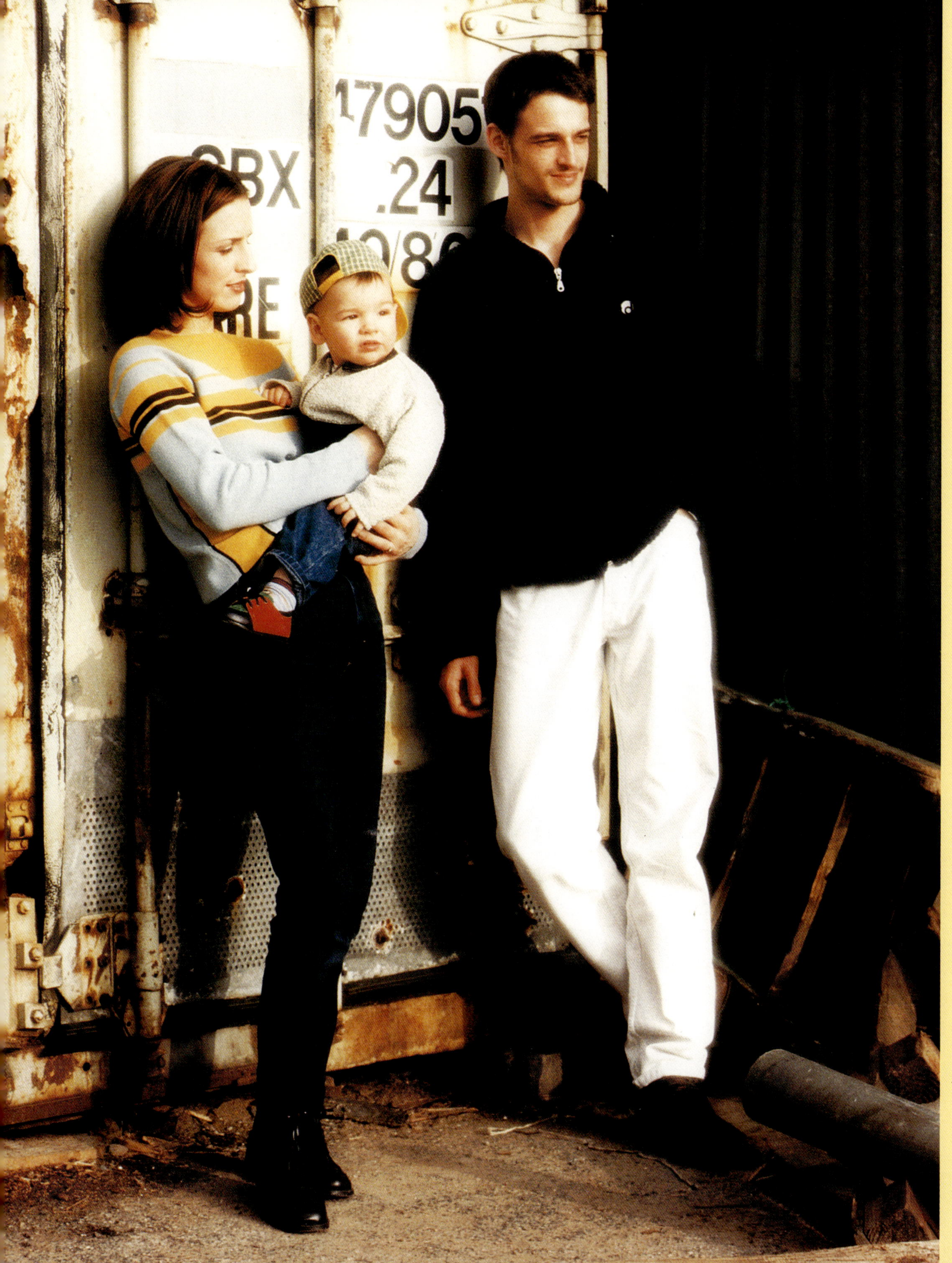

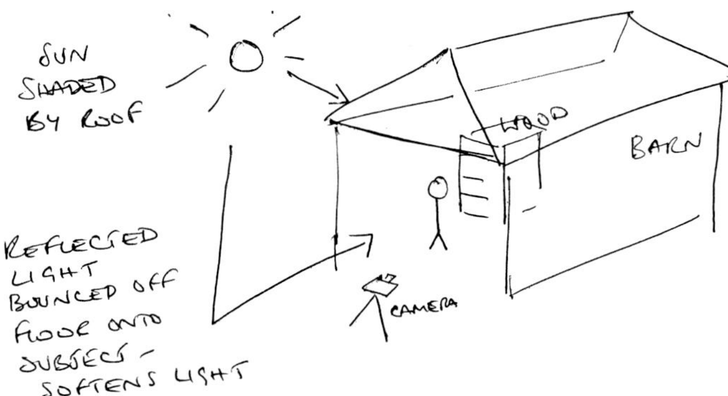

The most flattering way to deal with bright sunlight is to use top shade. By placing the subjects under some kind of natural shade, such as a porch roof or a tree, the light becomes softer over the face, but still maintains clarity and brightness from the reflected light of the sun (see picture below). Patches of light on the background or clothes often enhance the feeling of warmth and add depth to the picture.

The lighting for this picture is well balanced, even the area under the girl's hat that normally would have been in shade. It was simply a question of selecting the right lighting in the location: I positioned her in a space that was shaded by the roof of this building, and natural fill-in was provided by the light that was reflecting up from the floor in front of her.

Mamiya RZ 67, 150mm soft focus lens, Fujifilm Provia 400, cross-processed through C41 chemistry. Exposure 1/500sec at f/11

If it's not possible to find any top shade, ask your subject to move into an area where there's some shadow. The face is the important part of this picture to get correctly exposed, so take a reading from this area. Any highlight areas that are technically overexposed as a result will only add to the effect.

Canon EOS 5, 75–300mm lens, Fujifilm Neopan 1600. Exposure 1/250sec at f/5.6

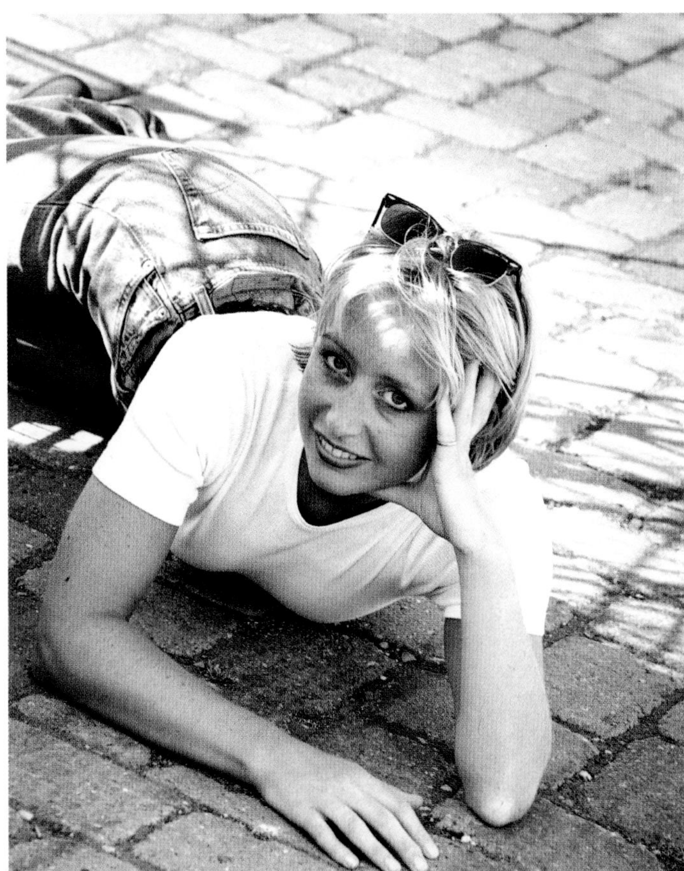

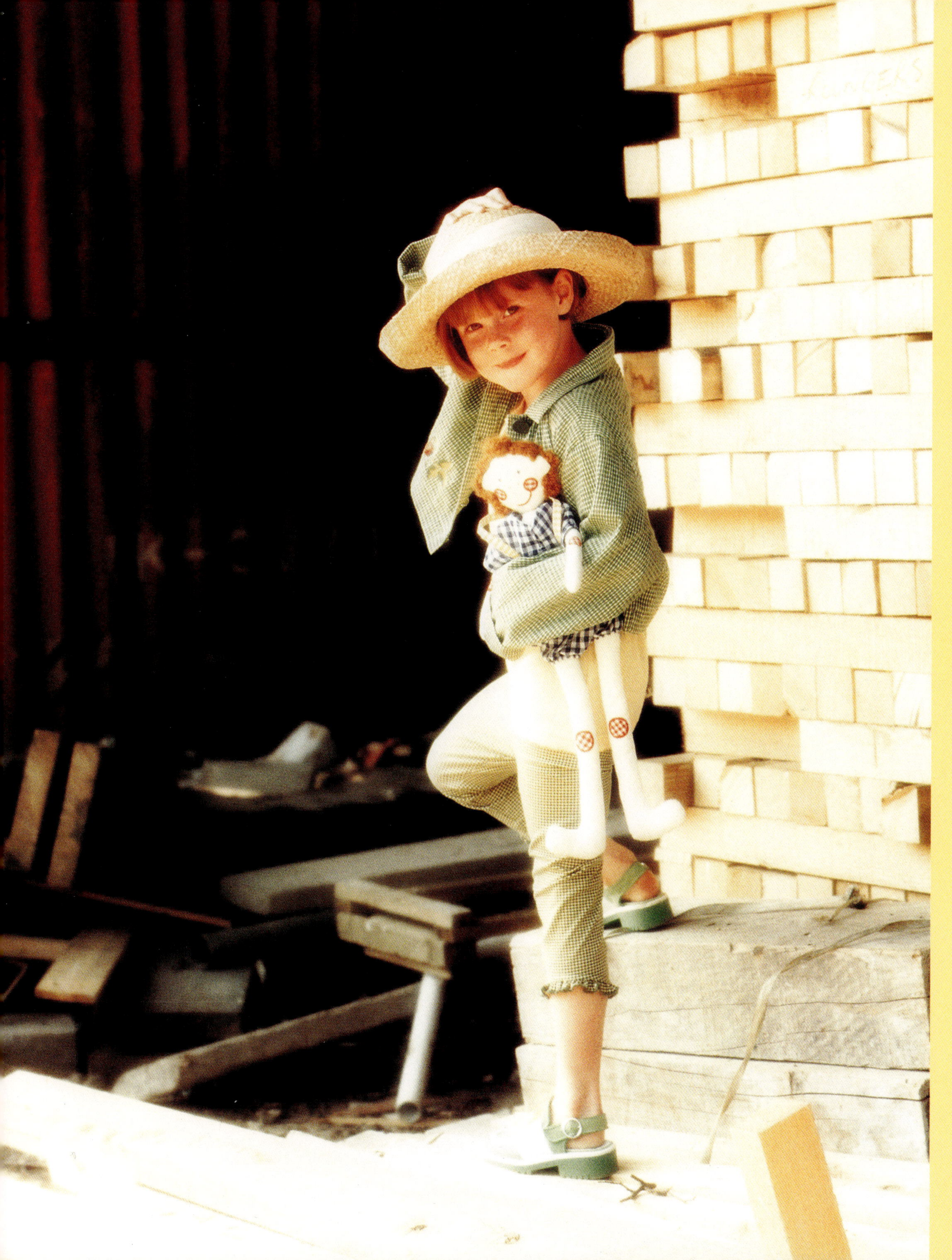

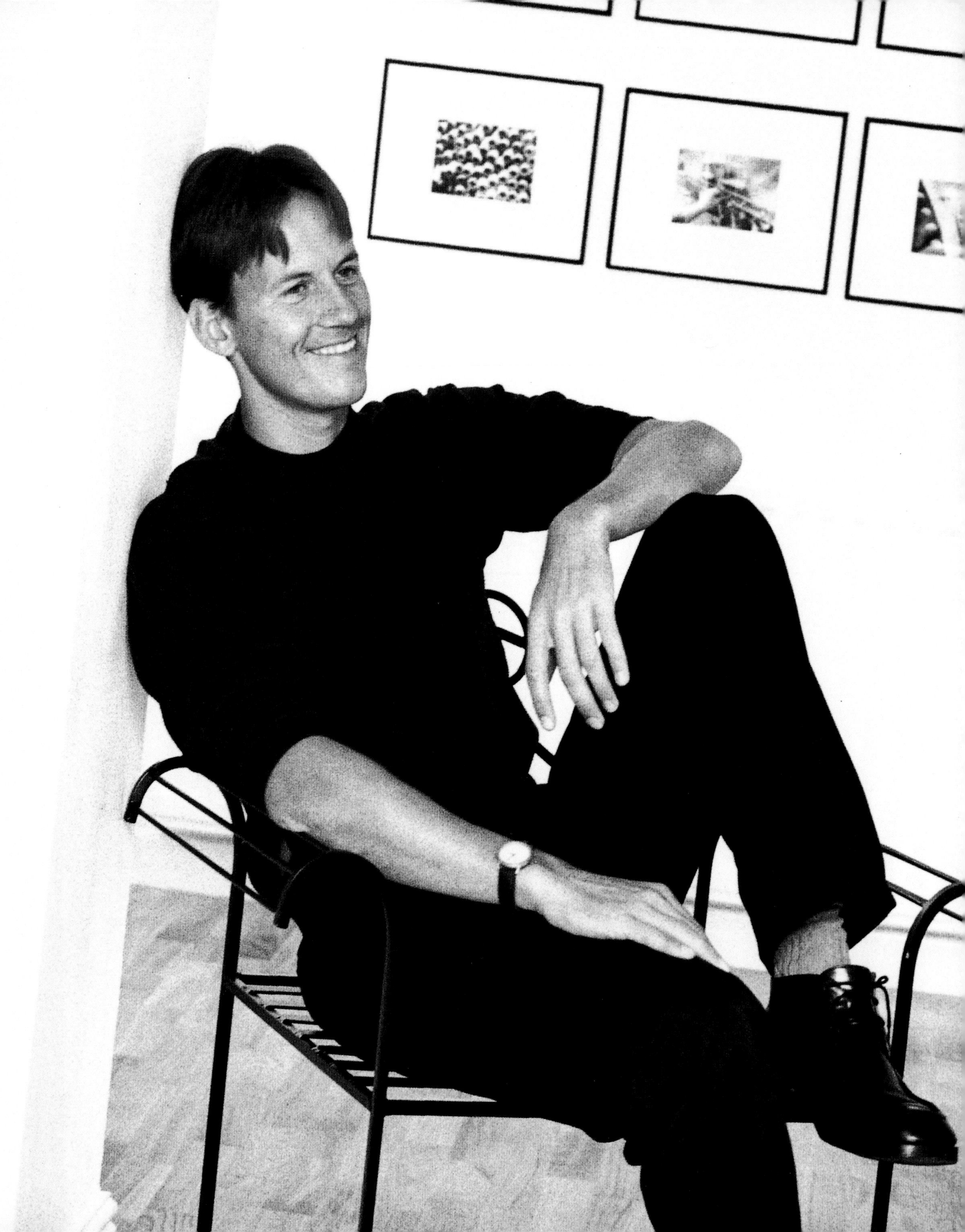

Many photographers imagine that once you venture into the studio, there is no alternative to using artificial light, but in fact the natural light that might enter the room through a window or a skylight can be just as effective if used carefully.

I also have a great aversion to fill-in flash, and never use it because I think it looks so artificial. I'm also reluctant to use reflectors because they tend to get in the way, although I will use one on occasions. I've tried to introduce natural reflection into my studio by painting the walls a neutral white, and this ensures that the maximum amount of natural light is spread around the room.

You must be careful, if you intend to shoot colour, to use only white on your walls. Light reflected from coloured walls will take on the colour, and will give your picture a cast. I also take care to position my subject well away from the window where the light is entering because, although this will mean that a longer exposure is required, it will even out the light that's falling on the face.

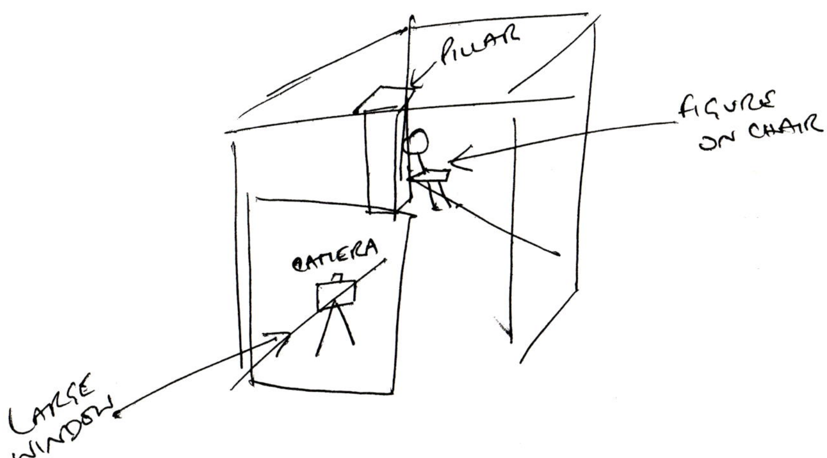

Although I had to use quite a slow shutter speed for this picture, it was still fast enough for the subject to be able to pose naturally. Modern emulsions can offer incredibly fast speed, and yet quality is still equivalent to that which you might have expected from a slow film just a few years ago.

Canon EOS 5, 75–300mm lens, Fujifilm Neopan 1600. Exposure 1/15sec at f/5.6

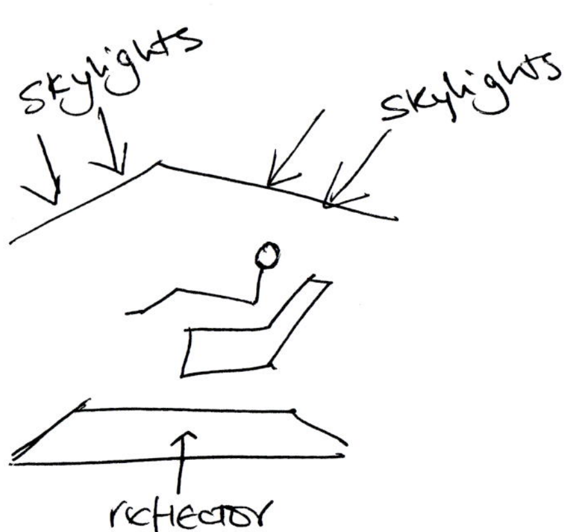

Overhead daylight, provided by a skylight or the glazed roof of a conservatory, can allow dramatic effects to be produced, enhancing not just the subject but the whole picture. I aim to keep the lighting in the area around the subject consistent, so that they have the chance to move around a little and relax without there being the need constantly to change things around and to interrupt the flow of the shoot. This is one of the major benefits of natural light: because you're not working with a bank of artificial lighting, you have the opportunity to see exactly what's going on, and to work with what you're being given. Often I'll work with the natural light exactly as it is, but here I did use a reflector on the floor in front of the chair to bounce some light back on to my subject. I've found small reflectors don't really throw back enough light when working with wider angles, so I use one called a Californian Sunburst which is six by four feet. Covered with gold and silver zig-zags, the light it throws back is very even and slightly warmed.

I find that I have to increase my exposure times to compensate for the fact that natural lighting has far less intensity than that provided by flash. Even so, I can usually work at around 1/15sec or above, which when I'm not trying to catch action is perfectly adequate. The pay-off is that the session is far more informal when natural light is used, and this is reflected by the way that my subjects react to the camera.

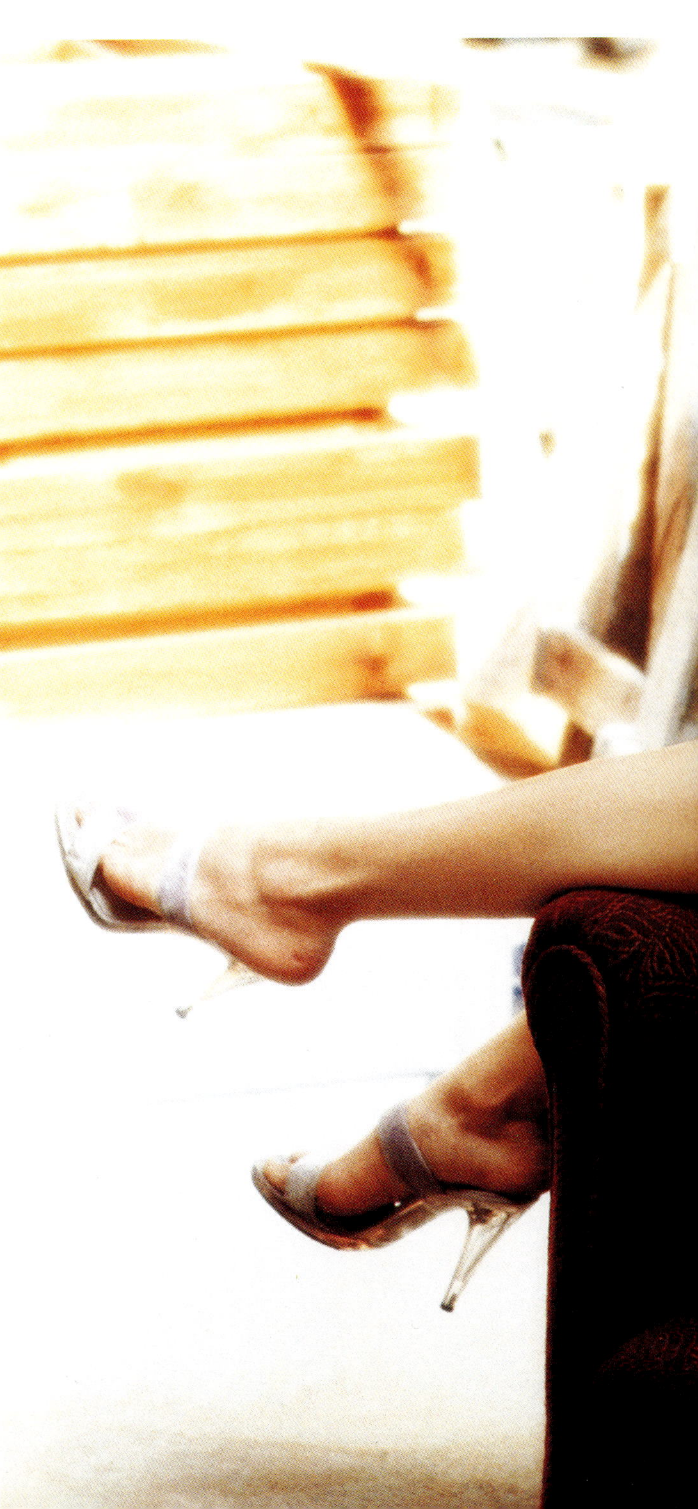

Chloe had booked a photo shoot to mark her 18th birthday. Before we started the picture session she went through make-up and had her hair styled, and was generally pampered to make her feel good. This helped to give her great confidence in herself before the camera ever appeared.

Mamiya RZ 67, 150mm soft focus lens, Fujifilm Provia 400. Exposure 1/15sec at f/5.6

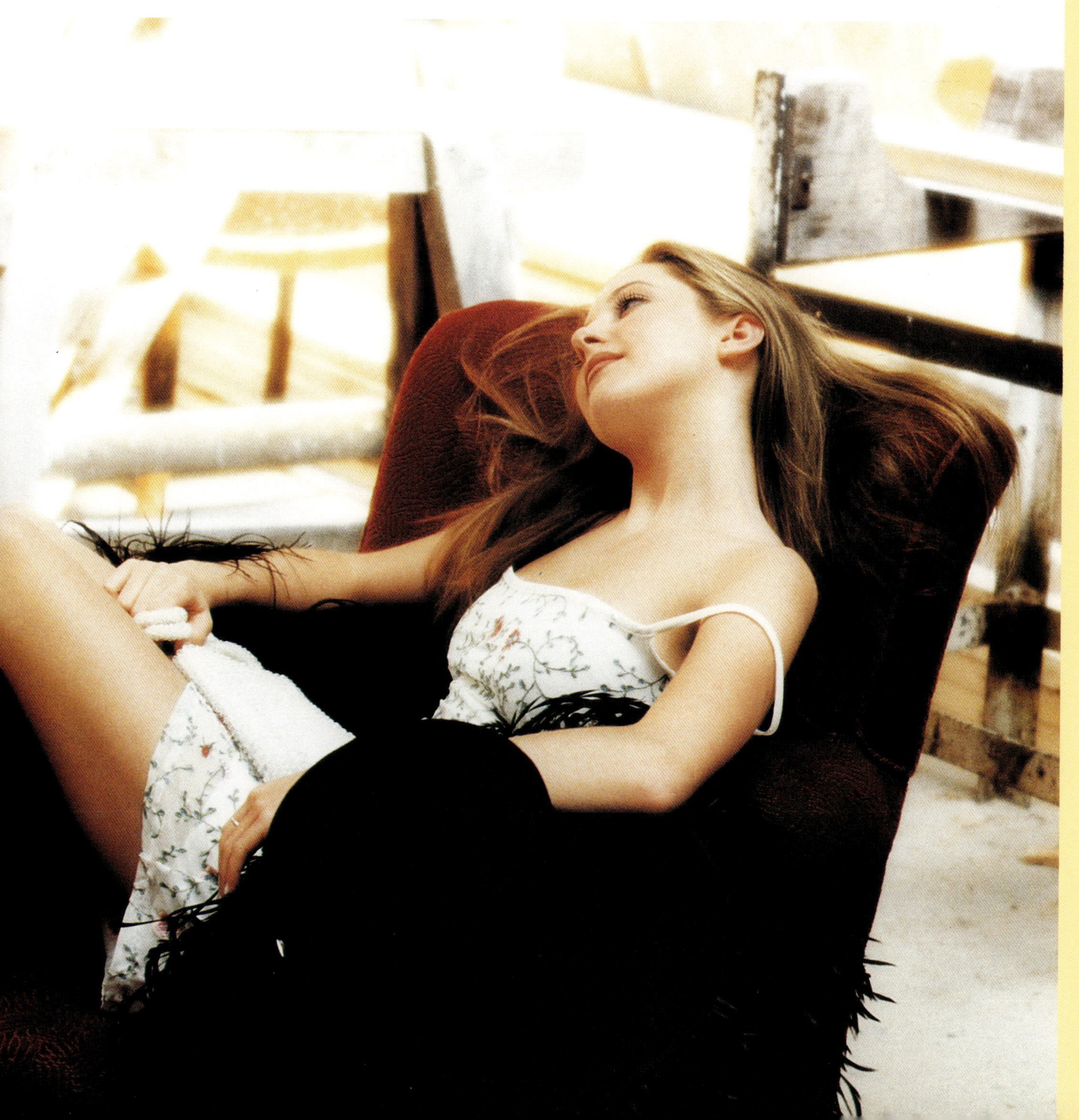

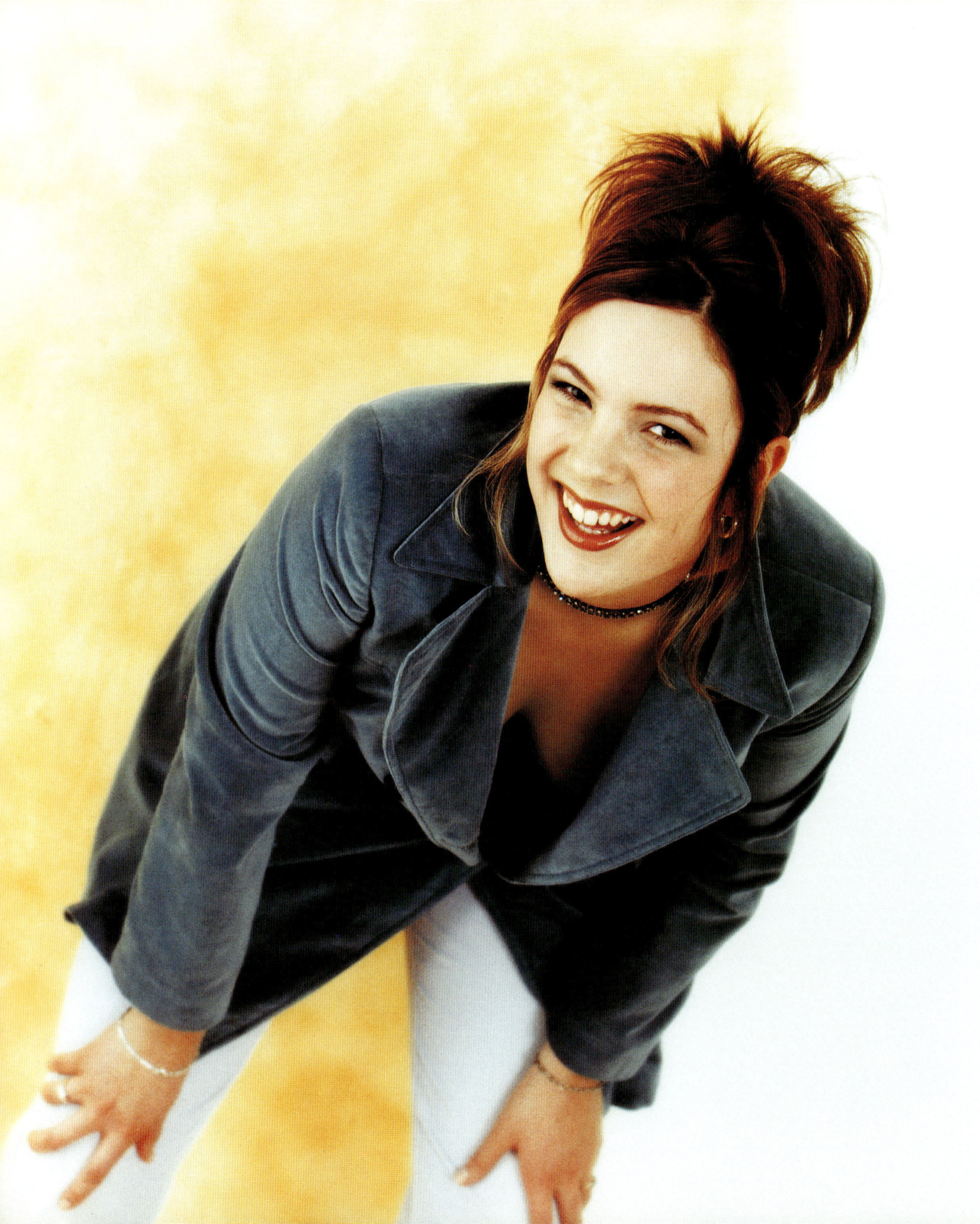

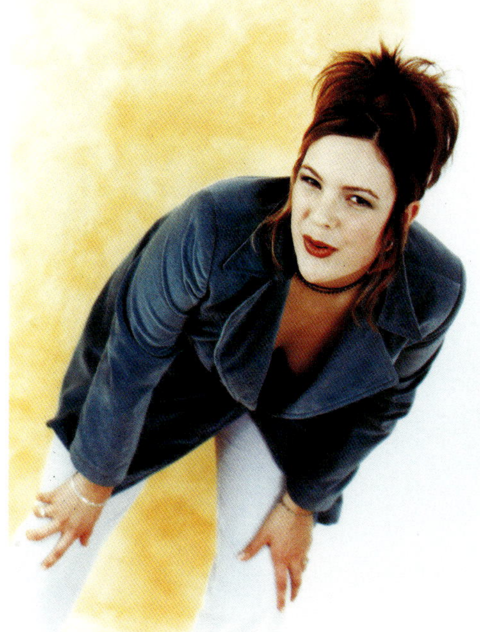

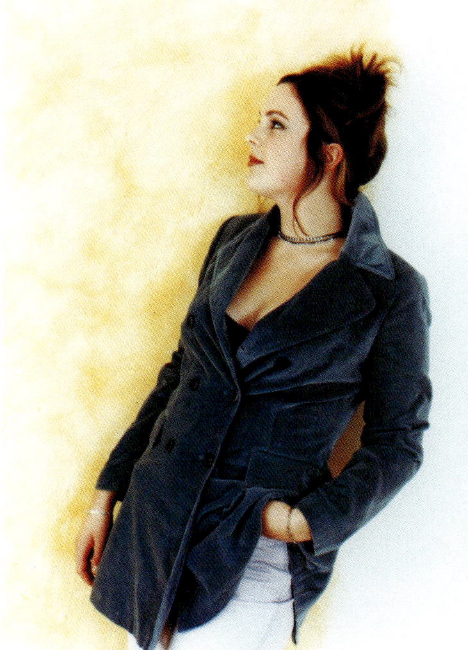

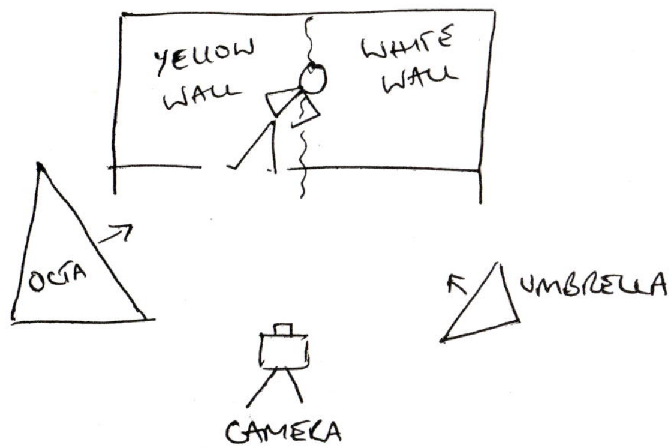

Studio lighting by its very nature can be intimidating to someone who is not used to being photographed, and is often perceived as creating a formal and artificial environment.

I try to make the studio as friendly and welcoming as possible by setting up lighting that is simple and unobtrusive. This will remain constant throughout the shoot so that I don't have to take time out from talking to the subject to change lights around and to check exposures. Instead I concentrate on the expressions I'm getting and making sure my subject is enjoying the session.

The main light I use is a very large softbox, an Octa, in combination with an Elinchrom 500. With a diameter of around five feet, the Octa is capable of throwing out a very consistent light over a large area. To soften the shadows I use a fill light, an Elinchrom 250, which is bounced back on to the set from an umbrella, ensuring that this light, too, is soft and even. The white walls of my studio also contribute to the even nature of the lighting I'm providing, giving me a wide area within which to work. This means that my subject has the freedom to move around instead of having to stay rooted to one point; this arrangement allows great flexibility too. If any shadows do find their way on to the background, this simply serves to add depth to the picture.

Because my lighting is so consistent, I find that I can work quickly and can produce pictures that have a very different feel while maintaining my camera position. This gives me a good variety of shots from a single session.

Mamiya RZ 67, 150mm soft focus lens, Fujifilm Provia 400. Exposure 1/30sec at f/5.6

"Go shopping! Look at window displays, furnishings and kitchen utensils to ascertain the colours and shapes that are influencing the latest generation."

Studio backgrounds need careful planning to create the right mood and atmosphere. The background should not take over, but rather complement the subject.

Historically, studio photographers used canvas backgrounds depicting clouds, outdoor scenes, library books etc., often because the Victorians saw this as a way of displaying wealth. Now we need to create images that remind us of our way of life today. Many current looks are dictated by trends in the media – ideas taken from magazines, CDs and videos can all be used to create contemporary pictures.

Whilst most photographs have traditionally been rectangular in shape, the trend is now towards square pictures, probably influenced by the shape of CD covers.

The board that I used against the background helped to break up the uniform colour, and saved the image from being boring. For added impact I placed my subject so that her head was seen against the light tone of the board, and then tilted the camera slightly to create some interesting angles.

Hasselblad, 50mm lens, Fuji Astia 100 slide film, cross-processed through C41 chemistry. Elinchrom 500 with Octa softbox and Elinchrom 250 with white umbrella. Exposure 1/30sec at f/5.6

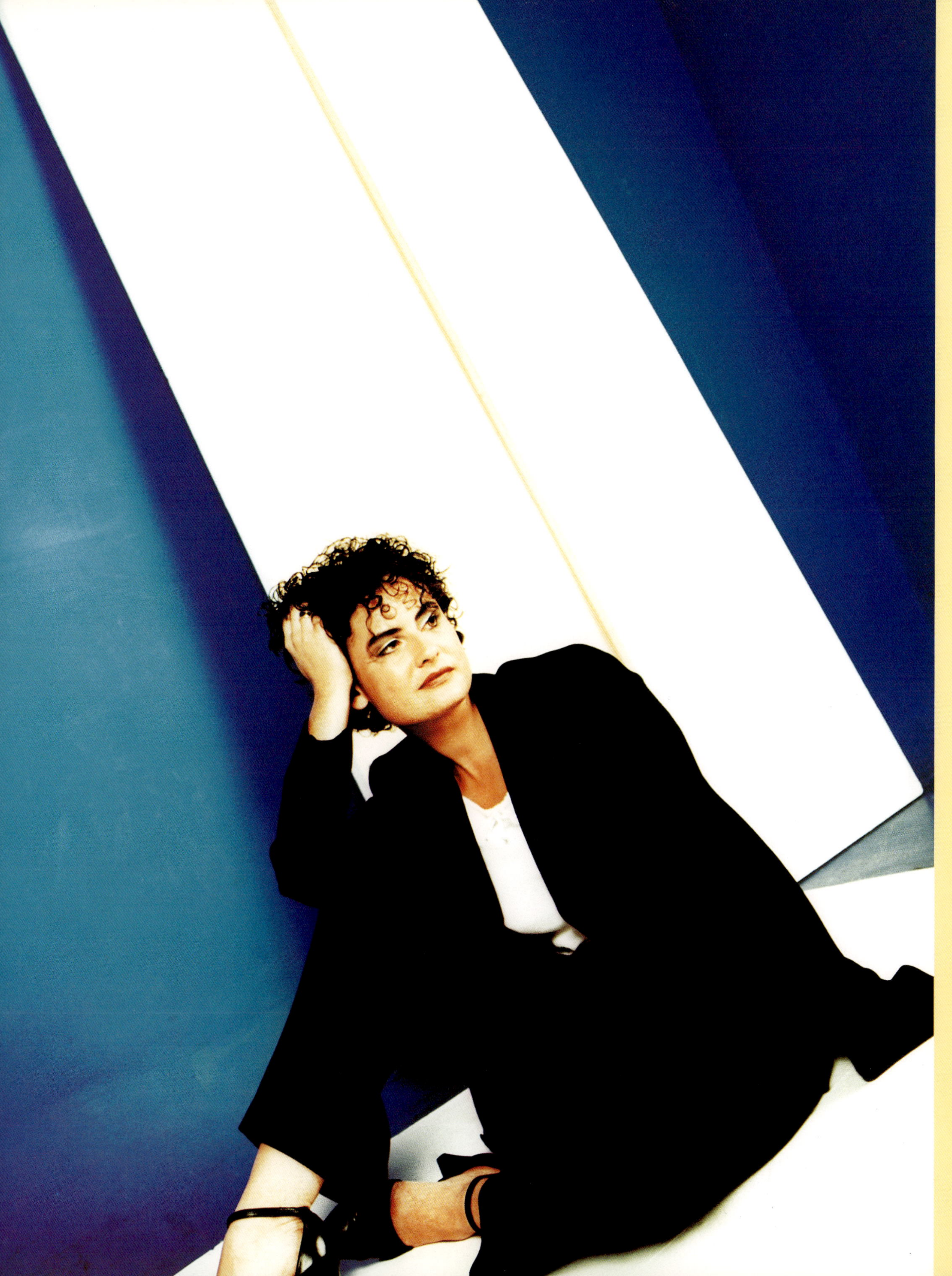

alternative backgrounds – studio

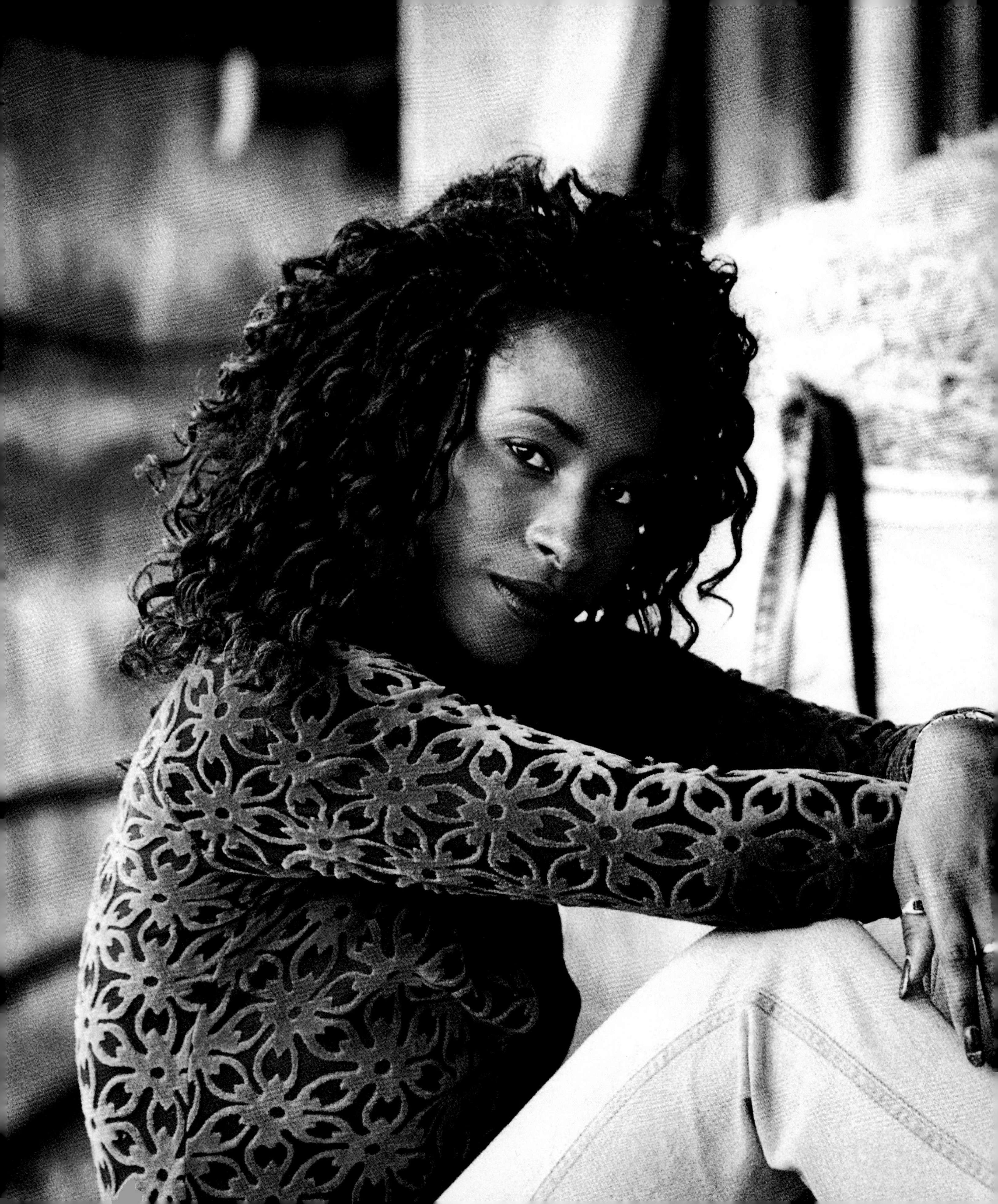

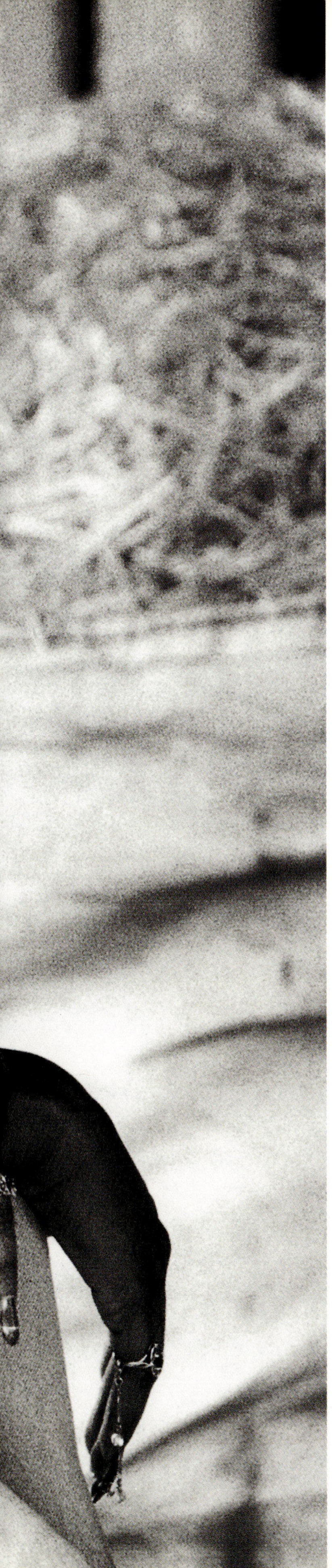

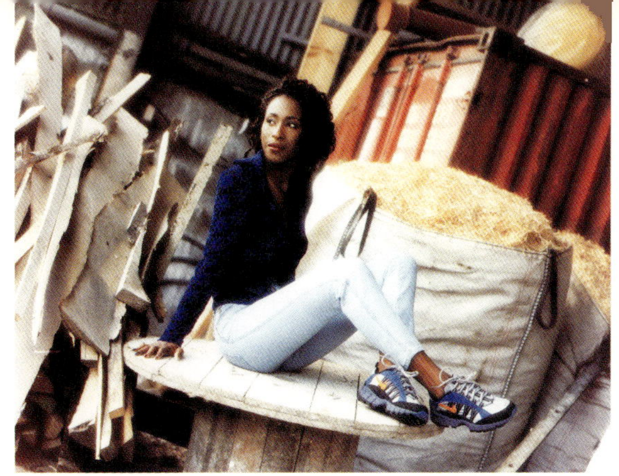

There is almost nothing that cannot be used in a picture. Here the background is made up of rubbish and items that might individually be seen as unacceptable. However, if we look at the background as nothing more than a series of shapes and textures, rather than letting the reality of what's really there cloud our vision, then it's possible to see the potential in virtually everything.

Here I used a 75–300mm zoom to move in closer to my subject. The natural tendency of the telephoto to compress perspective has brought up the shapes behind her, while the characteristic narrow depth of field that a long lens provides ensured that it was soft enough to be unrecognisable. The colour version of the picture gives more away.

Here you can see that what's actually behind my subject are piles of wood shavings and broken pieces of plasterboard, while the girl herself is sitting on a wooden cable container. The image still works, because it's so up-front that it's clear the surroundings were intentional, while the look of the girl is confident and she's clearly relaxed.

Same situation, two very different final results, and that's what it's possible to achieve if you think clearly about what a particular background can offer you. It took very little time to move between these two looks, and I was able to leave my subject undisturbed in her position while I changed cameras.

Colour: Mamiya RZ 67, 150mm soft focus lens, Fujifilm Provia 400, cross-processed through C41 chemistry. Exposure 1/60sec at f/5.6

Black and white: Canon EOS 5, long end of a 75–300mm zoom, Fujifilm Neopan 1600. Exposure 1/250sec at f/5.6

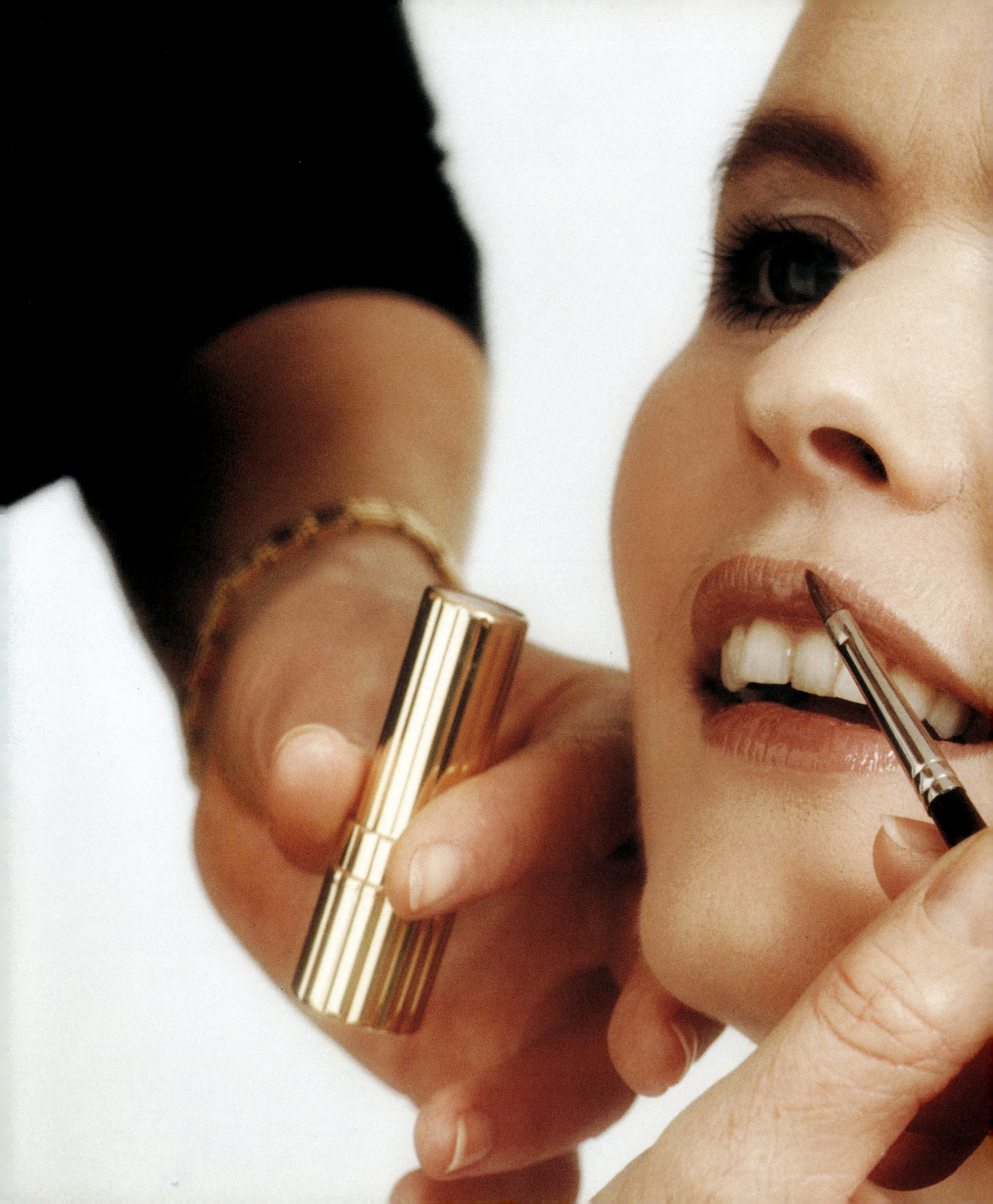

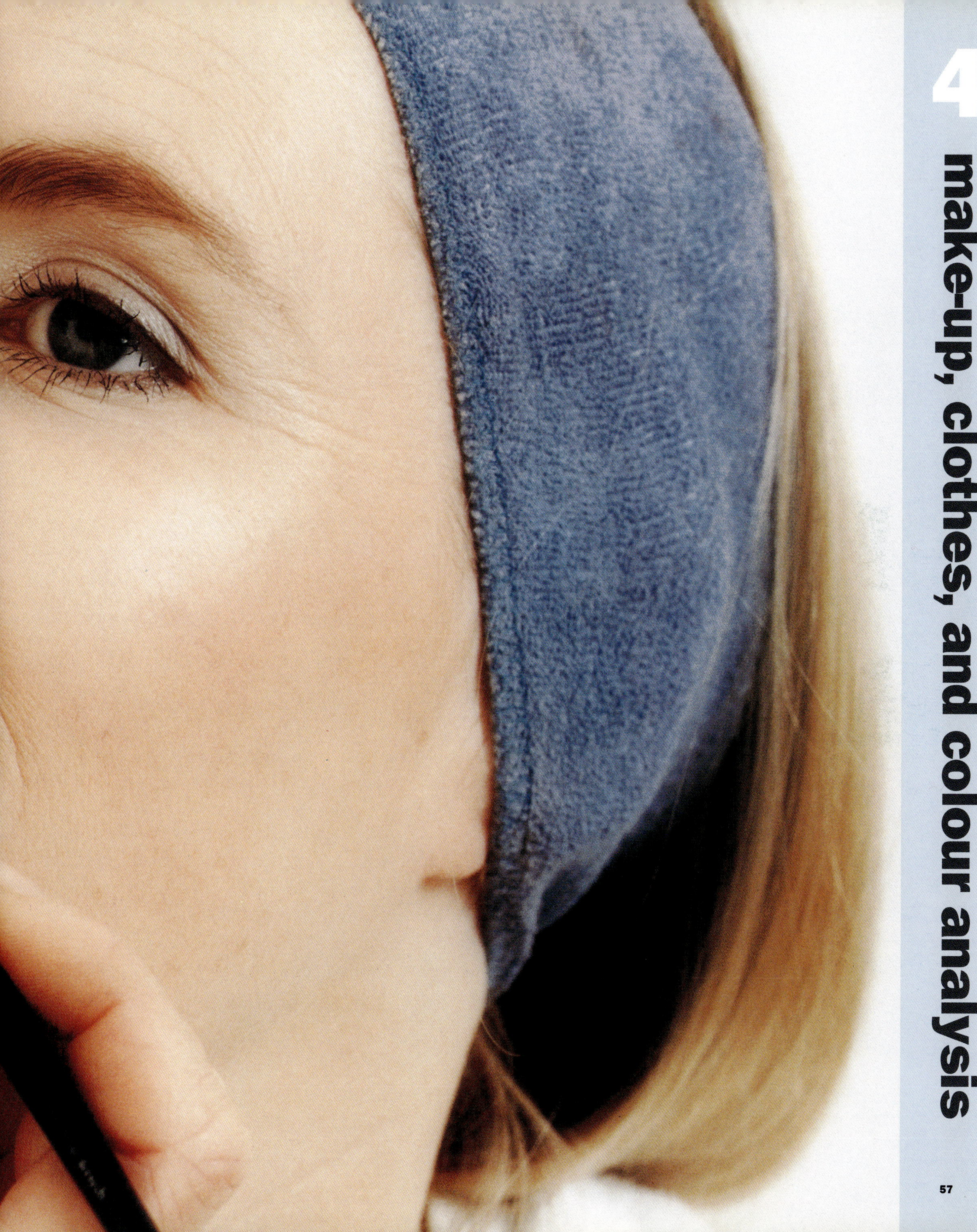

4 make-up, clothes, and colour analysis

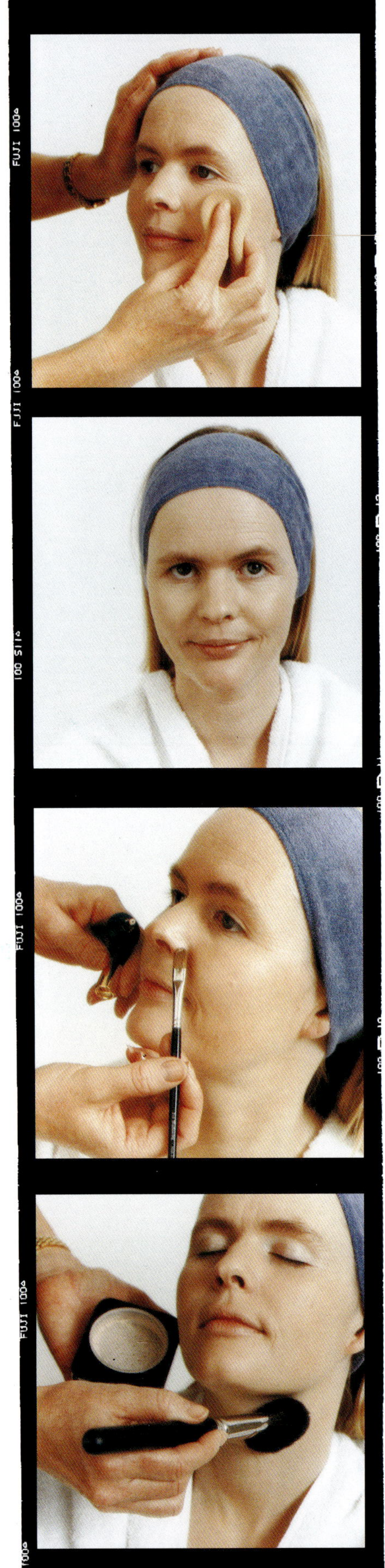

Hilary has arrived in the studio and without any make-up applied, I take a "before" picture of her. This is the kind of snapshot people usually hate of themselves, because most snapshots are taken in unflattering positions with no effort to enhance the subject's best features.

Involving a make-up artist in the shoot makes an enormous difference to the way that a subject feels about themselves. It could, in theory, be done in 15 minutes, but we make it last between 45 minutes and an hour simply because this is the ideal time to talk to the subject, to reassure them about the way they look and to make them feel pampered and relaxed. By the time I'm ready to start shooting, Hilary will look special and feel really good about herself, and that's exactly the frame of mind I want her to be in so that she feels confident in front of the camera.

9.30a.m. Hilary's face has been cleansed ready to start her make-up. The foundation is applied very lightly over the neck and face using a sponge.

Foundation evens out the skin tones, and acts as a base for the rest of the make-up.

9.40a.m. After applying foundation, Lucinda "retouches" any darker areas with a concealer to hide any problem areas such as broken veins, spots etc.

She then applies a matt translucent powder over the whole area to alleviate shine from the foundation, which would otherwise be unflattering under studio lighting.

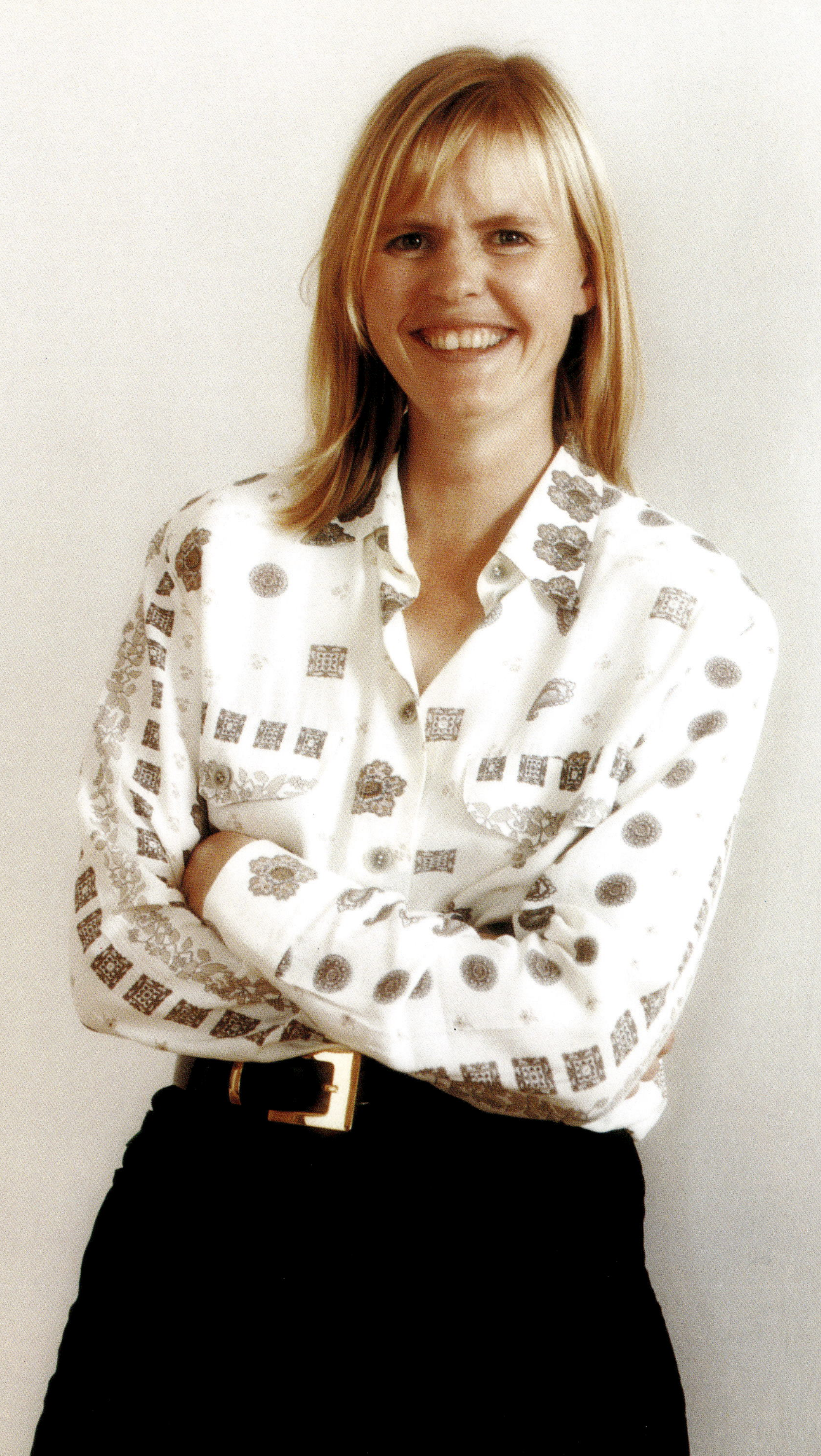

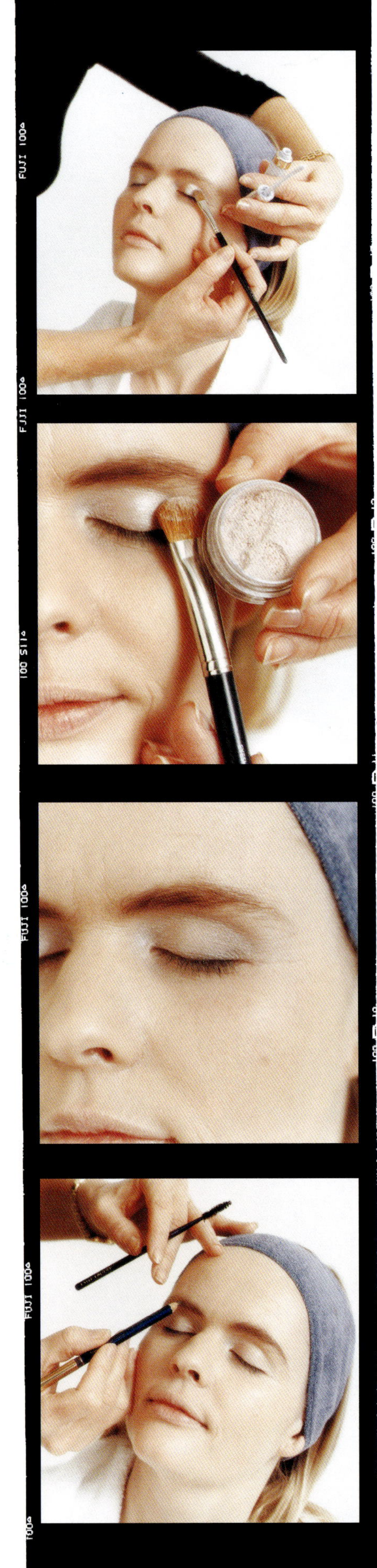

I've mentioned already that I always start the session with the most formal look, and this is the way that I began with Hilary. As the session progressed, I knew that she would become more relaxed and happy about being in front of the camera, and this would suit more closely the look that I was after as her clothes and appearance became more casual.

9.50a.m. Eyelid foundation helps to create a smooth base for the eyeshadow.

A light pink eyeshadow is applied as a base colour, followed by a darker grey eyeshadow on the outer area of the eye, which is then blended subtly.

A soft brown eye pencil is used to define the eyebrows, which will enlarge the eye area.

Positioning is very important; turning sideways on to the camera is more flattering than facing it. The film has been overexposed to lose the detail in the skin, which most women do not want to see!

Mamiya RZ 67, 150mm soft focus lens, Fujifilm Superia 100. Lighting from Octa softbox and umbrella fill. Exposure 1/30sec at f/5.6

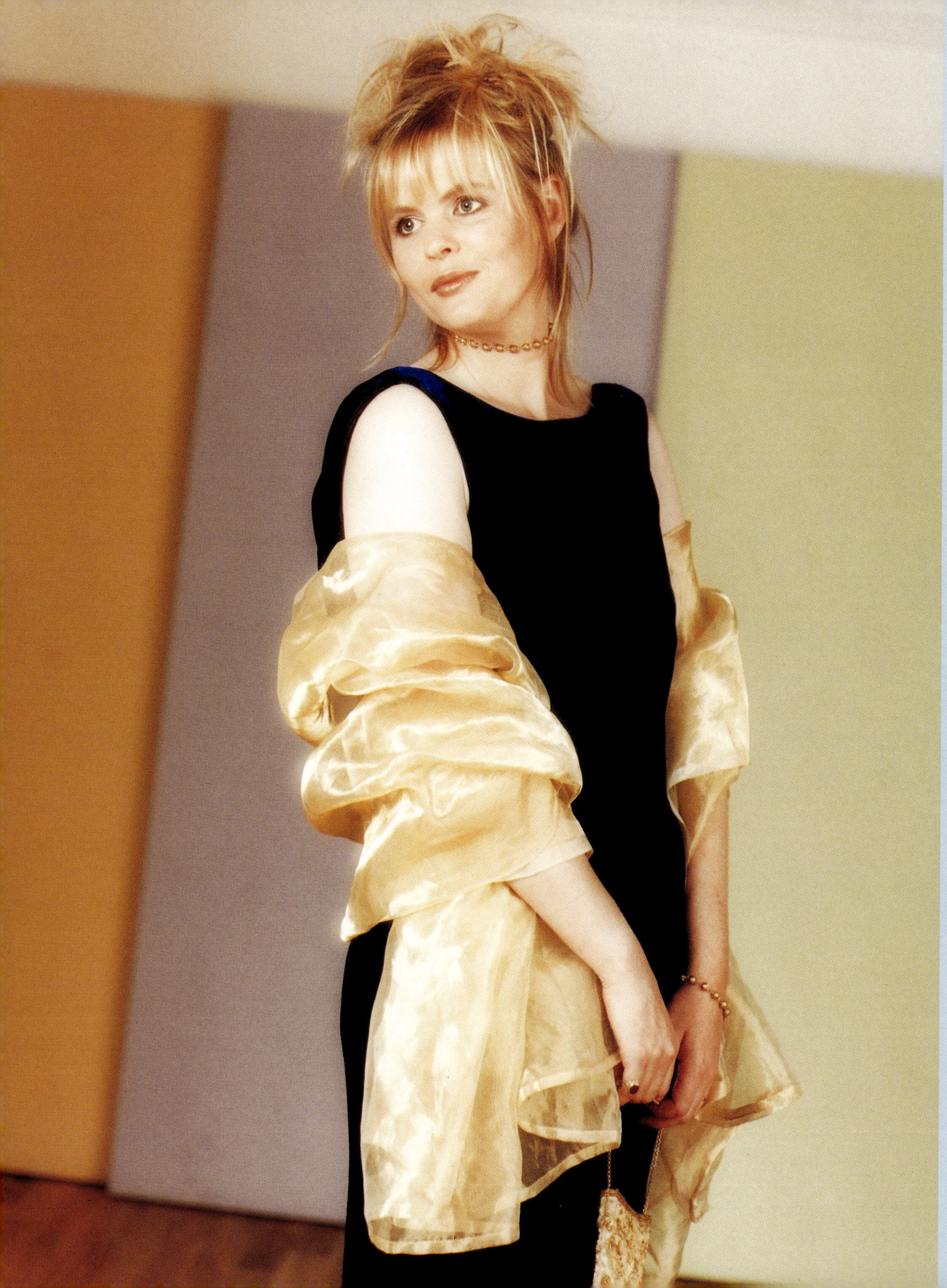

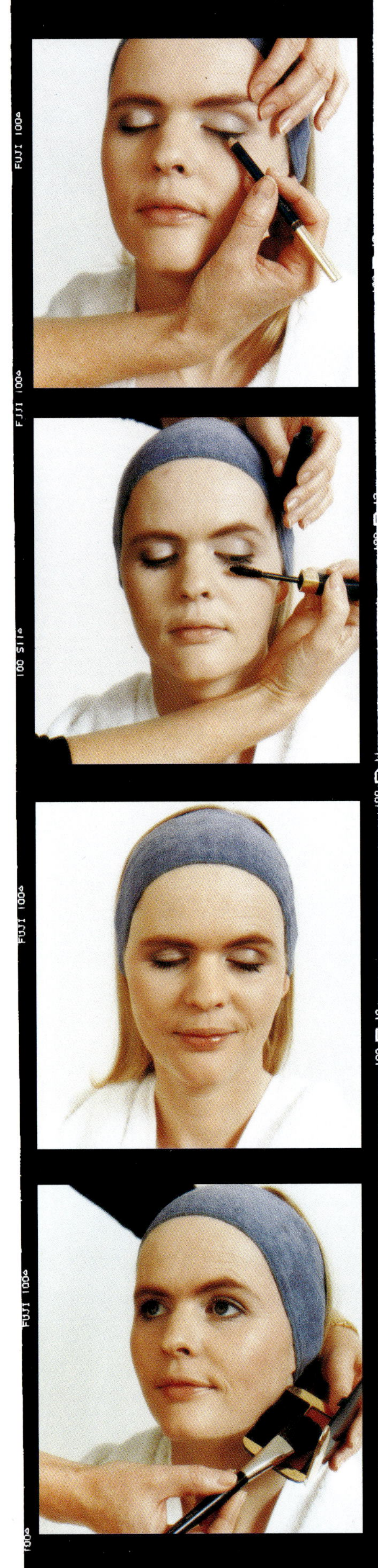

Hilary wore a long top that was the same colour as her skirt, and the combination of the two items helped to stretch her figure and to make her look taller.

Canon EOS 5, 75–300mm zoom, Fujifilm Neopan 1600. Lighting from the modelling lights of two Elinchrom flash heads. Exposure 1/30sec at f/5.6

10.00a.m. Soft brown eye-liner is applied to the outer edge of the eyelid to define the shape of the eye. Mascara is used to define and lengthen the eyelashes.

Blusher is applied to emphasise Hilary's cheek-bones and enhance her naturally good bone structure.

Very few people have perfect figures, and when I'm shooting clients in my studio I often have to work a little to make sure that their best features are emphasised while those that are not so good are disguised. After all, I want them to be happy with the results, and I think it's very important that whoever I'm shooting looks like themselves but also feels like a model.

Long, flowing clothes, for example, can hide the shape of hips, while a shorter top will emphasise that feature. Long jumpers will suggest a more slender figure, and can make a person look taller. I always ask people to bring a bigger selection of clothes with them than we're likely to need, and this gives me an opportunity to select things that I feel will help a person to look their best.

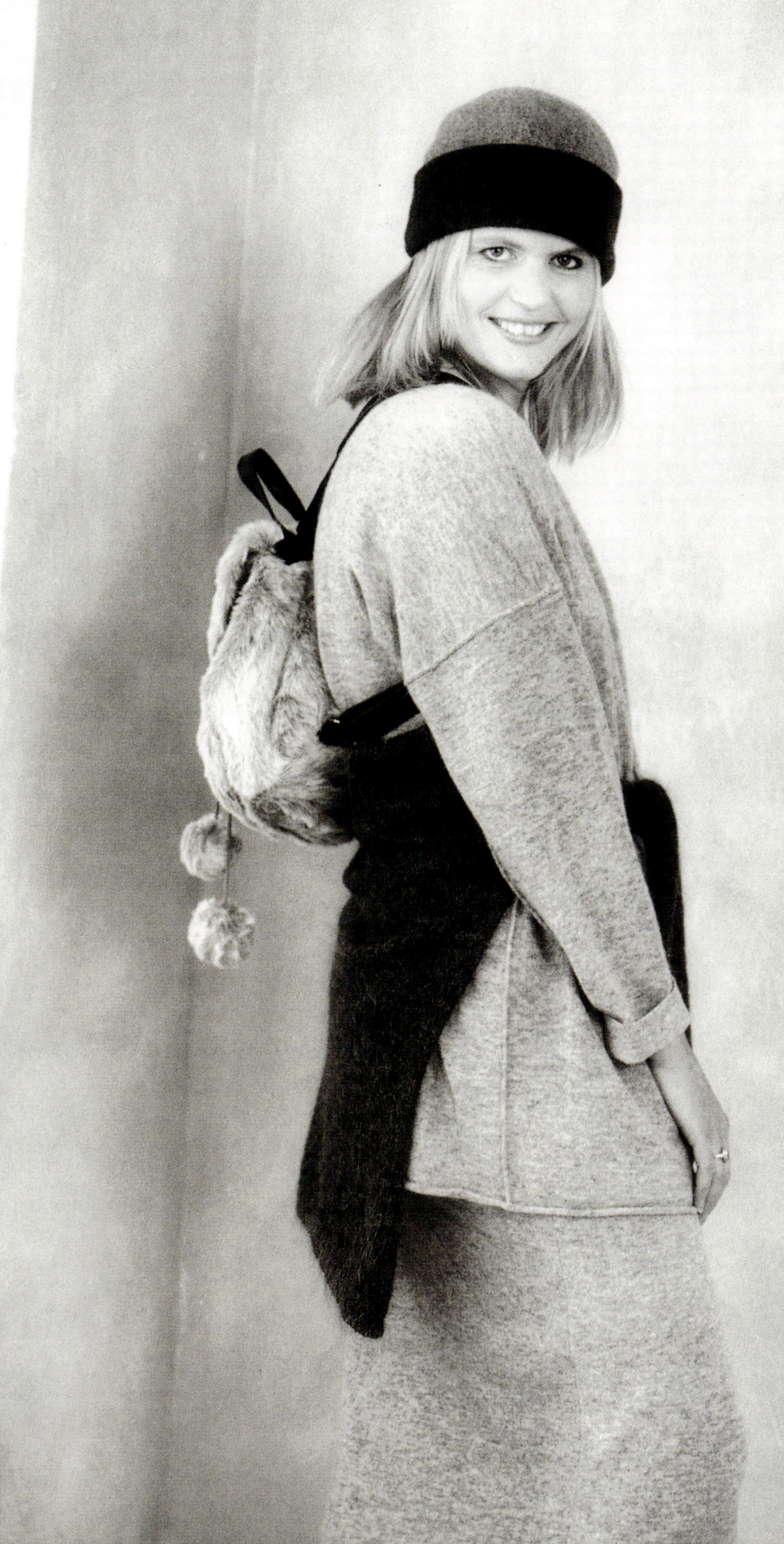

emphasising the best features

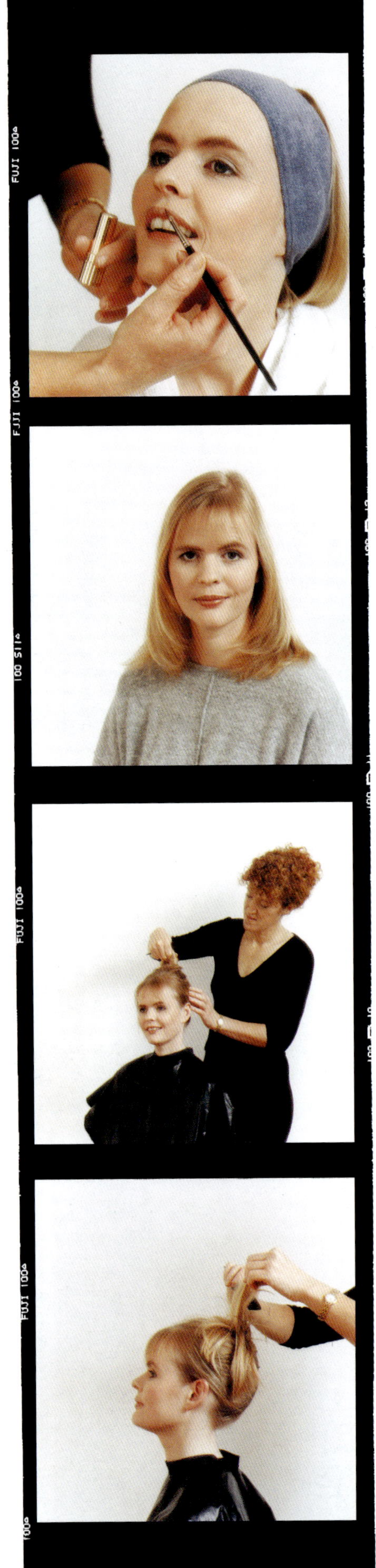

With long hair, I always start the shoot with the most difficult hairstyle as it is easier to take the hair down throughout the shoot, rather than put it up. The style here has been designed to be changed quickly and easily into other less formal styles, so that there is as little interruption to the shoot as possible.

Canon EOS 5, 75–300mm zoom, Fujifilm Neopan 1600. Lighting from the modelling lights of the two Elinchrom flash heads. Exposure 1/30sec at f/5.6

10.10a.m. The lipstick is applied using a lip brush to define the lip shape.

The make-up is now complete, and the client by now should feel happy and relaxed, and ready to face the camera. She will have seen the look coming together, and will know that she's looking beautiful, and this is an essential part of the day. Hair styling comes next and since the formal look is shot first, this is the style that will be worked on first and takes about 15 minutes to complete. As the session progresses and the approach progressively becomes more relaxed, the hair will be reworked, so that by the time the final set of pictures is being taken, the look will be a more natural one.

10.15a.m. Styling the hair for the first look, by twisting it up.

Backcombing the ends of the hair allows it to stand up on end giving height to the style.

10.30a.m. Ready to go!

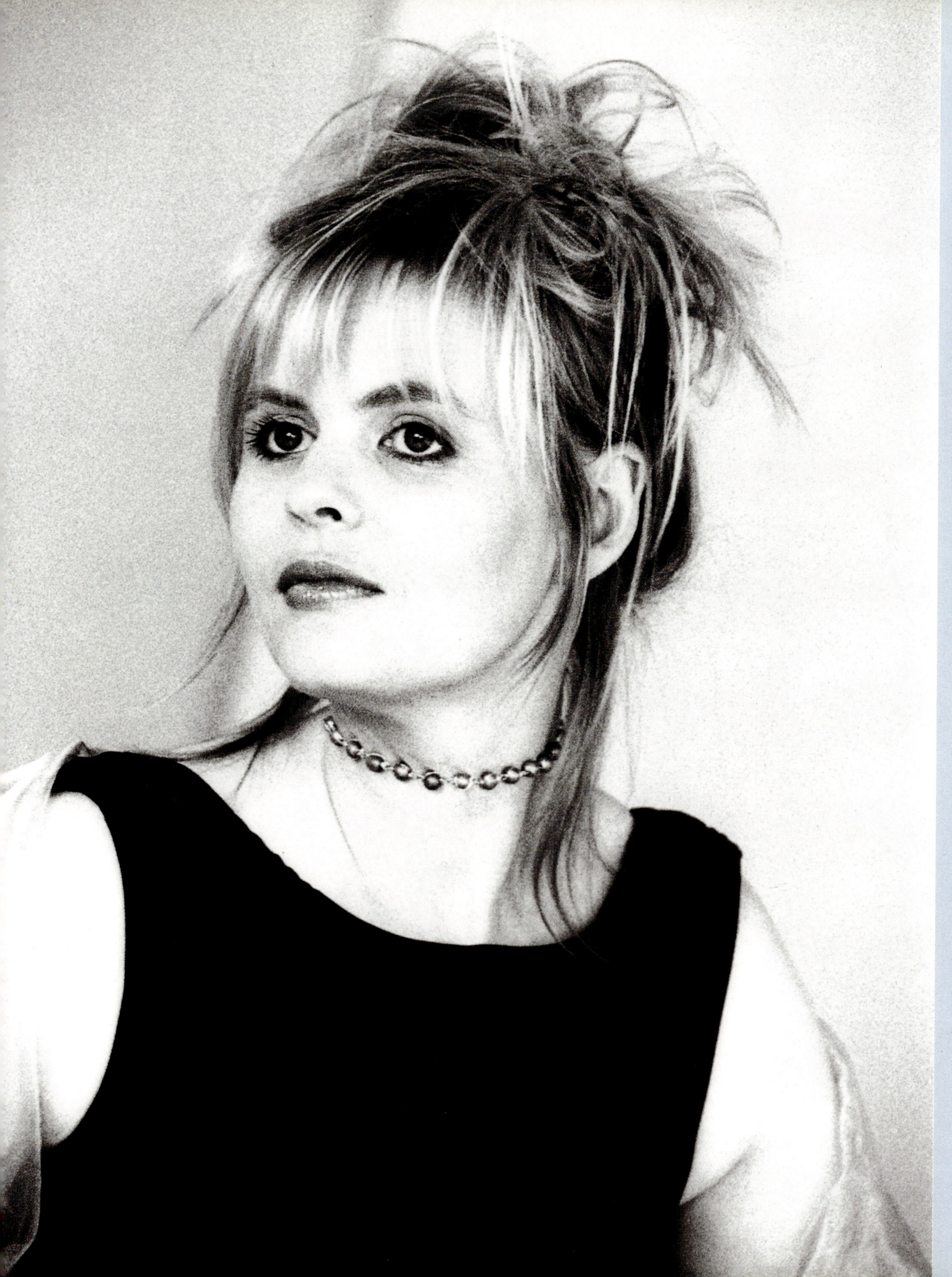

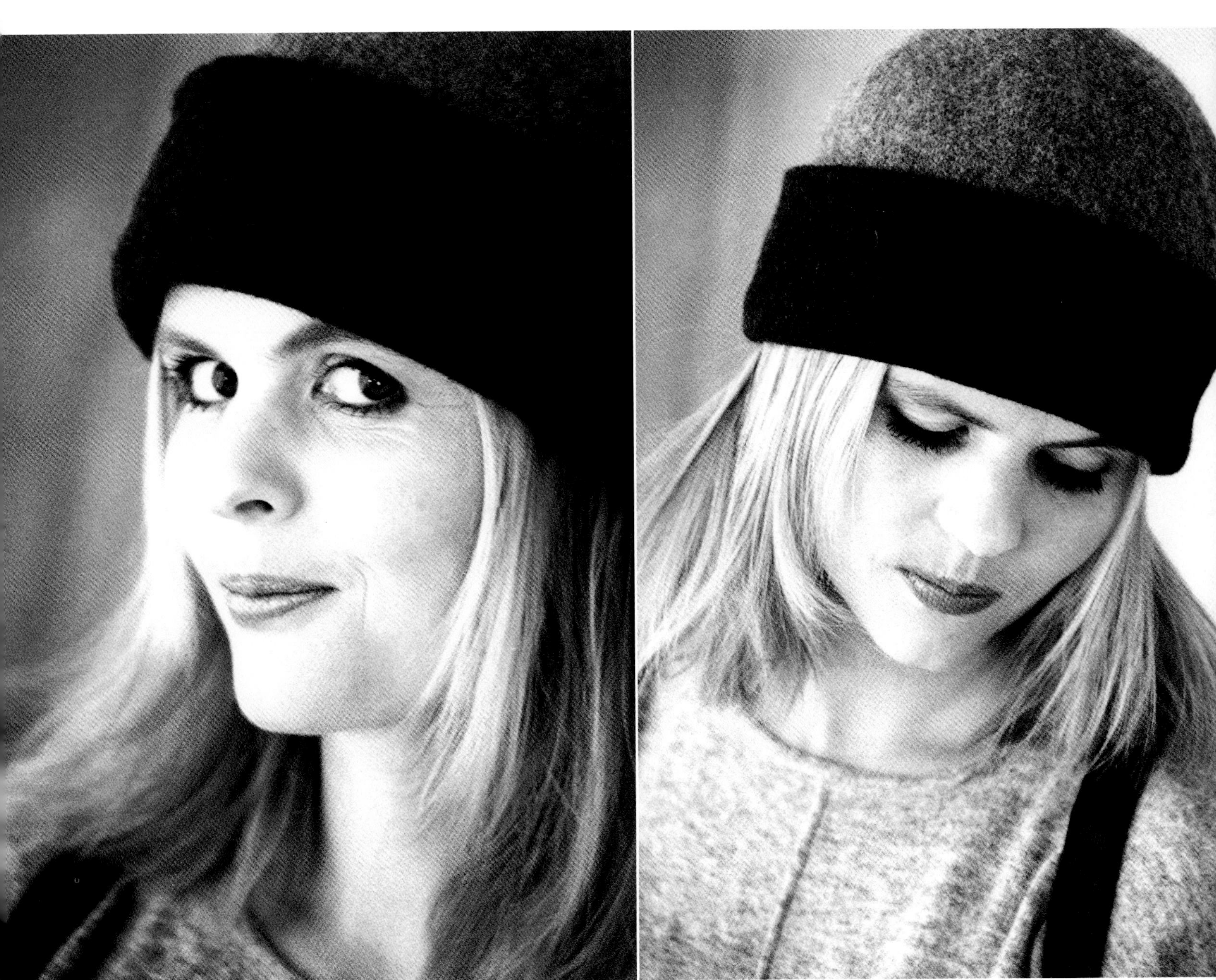

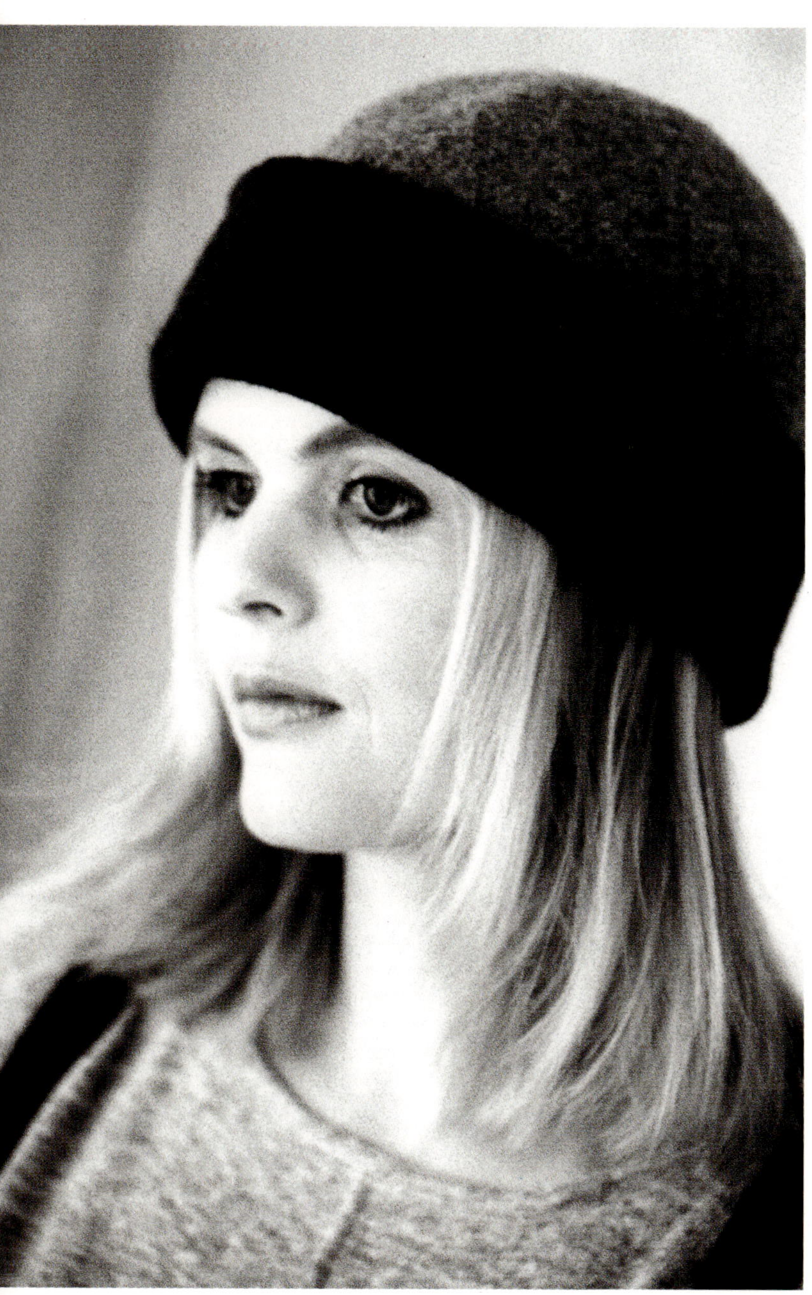

For the more casual photos I used the 35mm camera and zoom lens, and very quickly took a sequence of very informal pictures. Invariably, despite all the quality that a medium-format can offer, these are the pictures that the subject will like the best, because these are the photographs that show them as they really are.

Canon EOS 5, 75–300mm zoom, Fujifilm Neopan 1600. Lighting from the modelling lights of two Elinchrom flash heads. Exposure 1/30sec at f/5.6

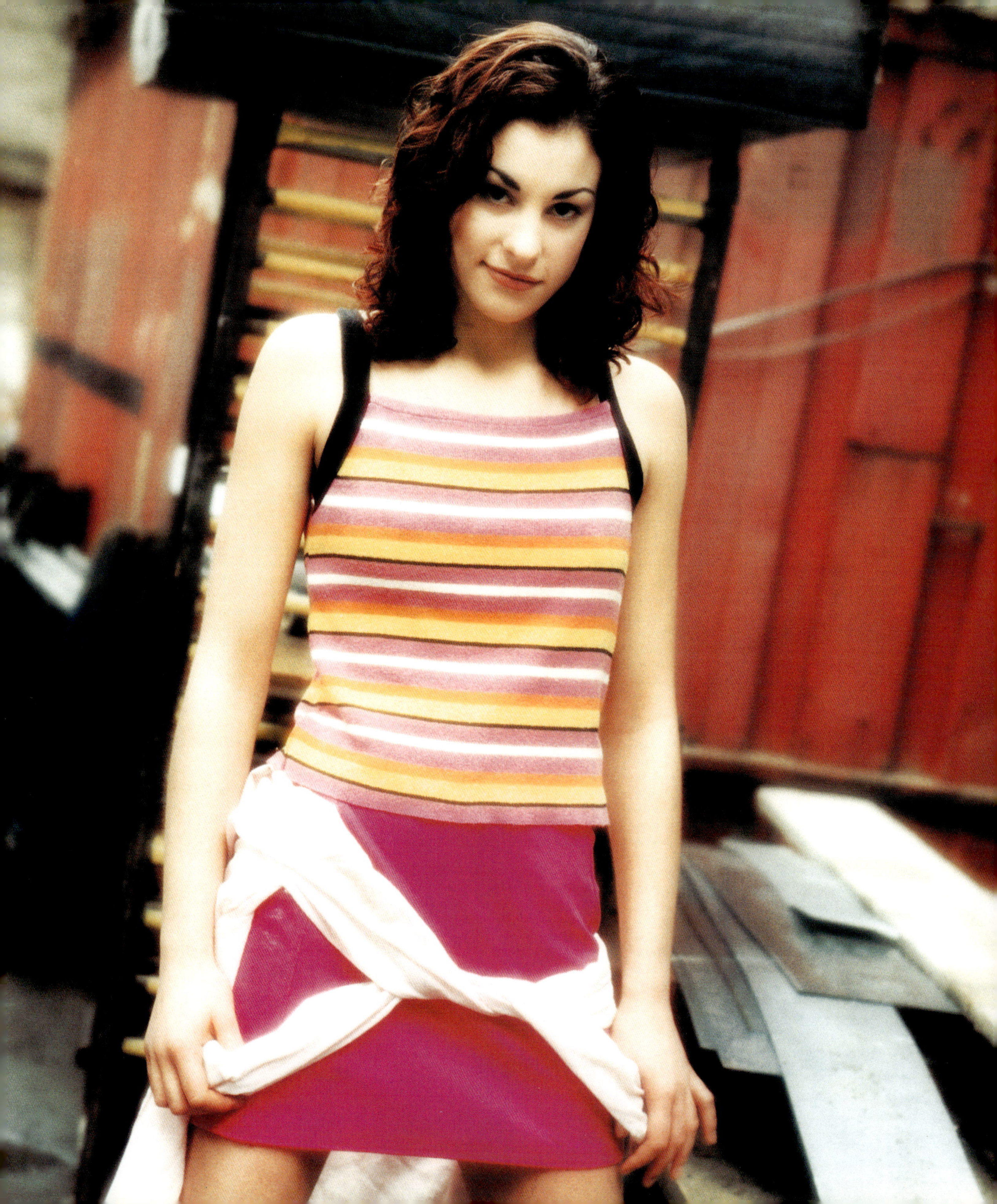

The way that a subject will work with their background is key to the success of a picture, and colour has a vital role to play in this. If the result is to have harmony, colours should be complementary, not fighting against each other, and this is equally true whether colours are bright or more subdued. Here the red of the girl's skirt, opposite, has echoed the colour of the container behind her. The sandy colour of the boy's trousers, below, is picked up by the hue of the wall behind him. When I go to locations I make it up as I go along and simply try to think on my feet. I'm looking for areas such as this that I know will work well with a particular subject and the clothes they're wearing.

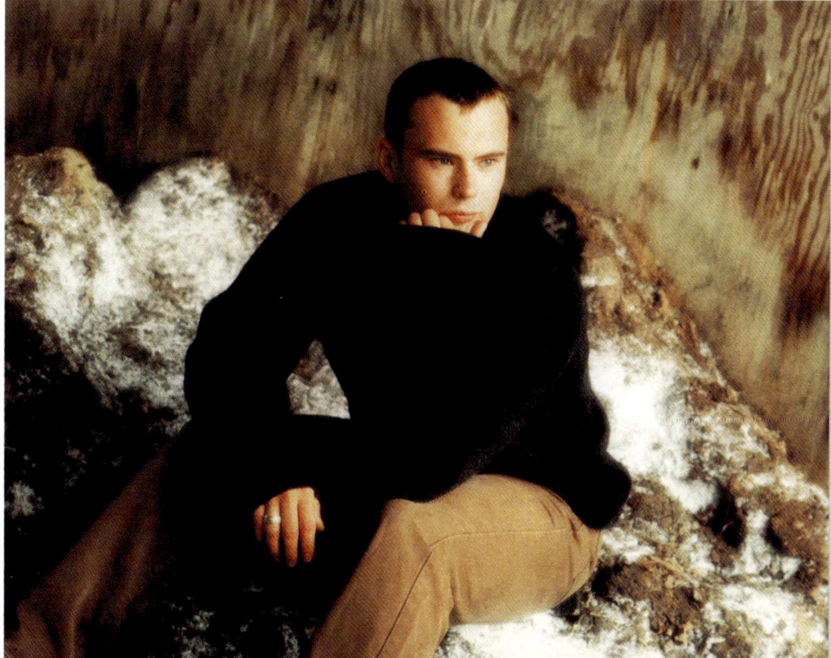

Both these pictures have made use of an unusual setting, but on each occasion the image is successful because the colours have worked together and created a good overall effect.

Both pictures: Mamiya RZ 67, 150mm soft focus lens, Fujifilm Provia 400. Exposure 1/30sec at f/5.6

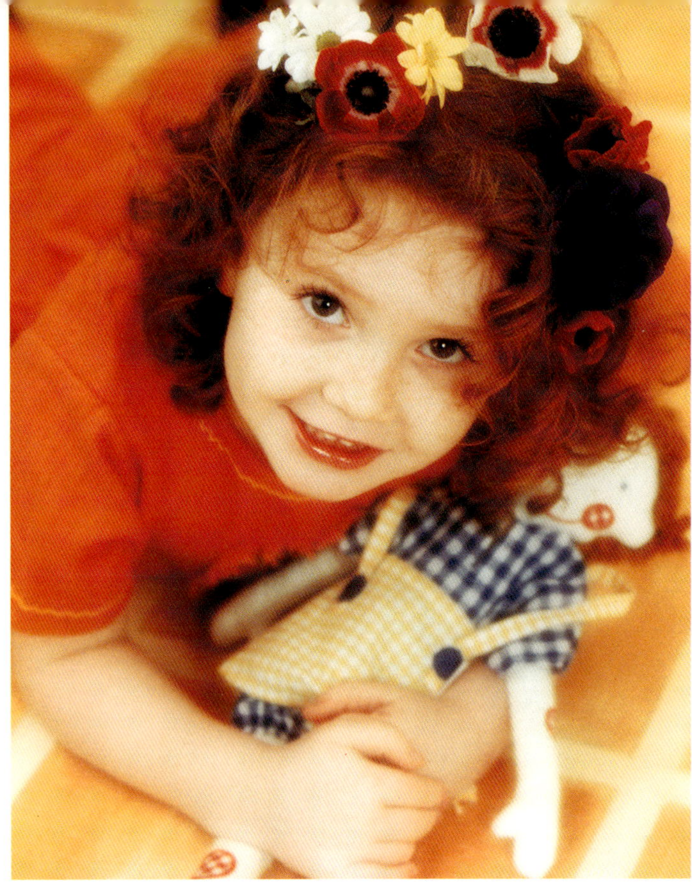

I don't often use props in pictures, but when I do I like them to be something that relates to the person I'm photographing. The parents of the girl with the tea cups and dolls, for example, run a shop that sells unusual items such as these. The result is a picture that's full of colours and textures, and involves objects which are familiar to the clients. The other picture uses a brightly coloured doll which complements the bright clothes and tiled floor.

The right prop can complement the colour in a scene, and can serve as inspiration for the final picture. If I use props at all, I'll usually find these around the house of the person that I'm photographing, so their use will be spontaneous.

Mamiya RZ 67, 150mm soft focus lens, Fujifilm Provia 400. Exposure 1/500sec at f/5.6

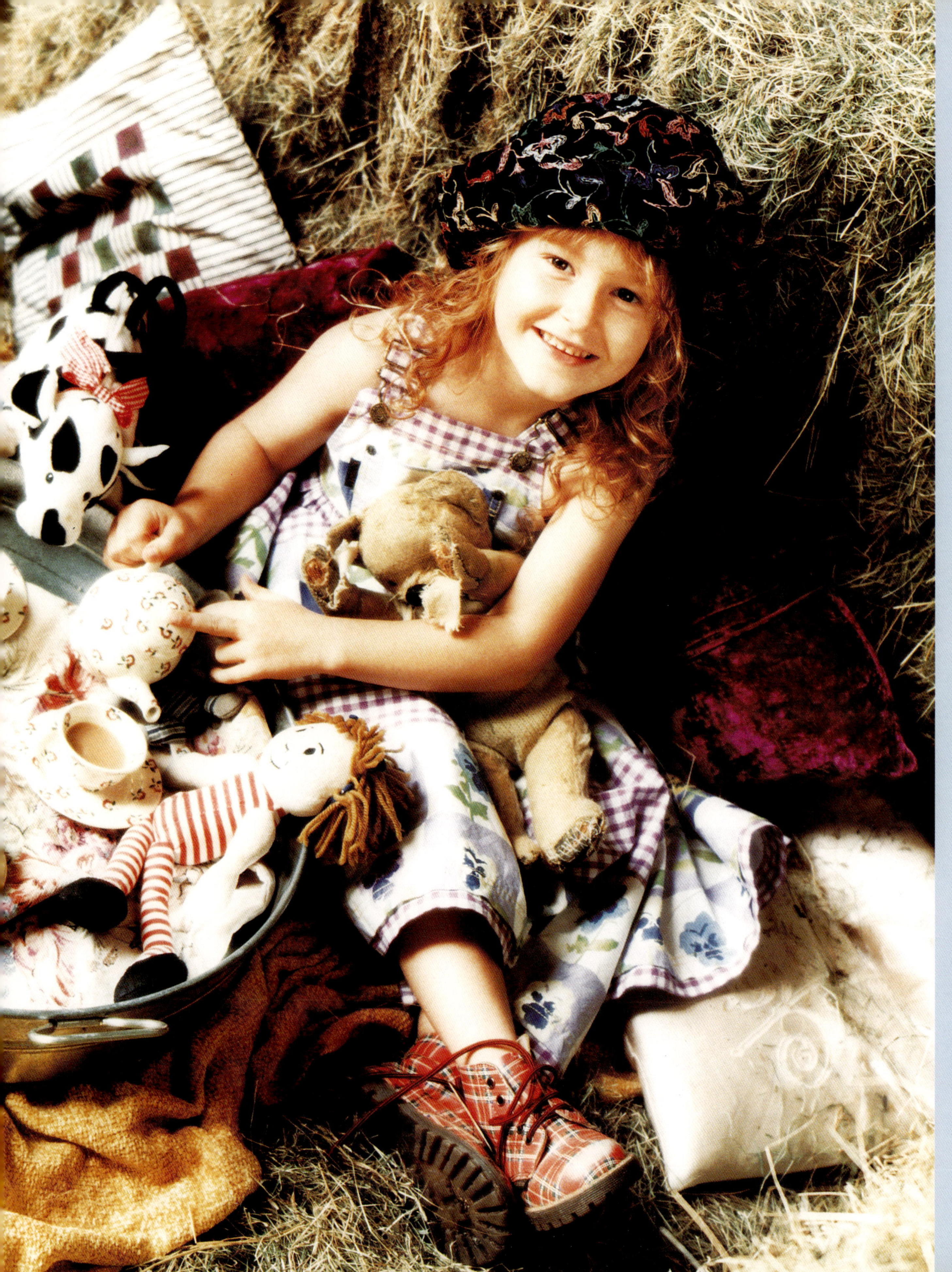

a few props can go a long way

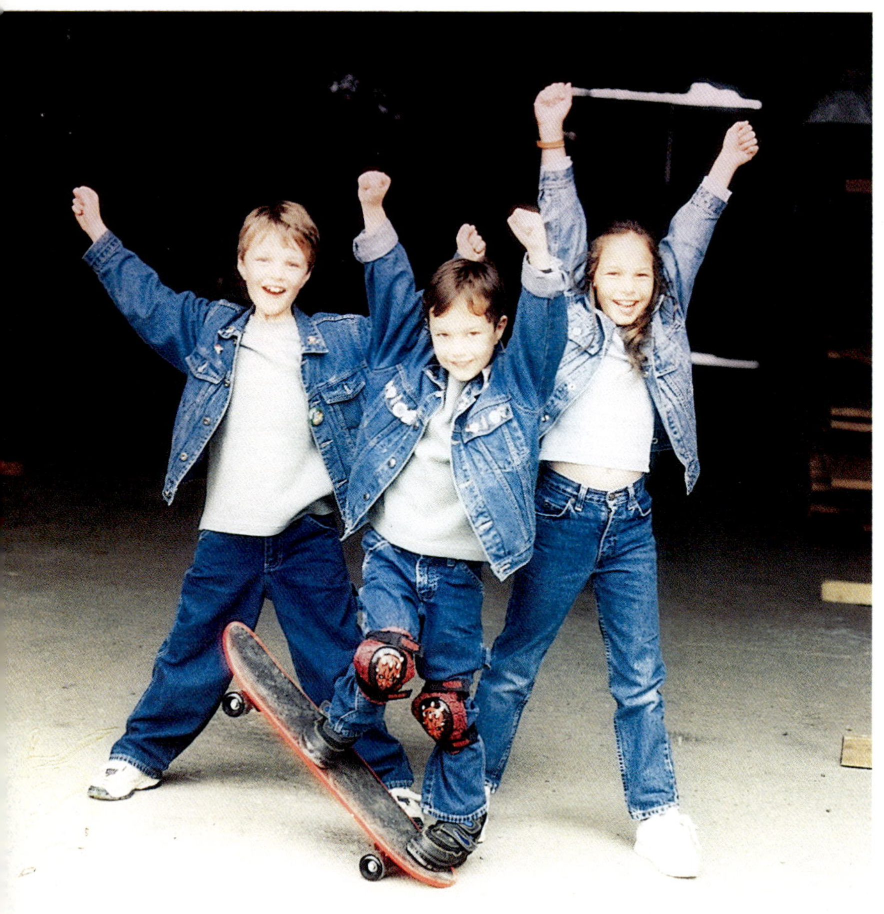

The colour of the clothes that the subjects are wearing should complement not just the surroundings, but also each other, so that there are no clashes in the picture. For the image of the couple on the right, I knew that their tastes were towards light and pale colours because of the décor of the house. It was a simple decision to ask them to dress in light clothes, and the beige and white work well together and also in the context of the setting, for a bright and airy picture.

Generally I like my clients to wear clothes that they are comfortable and happy with, but I'll advise when I feel that something isn't going to work in the picture. Had one of the couple, right, wanted to wear denim, for example, this would have ruined the harmony of the colours in the picture.

Mamiya RZ 67, 150mm soft focus lens, Fujifilm 800. Lighting: natural, from a set of French windows. Exposure 1/500sec at f/5.6

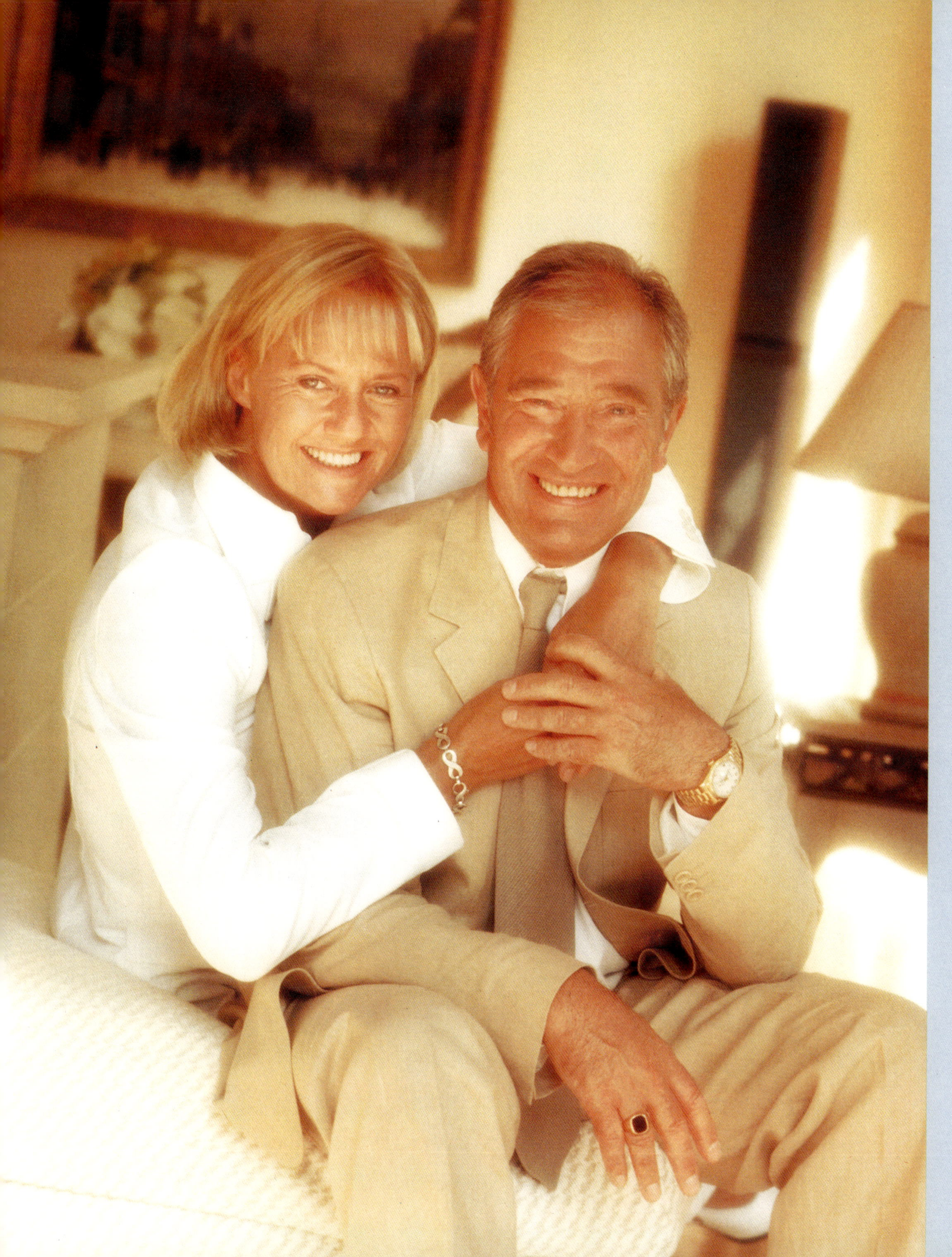

creating colour harmony in group compositions

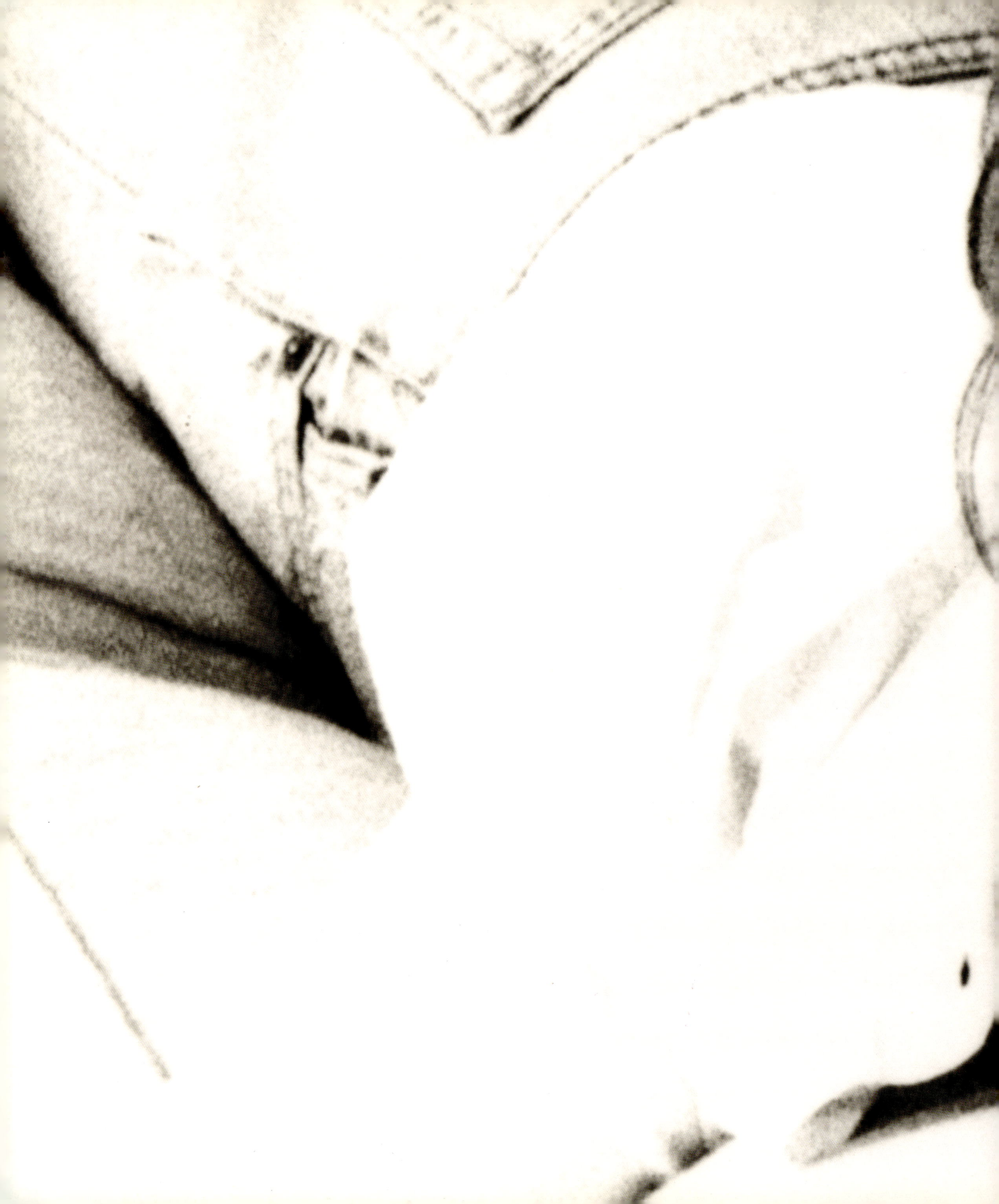

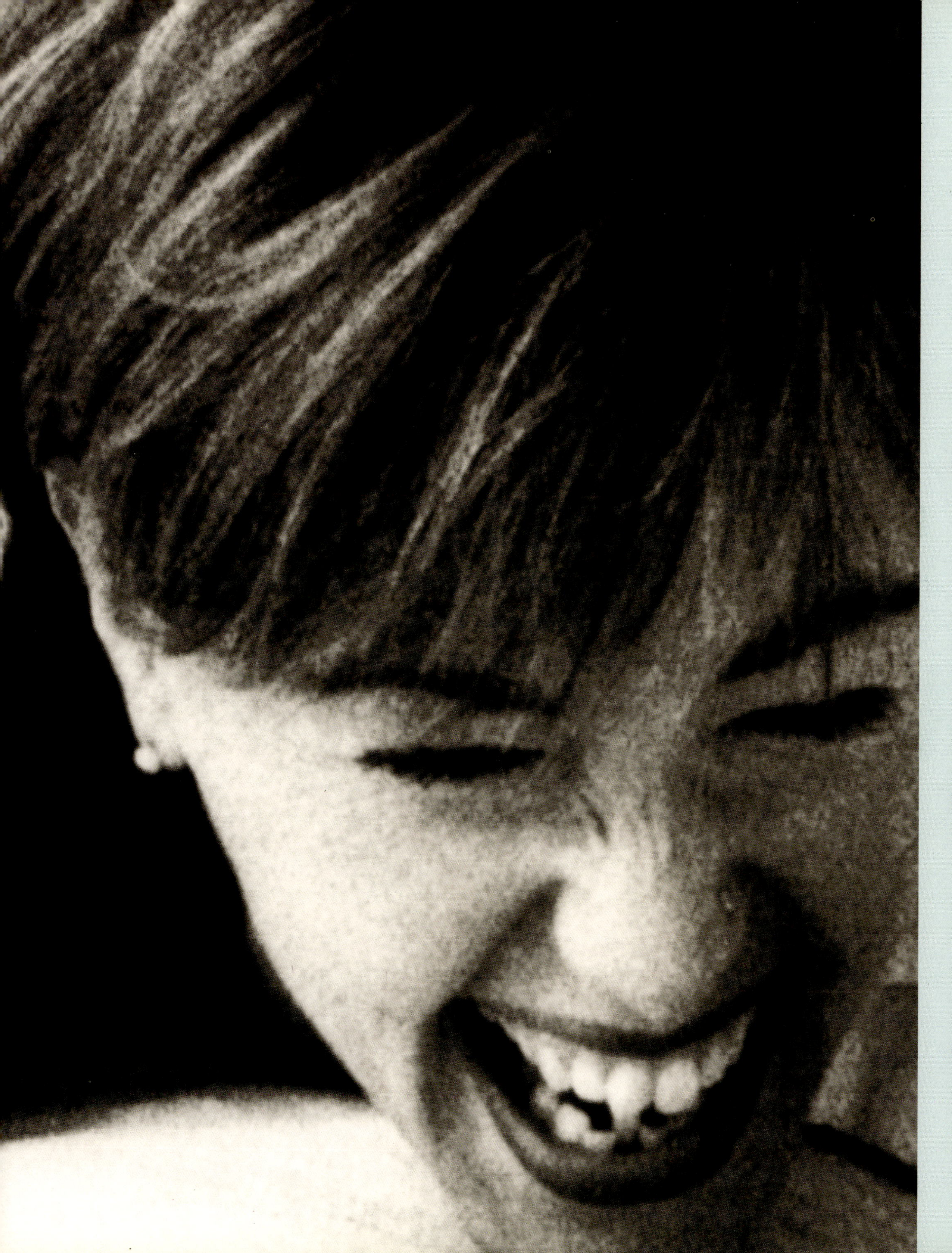

5 art directing and creating relaxed poses

"The essence of a relaxed picture is the result of understanding how a person feels as well as how they look."

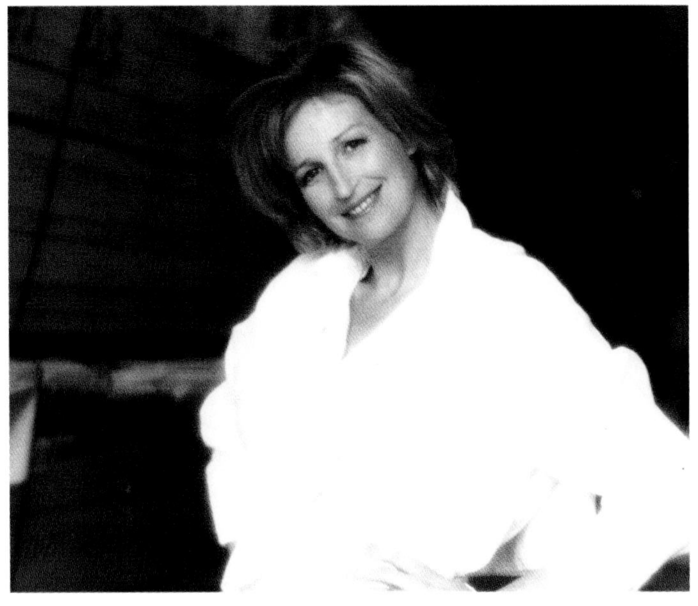

Careful positioning of the person is the key to a successful photograph. Today's clients want to look natural and unposed, but without careful positioning the photographs will enhance the very features they want to hide. Therefore we have to be acutely aware of placing certain parts of the body to enhance the subject's best features and detract from those they dislike; whilst keeping the result from looking false or over posed. When people look at photographs of themselves, they tend to be very self-critical, and no matter how good the lighting, clothes, make-up and backgrounds are, if their posture and expression are not attractive they will not like the photograph.

Positioning a subject so that their body is at a slight angle will give a more flattering result, and will also lead to more vibrancy and life in the picture.

Canon EOS 5, 75–300mm zoom, Fujifilm Neopan 1600. Exposure 1/250sec at f/5.6

The Warmsley sisters could not appear more relaxed as they stand together in the garden, arms around each other. By photographing them together, they feel more confident and relaxed – safety in numbers!

Canon EOS 5, 75–300mm zoom, Fujifilm Neopan 1600. Exposure 1/250sec at f/5.6

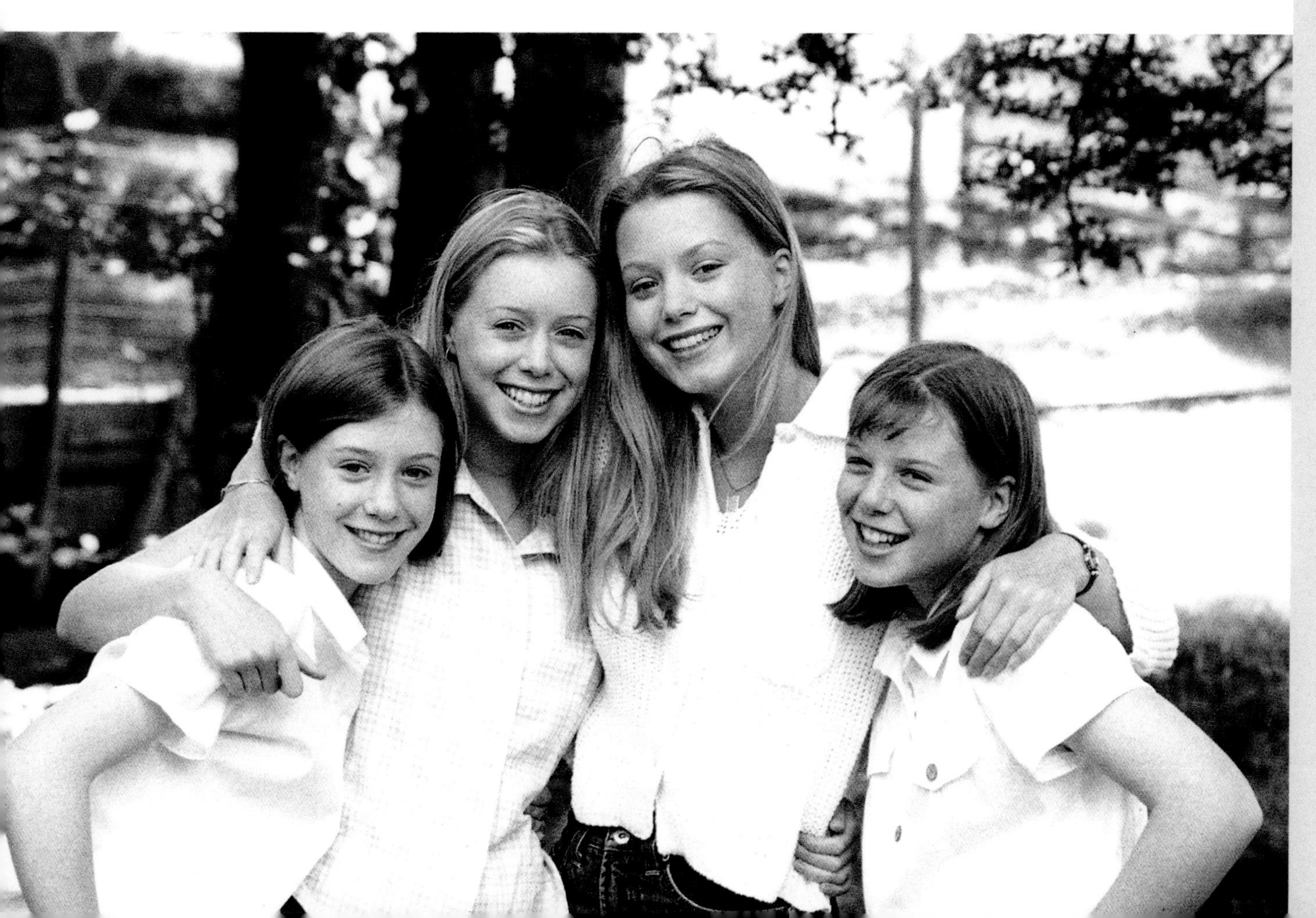

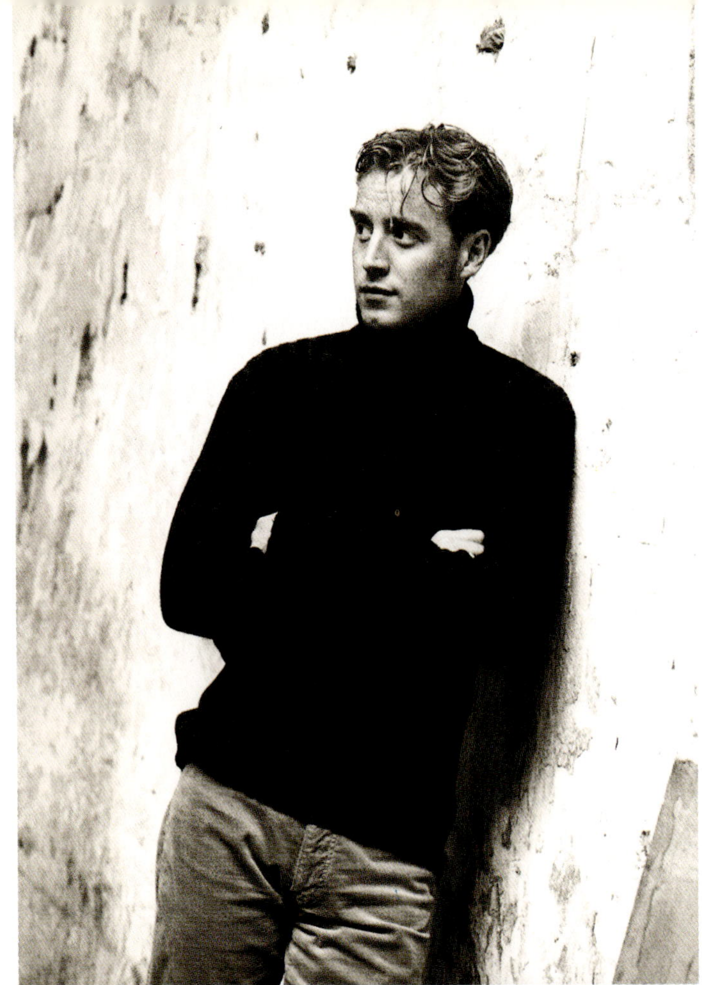

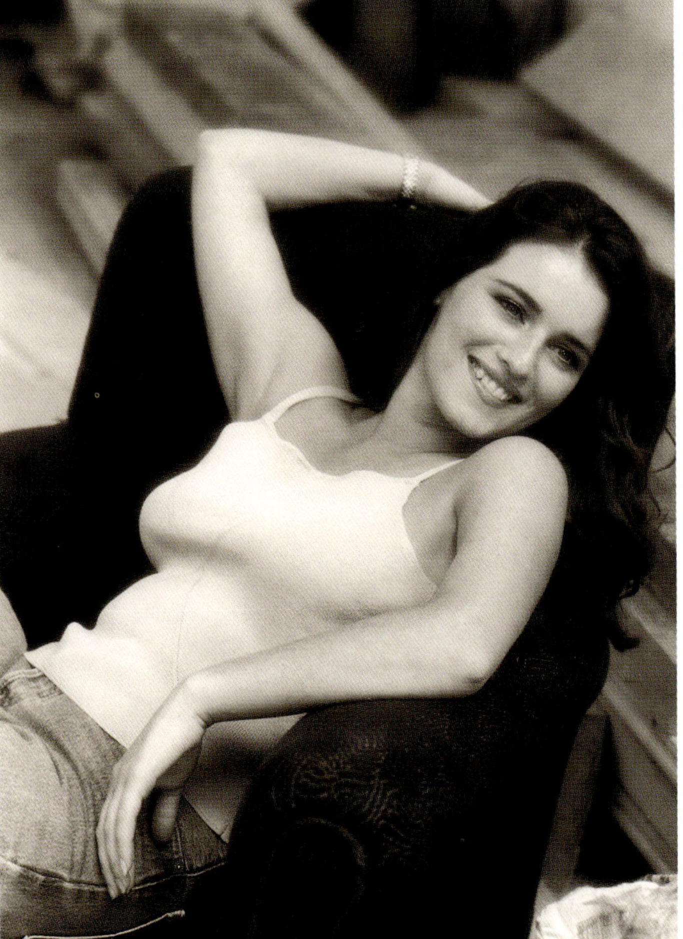

In order for the client to feel comfortable and relaxed we need to direct them into positions which feel natural to them, i.e. leaning on a wall, hands in pockets, lying on the floor, sitting with their feet under them, lying on a sofa hugging a cushion – doing things they are used to doing every day. Sitting people in an alien environment – for example on high stools or standing them in open spaces – causes tension and anxiety as they feel exposed and unsure about what you expect of them.

Right: When I'm positioning subjects, I like to start by asking them to do something that they would almost certainly do naturally. With this little girl, it was easy for her to lay on the floor like this and to flick her legs up behind her, because that's how she relaxes at home.

Canon EOS 5, 75–300mm zoom, Fujifilm Neopan 1600. Exposure 1/30sec at f/5.6

Left above: Andrew has the security of a wall to lean on, whereas had he been standing in an open space he would have looked less natural.
Left below: Grace sat in an armchair and instinctively relaxed, able to relate immediately to an everyday situation.

Both pictures: Canon EOS 5, 75–300mm, Fujifilm Neopan 1600. Exposure: top picture 1/15sec at f/5.6, and bottom picture 1/250sec at f/5.6

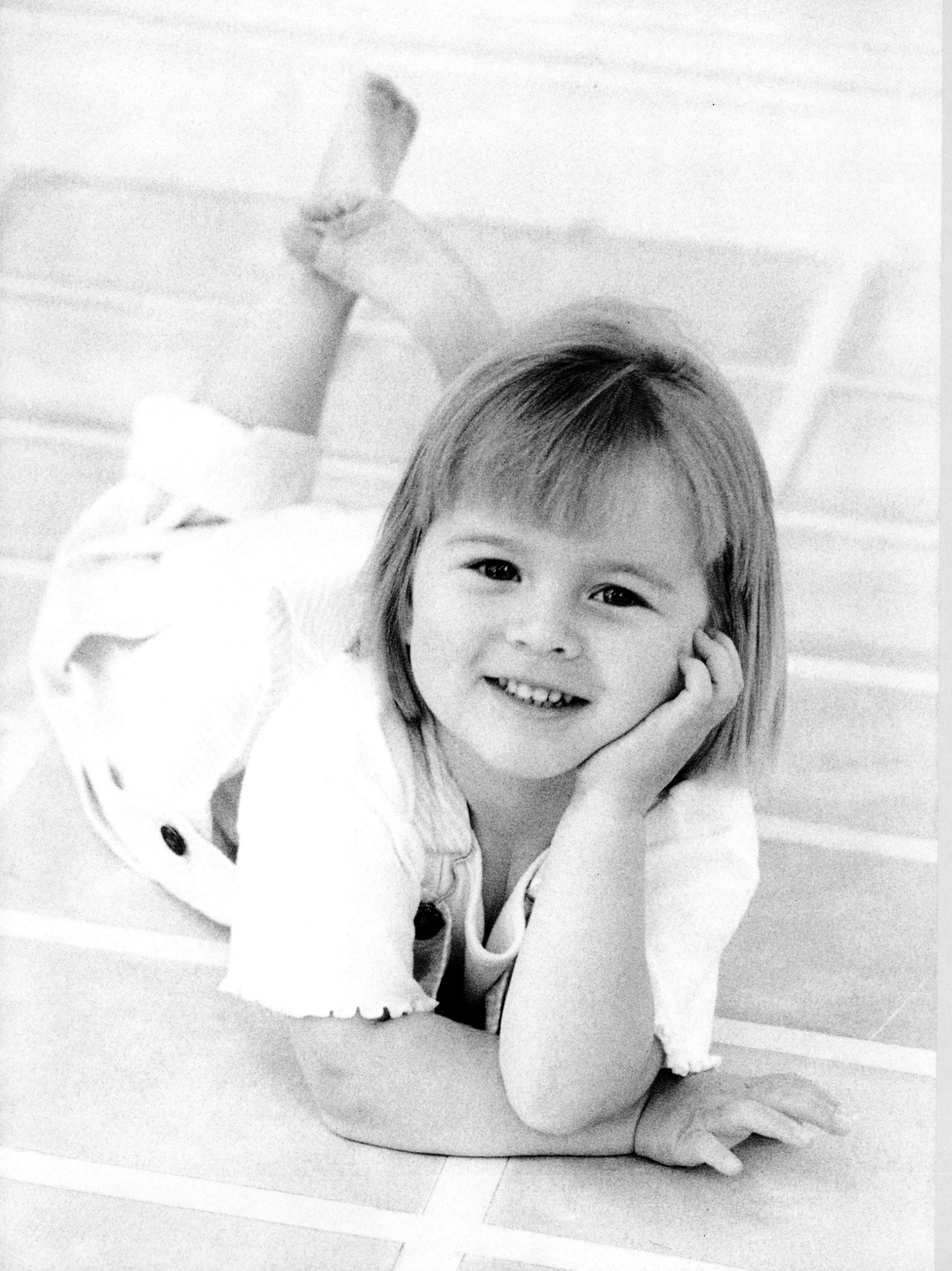

relaxing positions that look good and feel good

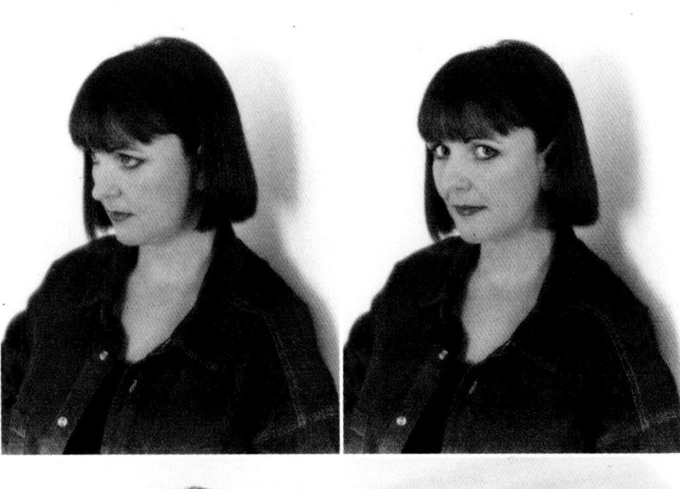

1 **Nobody likes double chins! Always ask the client to push her chin forward slightly, which will create a firmer jaw line.**

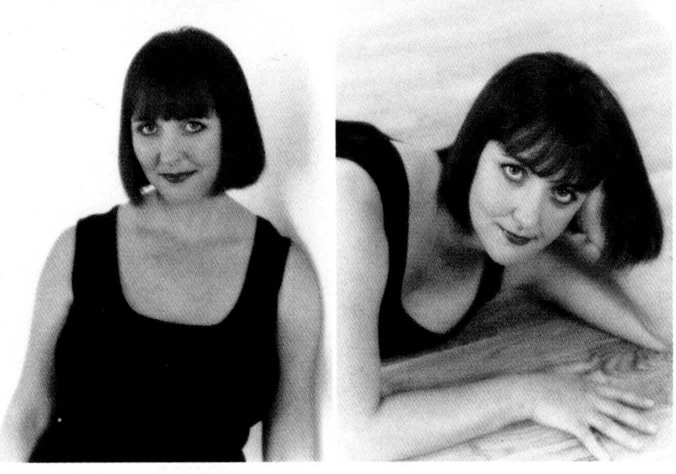

2 **Lying the subject down will create a much more flattering head shot than photographing them standing, facing the camera.**

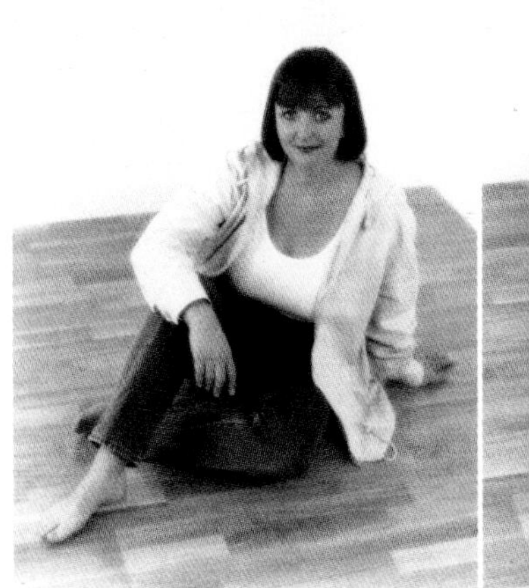

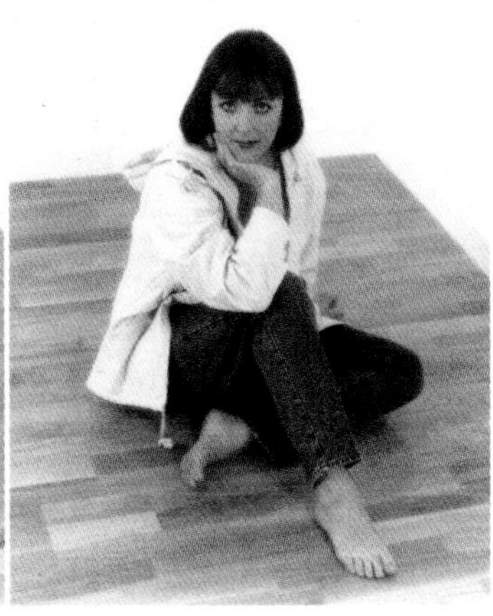

3 **Leaning on one hand and turning around slightly makes the subject look slimmer. Most clients love this pose, and you can adapt it by asking them to move to their left or right, which will allow you to enhance or to take attention away from features.**

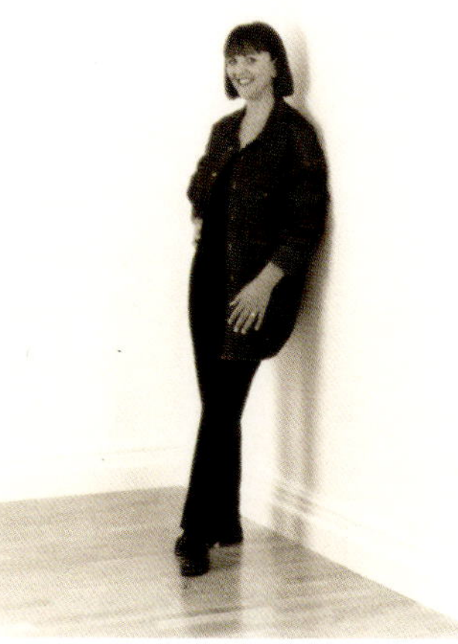

4 To make small people appear taller, crop the photograph through the thigh, to give the impression that the legs are much longer. A full-length shot of a small person will only make them look smaller.

5 Bare skin against black clothes will make the client appear larger. Careful positioning of similar coloured clothing, such as a shirt, will slim the body down.

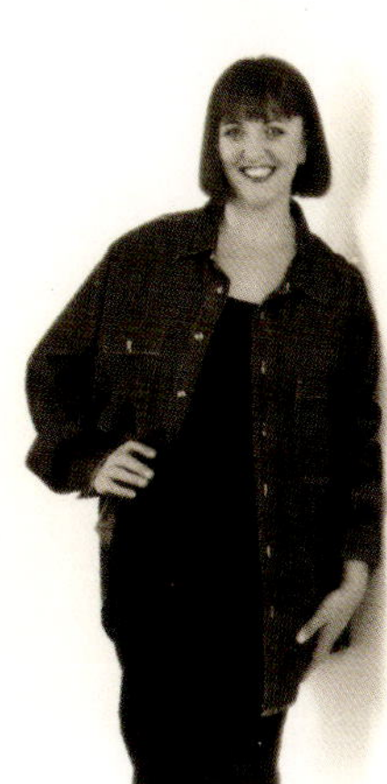

6 Women can look wider than they actually are when photographed facing straight towards the camera. Avoid this by turning them slightly sideways and creating an "S" shape.

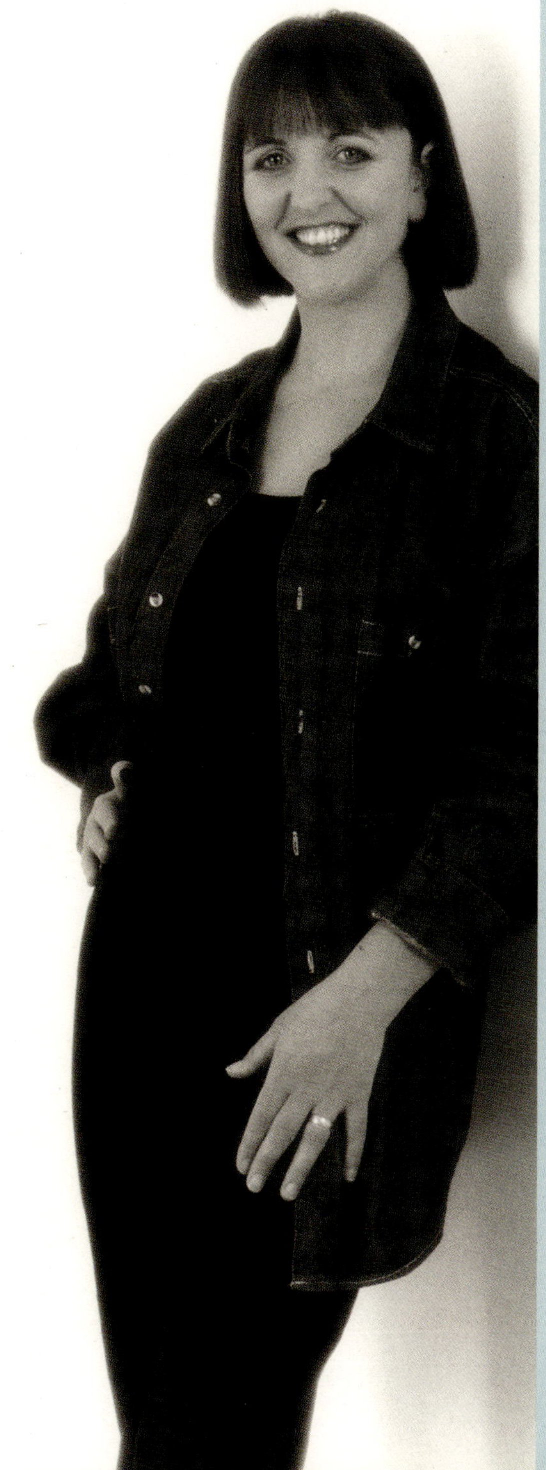

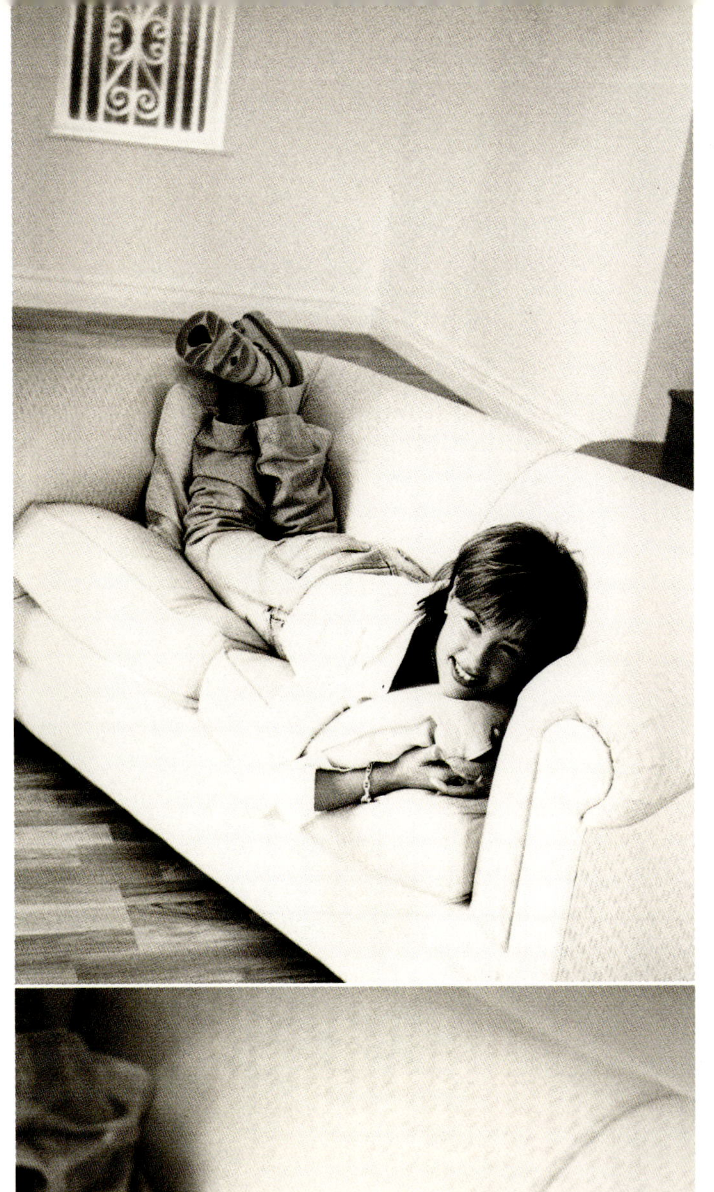

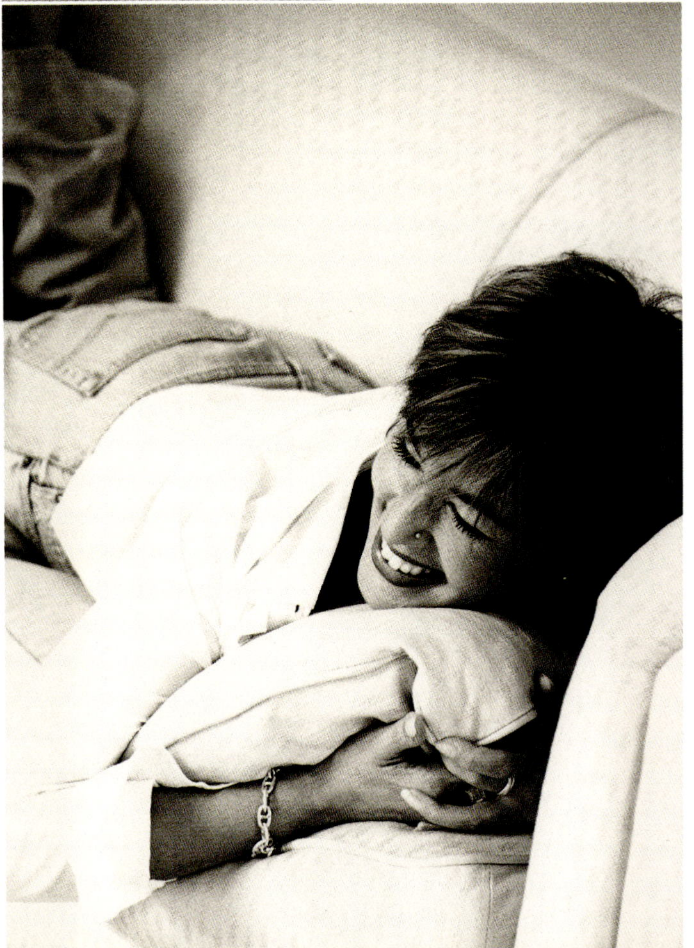

When people are enjoying themselves and starting to relax in the studio, make sure that you're ready for spontaneous shots with a 35mm camera, because these are the ones that will inevitably be the most in demand later. Something just appealed to my subject here, and she suddenly burst into fits of laughter. It was a wonderful sequence, and I just grabbed my camera and took pictures. The use of a zoom lens is invaluable in these situations because it allows such a rapid change of focal length, and the fact that I was able to hand-hold the camera because of the fast film I was using was also critical. With pictures like this, even a little blur would be acceptable: it's the moment that will captivate people, not the technical quality.

Geraldine started off by trying to pose, but was so relaxed that she soon found herself laughing uncontrollably. The sequence of shots tells a story and shows her in natural, unforced circumstances.

Canon EOS 5, 75–300mm, Fujifilm Neopan 1600. Exposure 1/30sec at f/5.6

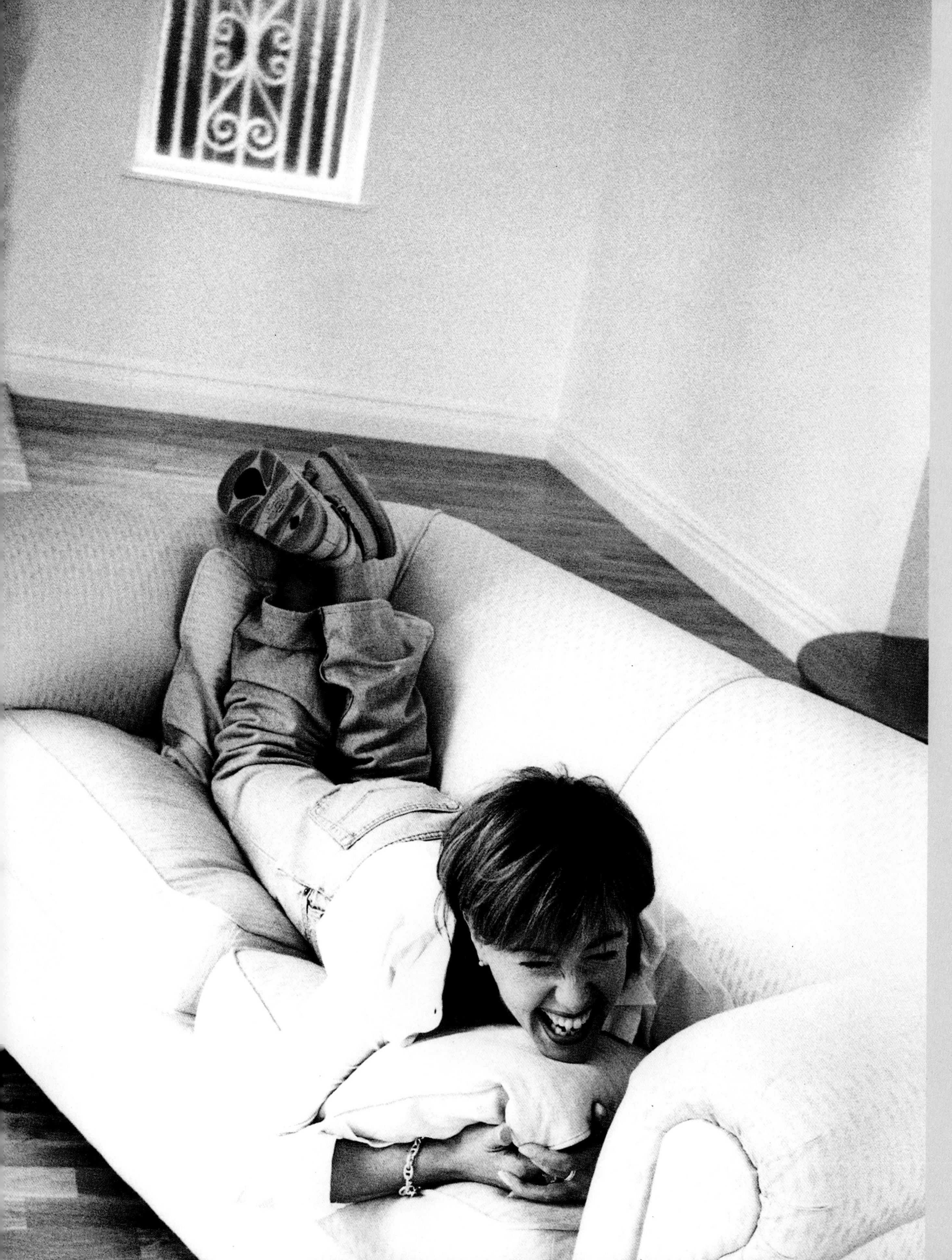

capturing a moment in time

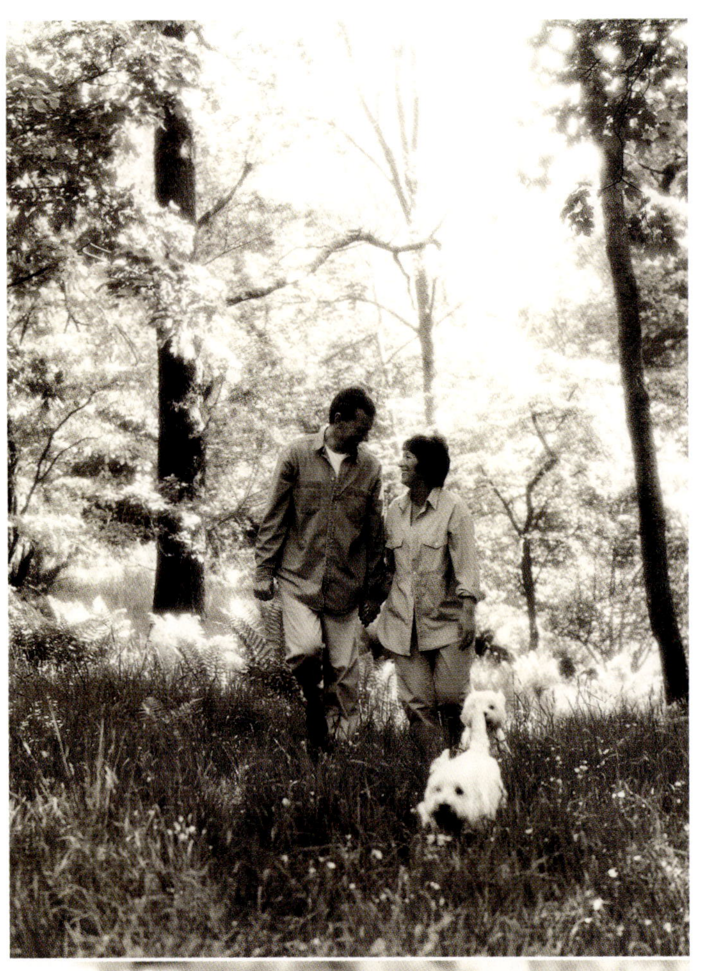

"Each of these images is equally powerful, because they are saying different things about the same subject. Whilst one is a classic portrait, the others are more relaxed and spontaneous versions."

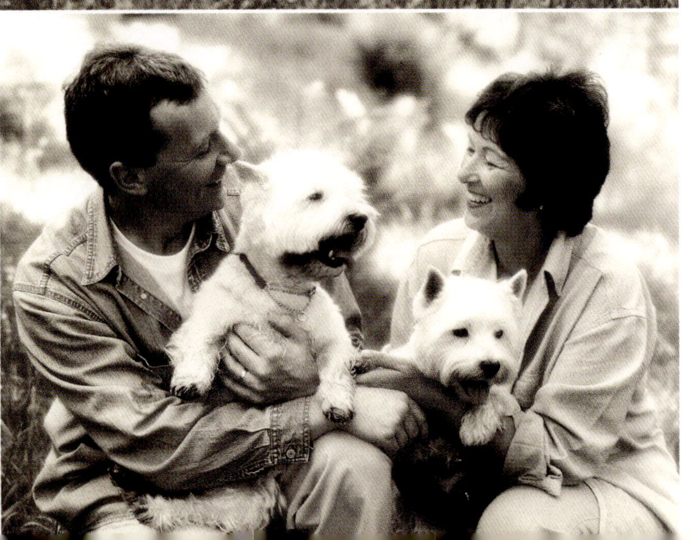

The classic portrait on the right, is the one that most people expect they will want. It shows two happy and relaxed people, while the inclusion of the couple's dogs in the picture adds the final touch. This is the picture that has to be taken, but once it's in the bag you should always try to produce some variations, which will often appeal more to the subjects because they show a more informal side of them. Try to introduce some action into your pictures, and make your pictures say something about the relationship between the subjects that you're photographing.

Mamiya RZ 67, 150mm soft focus lens, Fujifilm Neopan 400. Exposure 1/500sec at f/5.6

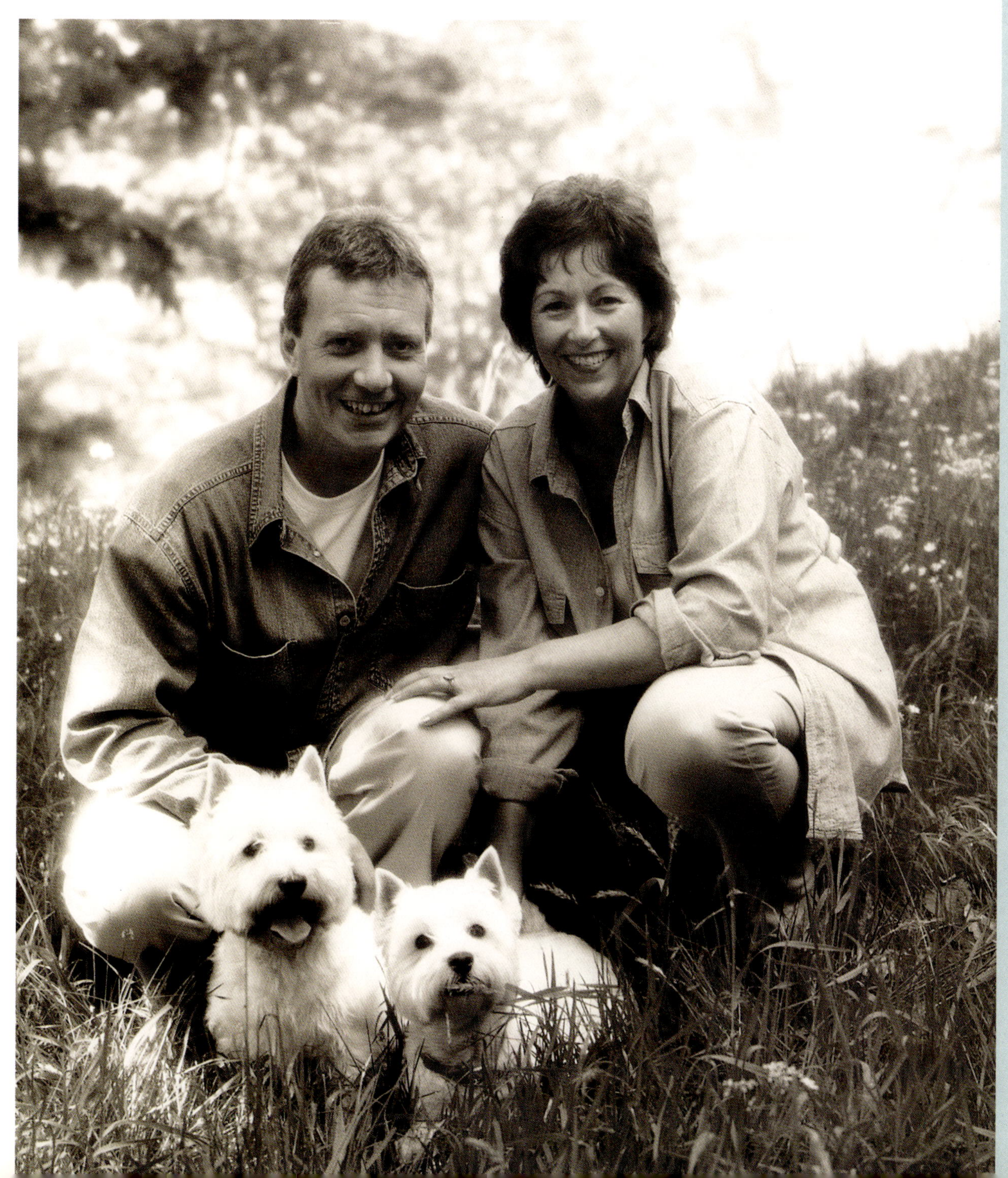

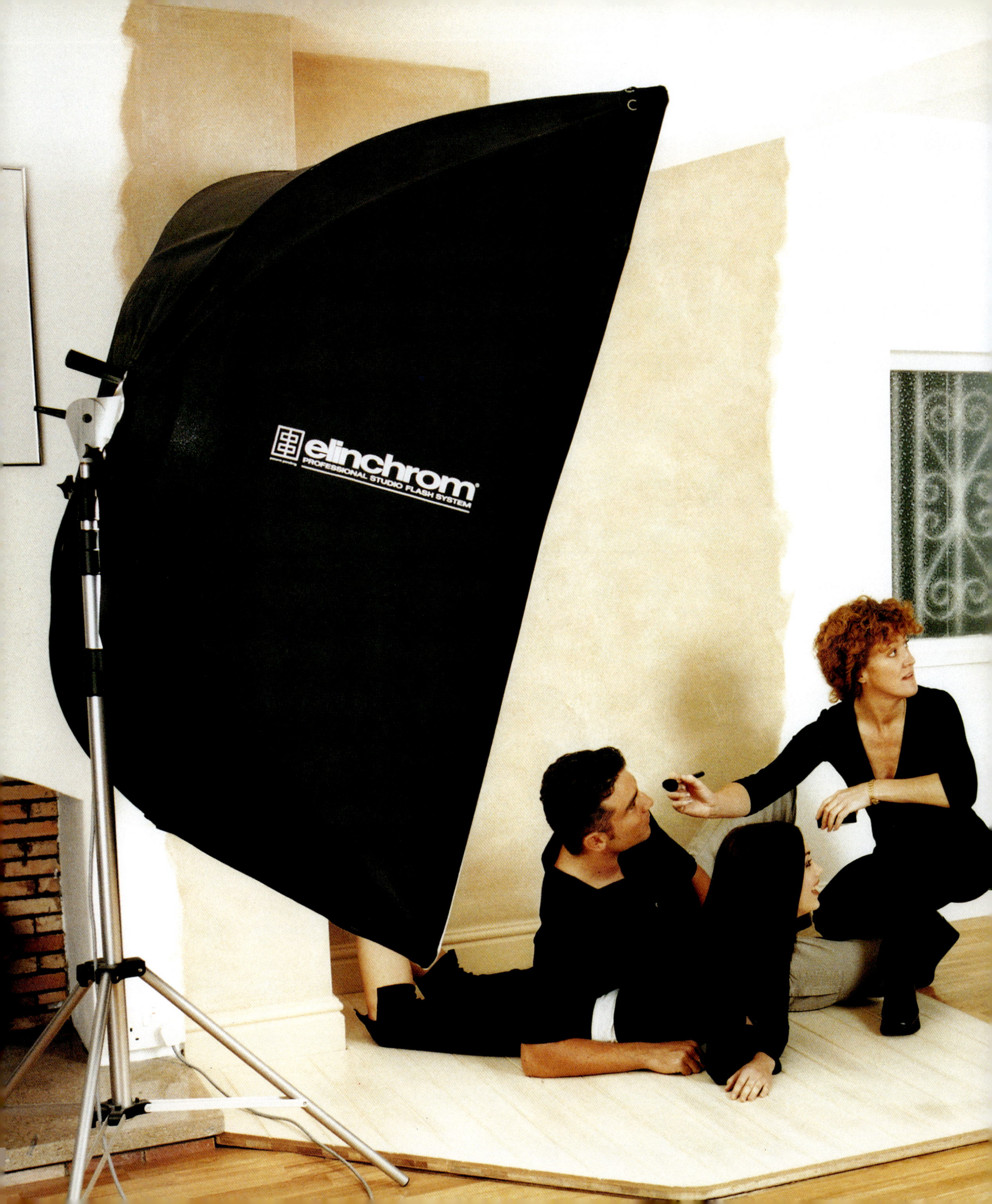
elinchrom
PROFESSIONAL STUDIO FLASH SYSTEM

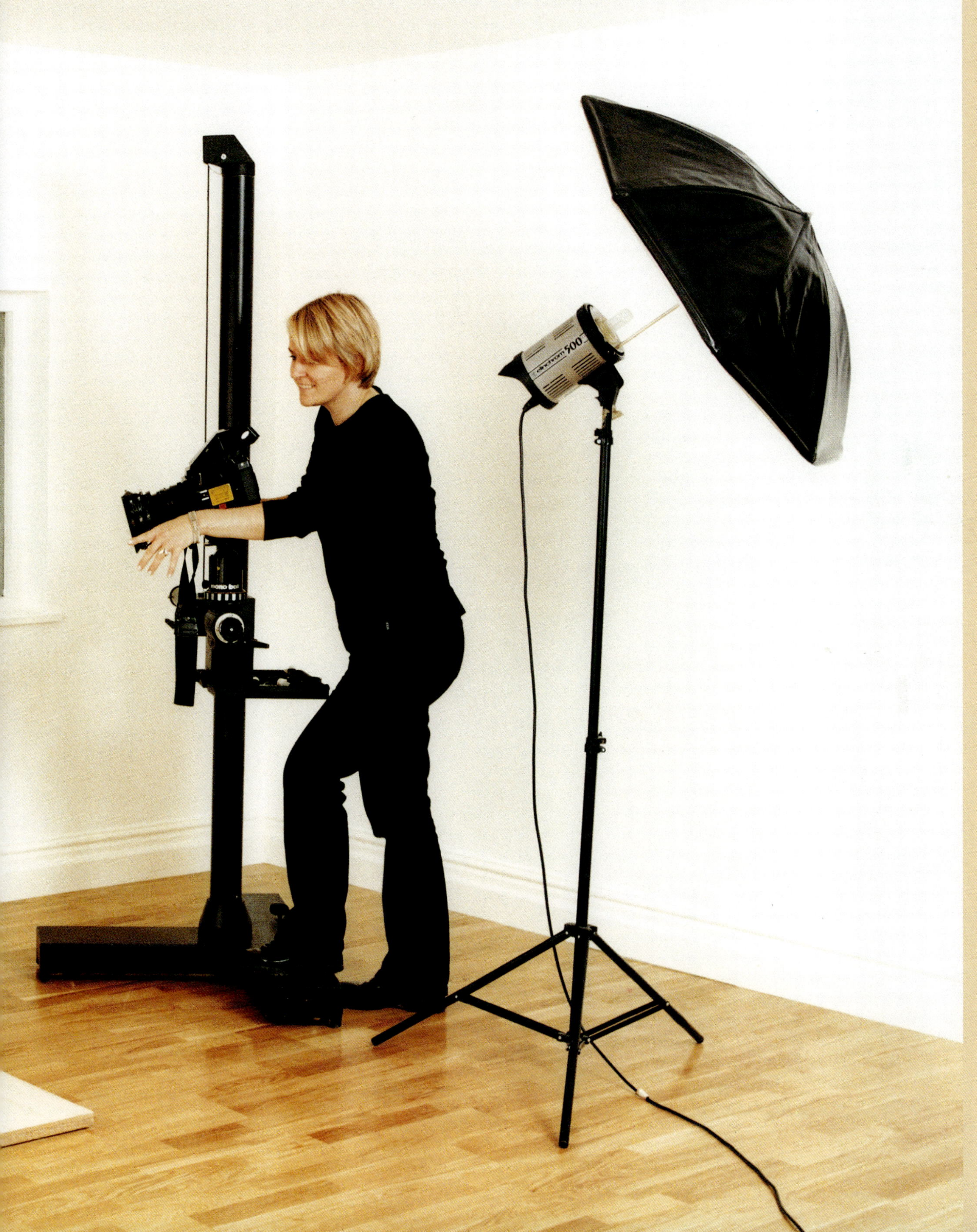

6 real-life shoots

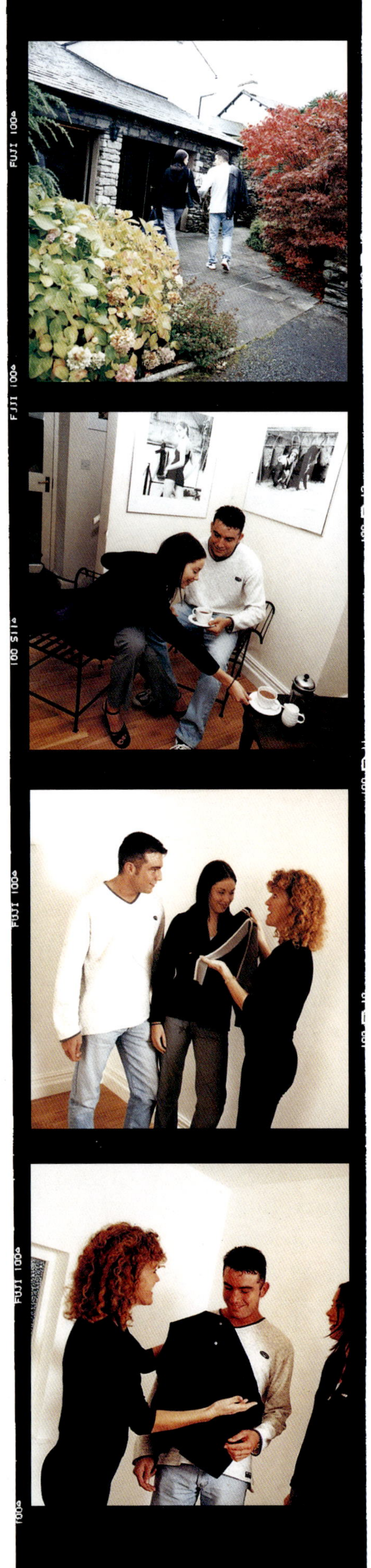

9.30a.m. It's the start of the day, and Lisa and Scott are arriving for their session feeling excited but a little nervous. The first step is to make them feel comfortable and to start the process of relaxing them, and a simple cup of coffee helps them to settle into their surroundings.

9.45a.m. Moving through to the studio, the couple meet stylist Lucinda Hayton, who chats through clothing that will be worn for the shoot and the kind of look that Lisa and Scott are hoping to achieve. For the session in the studio it's decided that both of them will wear black tops, which will ensure a stylish and contemporary look. Black is always in fashion, and usually flatters the wearer, and by asking the couple to dress the same it has given harmony to the picture and emphasised the relationship between the two of them.

The black clothing that Lisa and Scott chose to wear has ideally suited the black and white film used here. Had one of the couple worn a lighter shade, there would have been the chance that the picture would have looked very disjointed.

Canon EOS 5, 75–300mm zoom, Fujifilm Neopan 1600. Illumination from an Octa softbox and umbrella fill, but only modelling lights used. Exposure 1/30sec at f/5.6

before we begin

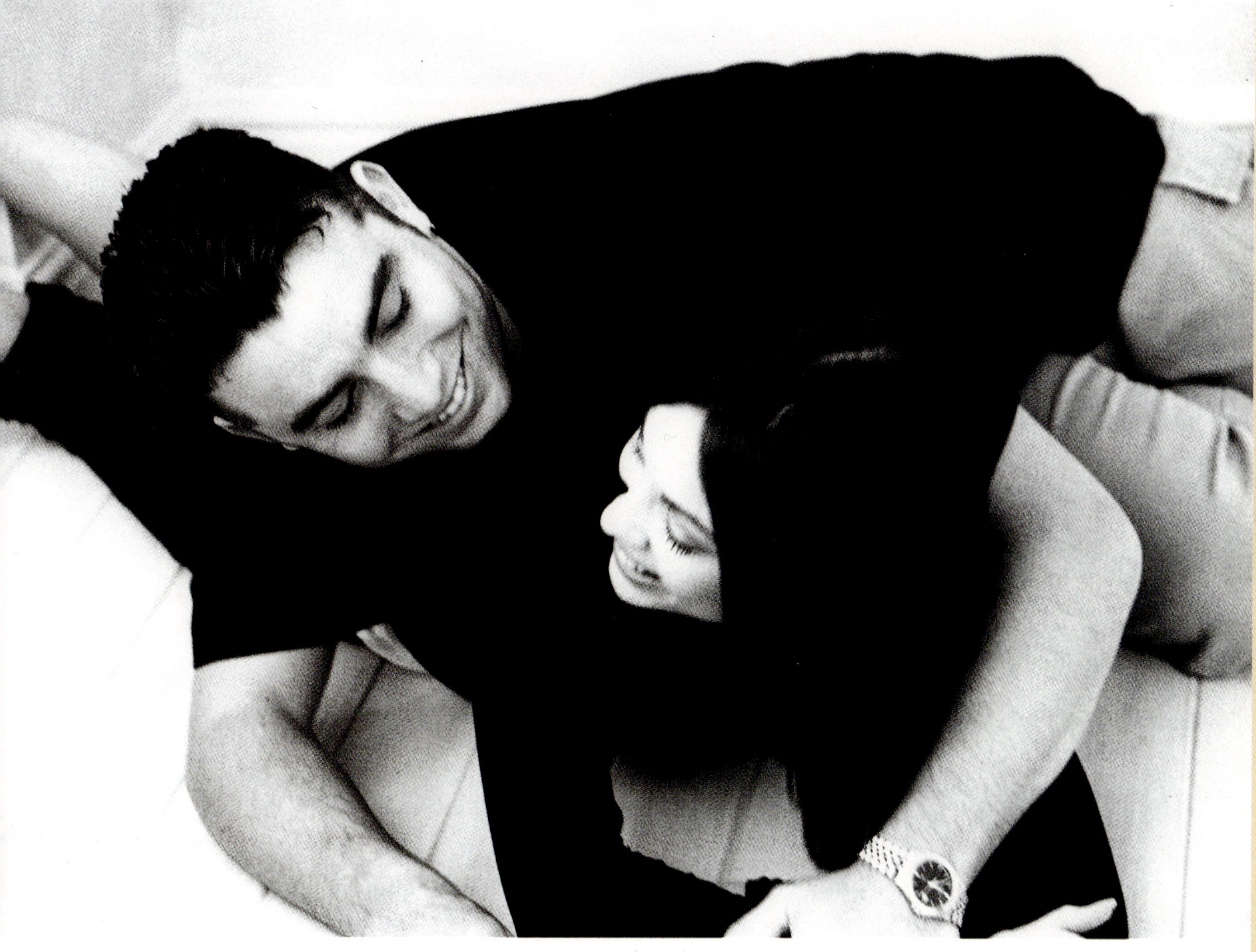

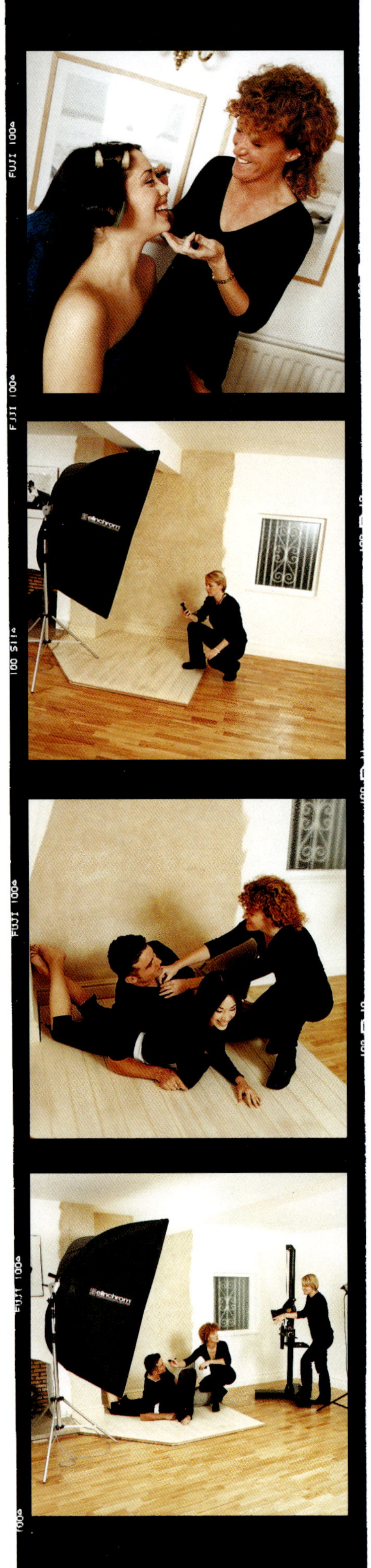

10.00a.m. The make-up session follows next, and this should be a relaxing and enjoyable part of the day. This is an opportunity to get all those fears out of the way, so that any worries and tension have disappeared by the photo stage. Having make-up applied by a professional make-up artist is a very relaxing experience and makes the clients feel completely pampered.

Meanwhile, Annabel checks all her lights and sets, so that she can concentrate on the client rather than the equipment during the shoot.

Annabel positions Lisa and Scott on set while Lucinda checks the make-up under the studio lighting and makes final adjustments to the clothing.

11.00a.m. The first photos are taken lying on the floor, to allow the clients to settle into the shoot, and to gain confidence. The positioning is simple and natural so the clients can relax and realise that it's not going to be hard work!

By asking the couple to lay on the floor for the first set of pictures, I was able to take an elevated view and use the floor itself as a simple, uncluttered background for this picture.

Canon EOS 5, 75–300mm zoom, Fujifilm Neopan 1600. Illumination from an Octa softbox and umbrella fill, but only modelling lights used. Exposure 1/30sec at f/5.6

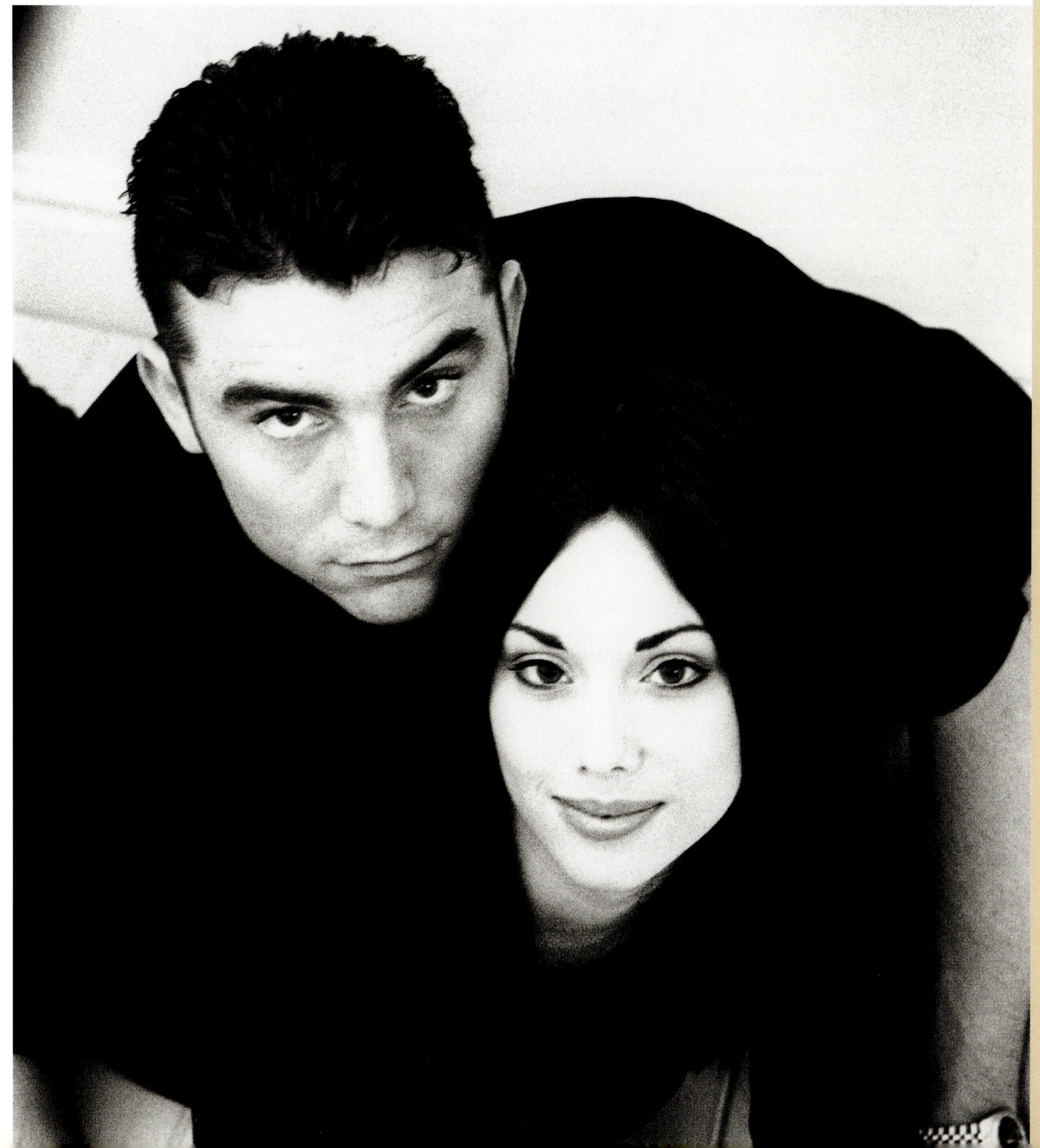

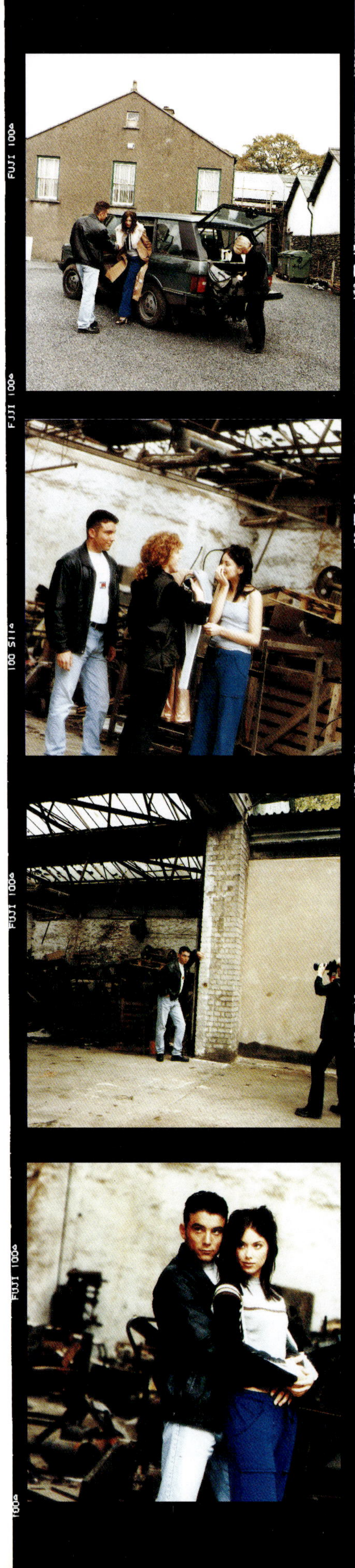

Even though this session took place in November, I still went outside for location pictures, because the light at that time of year can be fantastic. The downside is the cold, but if clients are enjoying themselves they will be quite happy to co-operate and to brave the elements.

Canon EOS 5, 75–300mm zoom, Fujifilm Neopan 1600. Exposure 1/30sec at f/5.6

11.30a.m. Then it's off on location! Today, it's an old bobbin mill and industrial estate, full of amazing potential, adding a new dimension to the shoot – it's not everyday you have your photos taken against a rubbish tip, or pile of sawdust!

Lisa and Scott are now really enjoying the shoot, as working in this location is new and exciting and they don't quite know what to expect next. Lisa is freezing, so Lucinda allows her to wear her jumper: providing it suits the feel we're trying to achieve, there's no problem adding elements like this to the picture. It's obviously easier to handle in black and white as well, because there's no danger of a colour clash.

The colour pictures set the scene, and the 35mm black and white allows movement and variety in the shots.

Standing further away with a long lens throws the background out of focus, placing more emphasis on Scott, and the use of black and white grainy film turns the junk into a series of interesting shapes and textures.

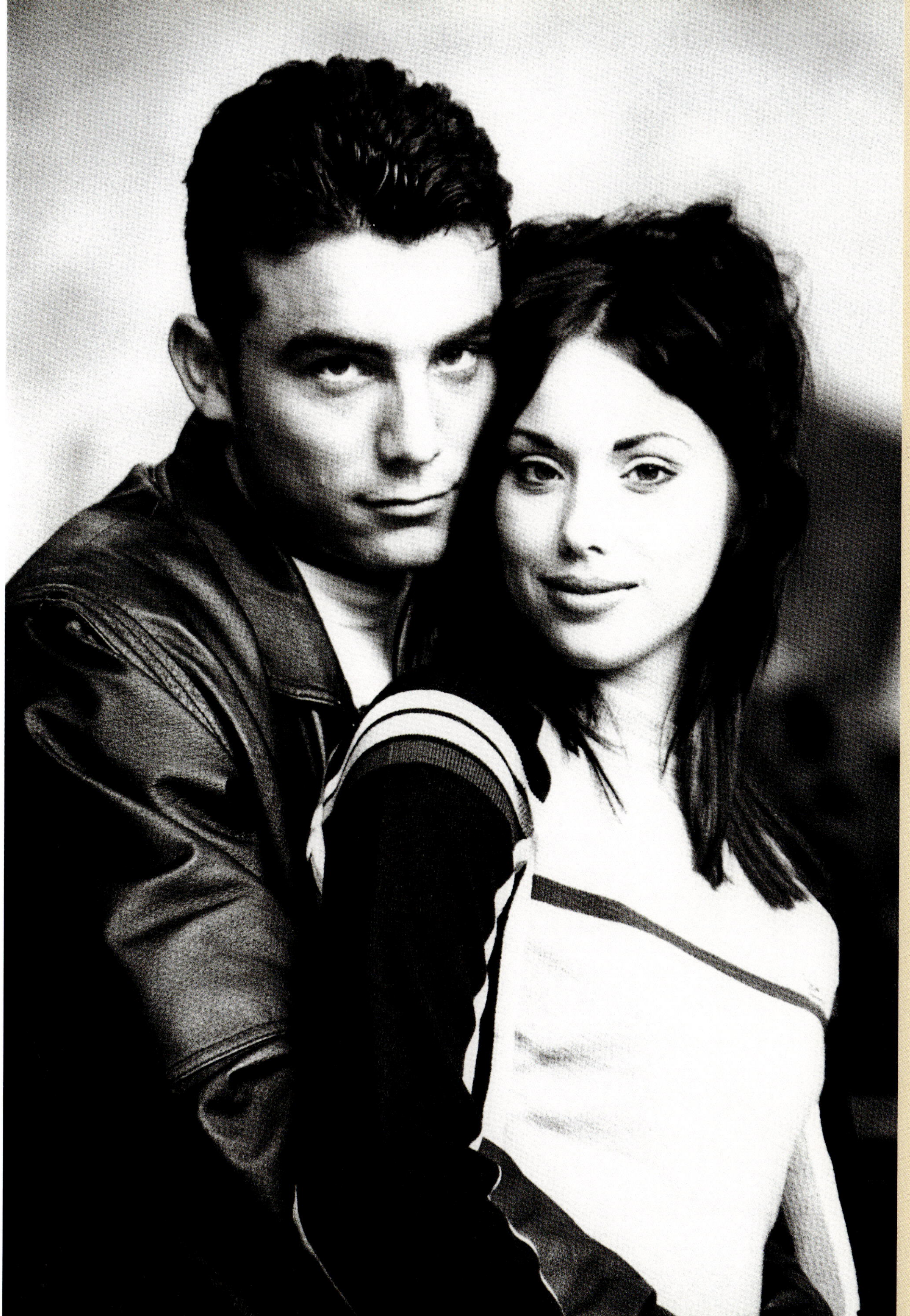

a new and exciting location

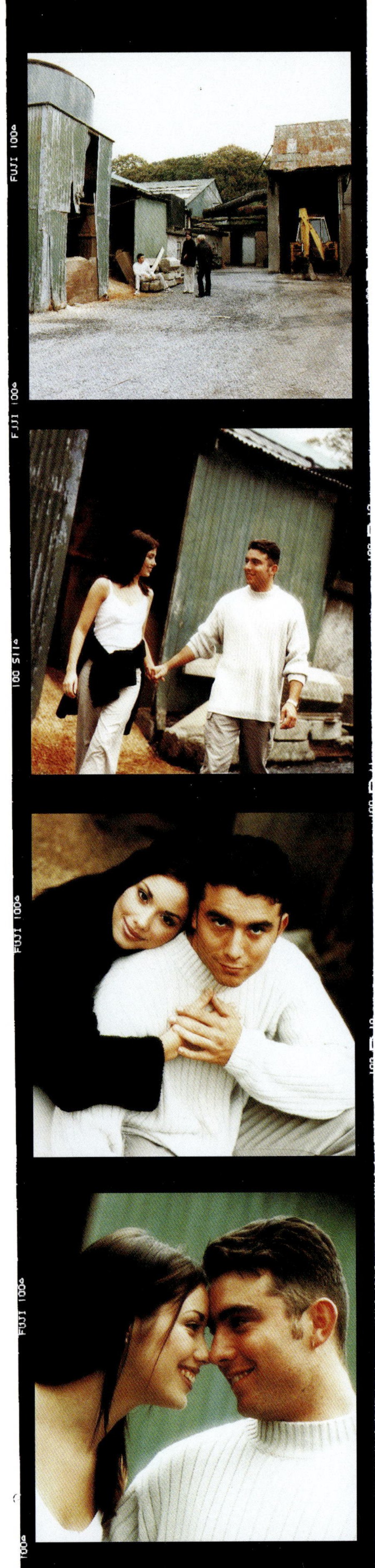

The juxtaposition of the two heads and the touch of the hands suggest a close relationship, a feel that's been emphasised through the use of the long end of the zoom lens to compress the perspective and a tight crop in-camera.

Canon EOS 5, 75–300mm zoom, Fujifilm Neopan 1600. Exposure 1/30sec at f/5.6

12.00p.m. It's always good to have a few changes of clothes to hand, so that other ideas can be tried out throughout the session. Lisa and Scott also needed to wear something outside that would keep them warm and comfortable, although for short periods it is possible, even in November, to wear some lighter clothing. On location the only changing facility to hand is generally the back of the car and today is no exception, but fortunately the session is going so well that no one complains.

Annabel directs Lisa and Scott into an area chosen for the warmth of colours in the background, which will complement the feeling of warmth in the fluffy jumpers. Lisa and Scott are still enjoying every minute, despite occasionally being blasted with sawdust from a fan close by!

The pictures to the left show how the colour side of the shoot developed throughout this period. The style is still informal; although it's medium-format the camera is still hand-held, and the aim has been to establish the relationship between the couple through the intimacy of their body language. The chance has been taken to add extra vibrancy to the pictures through subtle tilting of the camera. At times, straight lines can look too conventional, while angles within a picture suggest a contemporary feel.

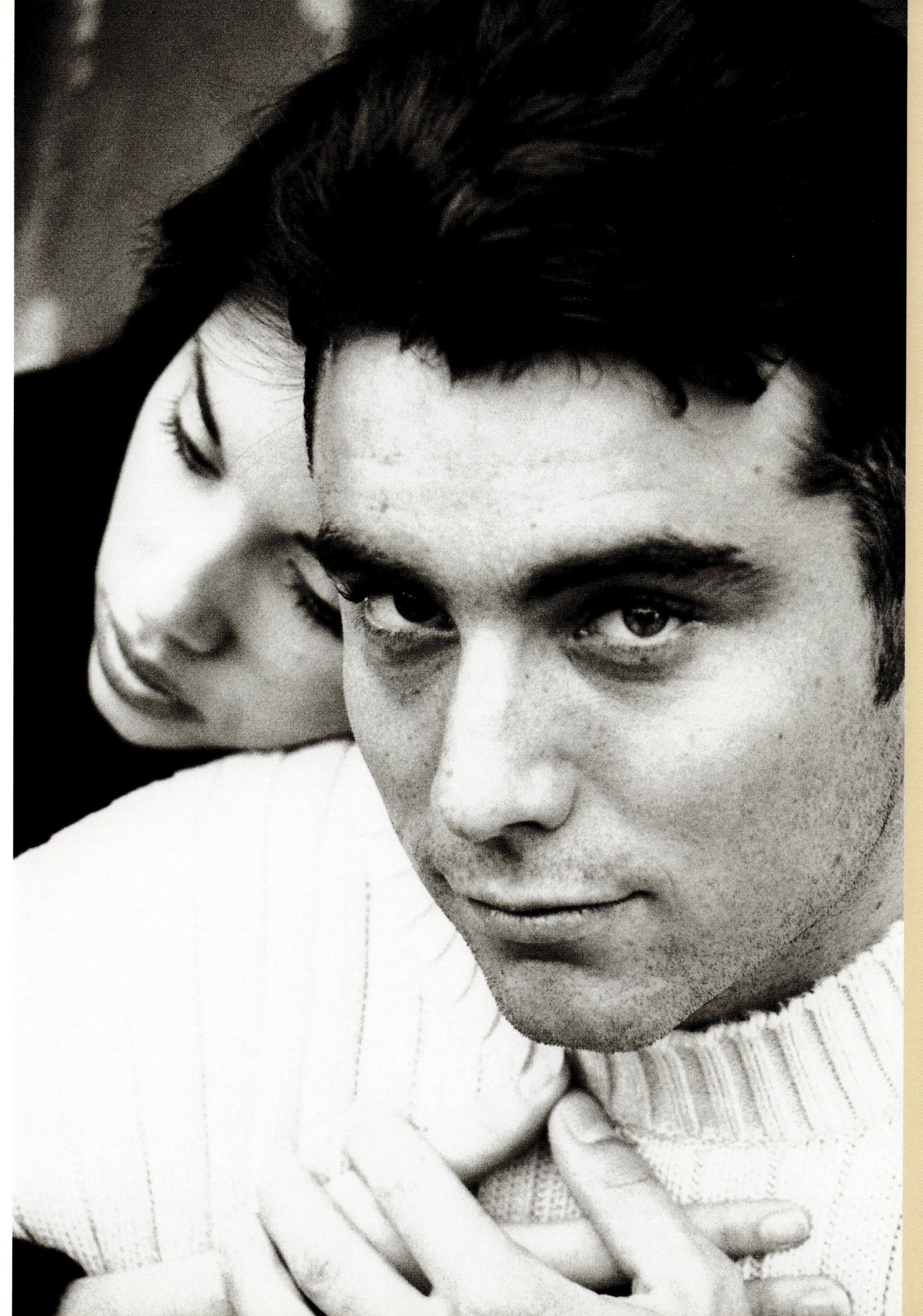

a new set of clothes

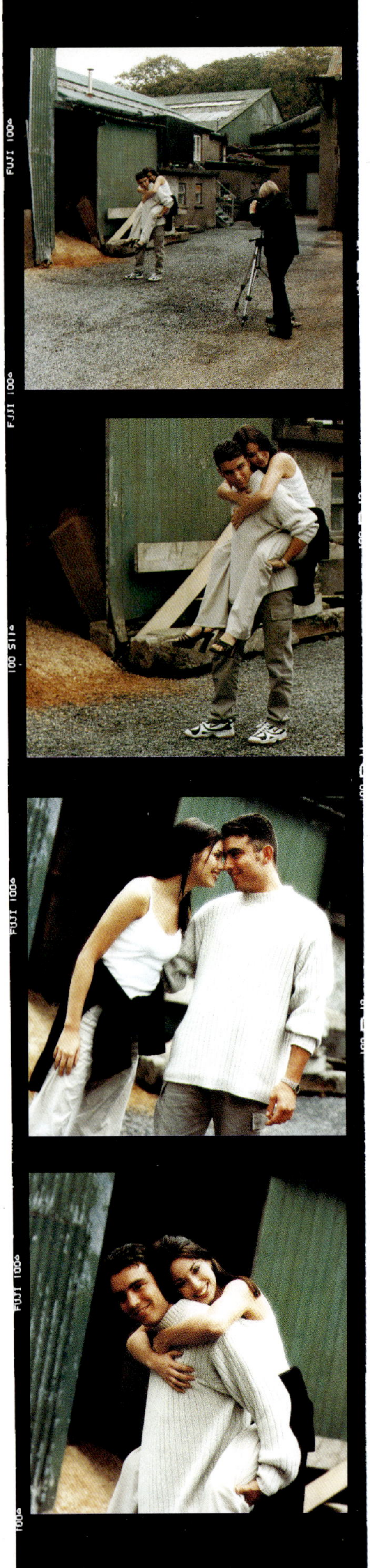

12.45p.m. Some of the best shots from a session often occur right at the very end, when everyone is at their most relaxed. Annabel keeps her camera to hand and her shooting instincts on alert so that, even when Lisa and Scott think it's all over, there's still the chance of more pictures. Annabel is still mixing colour with black and white to ensure that she gets the overall coverage that the couple is looking for and, when a picture is working particularly well, she makes sure that she shoots versions on both.

The session ends on a high note, with the clients feeling exhilarated and declaring that they want to come and do it all again soon. It's how it should be: when a shoot becomes a chore or never moves beyond the stage where the participants are feeling mildly embarrassed throughout, then it's going to show and results are never going to be satisfactory.

1.00p.m. Time for lunch!

A tight crop and the use of a doorway as a natural dark background has made this a strong picture in black and white as well as colour. The final element is a slight twist to the camera to allow the angles of the doorway to move away from the vertical. If the subjects are enjoying the shoot then it's possible, even in winter, to shoot without layers of clothing.

Canon EOS\5, 75–300mm zoom, Fujifilm Neopan 1600. Exposure 1/30sec at f/5.6

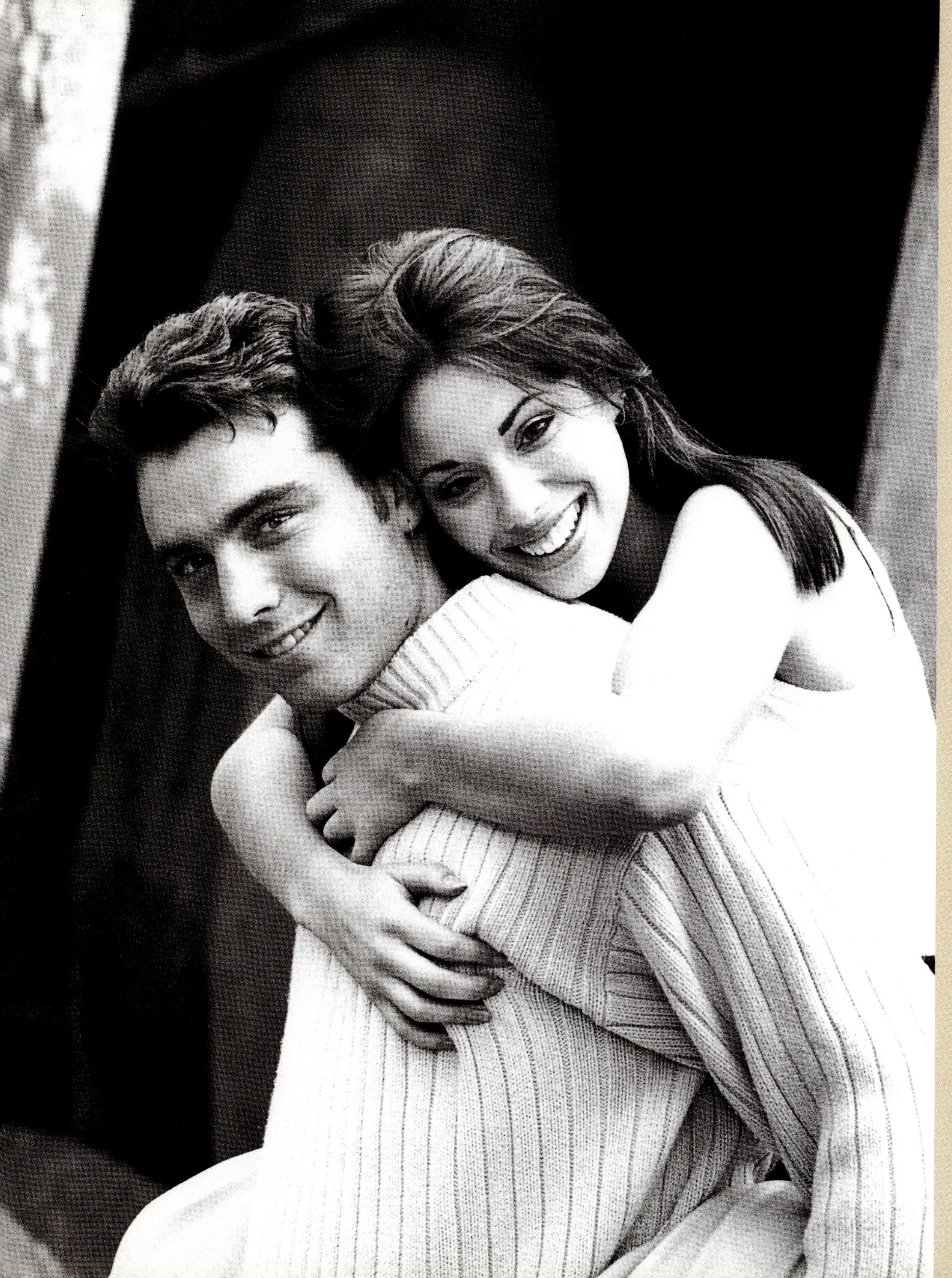

finishing on a happy note

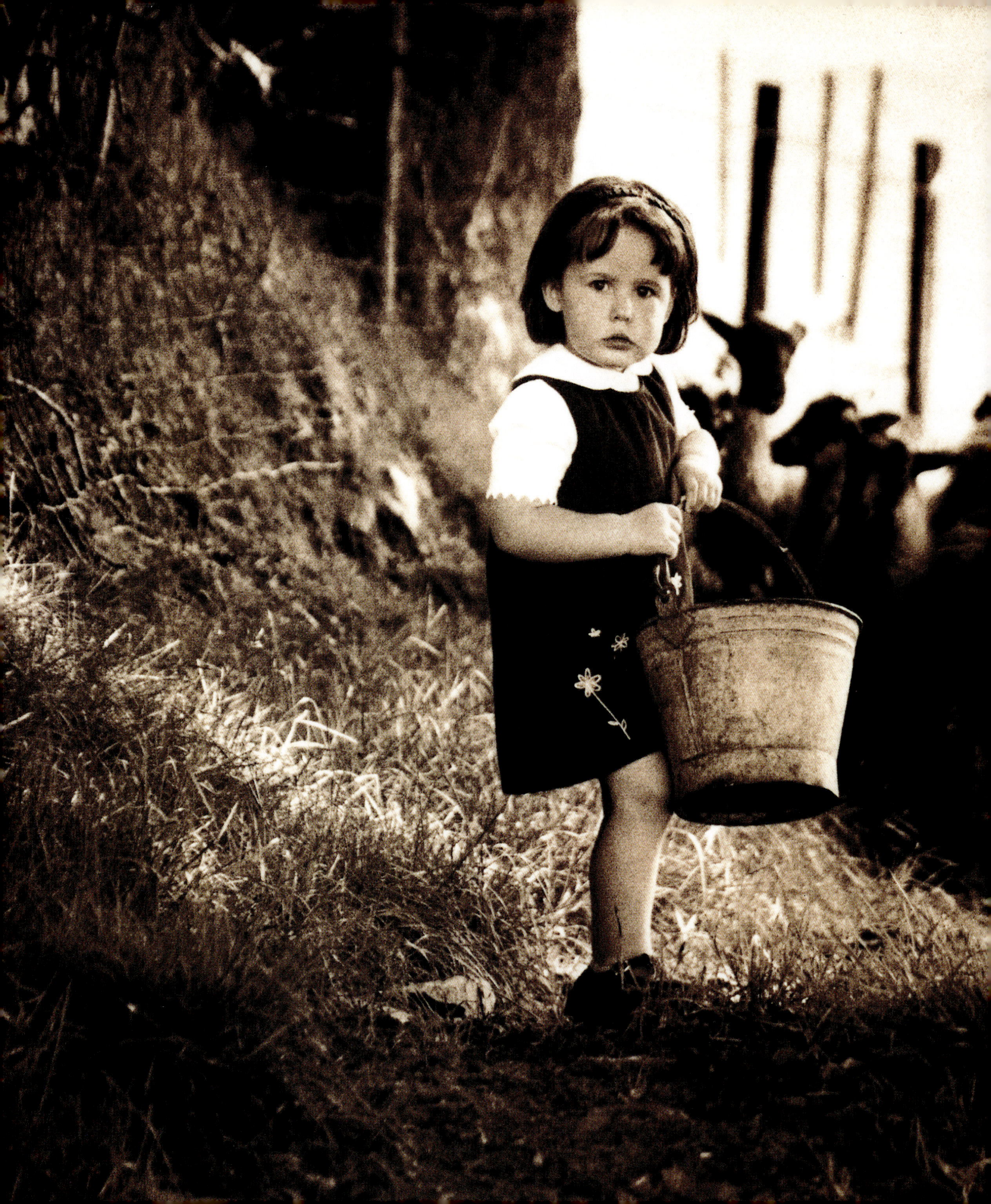

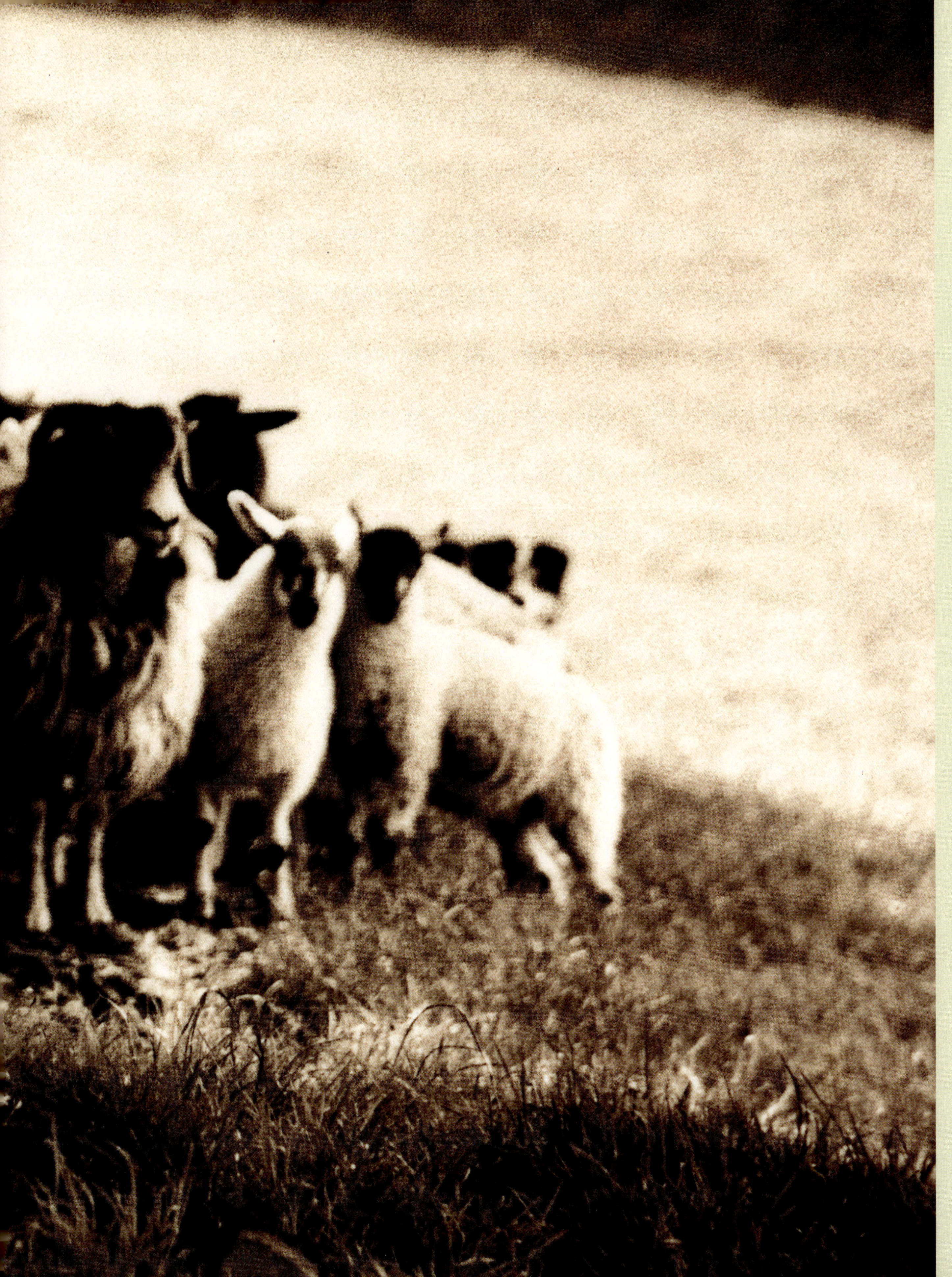

7 working with children

Great photography has less to do with the equipment you're using than it does with your approach to your subject. How quickly you can build a rapport with someone you may never have met face to face before is what will decide how successful the pictures are going to be.

These skills may well be tested still further if the subject you're photographing happens to be a child, and if you've decided that you're going to be taking your pictures on location. With the set of pictures featured throughout this section I even managed to add one further unpredictable element, a dog, and so I really had taken on a challenge!

To break the ice at the start of the session you have to take it slowly and be prepared to spend time getting to know your subject. See things from their point of view: to a child particularly as you'll be a stranger and a little frightening as a result, while posing for pictures sounds as though it's going to be boring. You have to be friendly and to try, in a subtle way, to "sell" the idea of the session to them, and to make it sound like fun and something that they can contribute to.

Once things start it invariably gets easier, and the up-side is that children and animals will often react with each other so well that they serve to put each other at ease. You can help things along by varying the location you use and the clothes that the child is wearing.

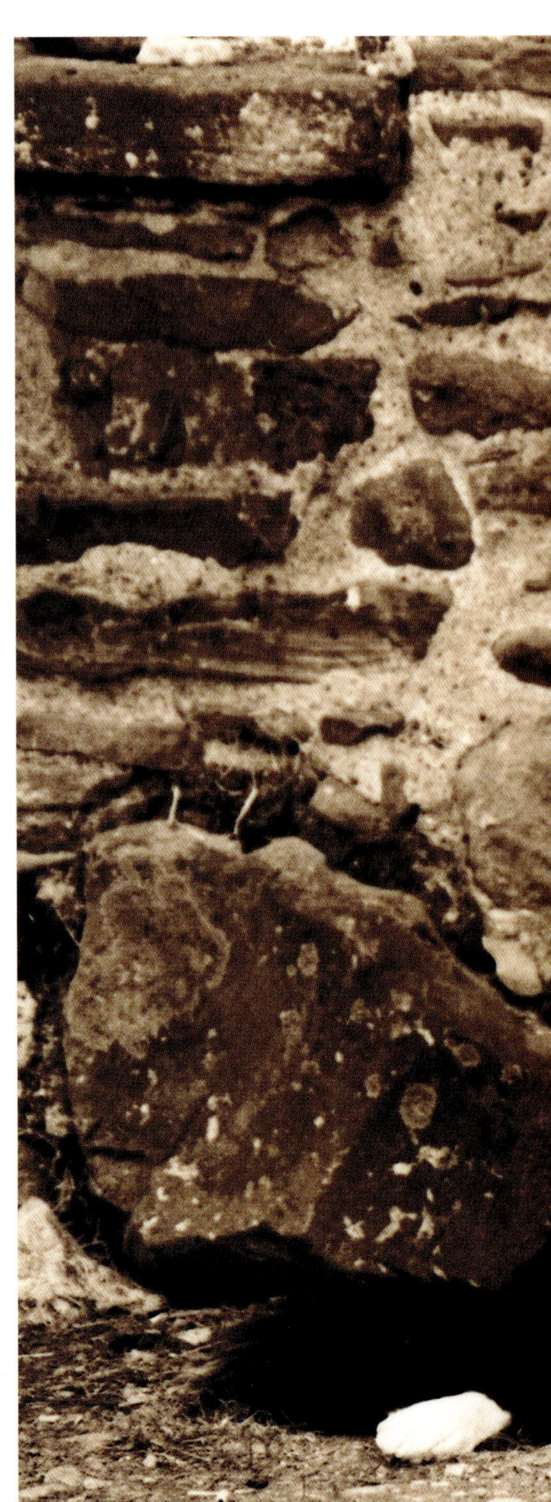

"Don't talk down to your subject because they happen to be a child. It's important that you make them feel involved and that you listen to what they have to say, and make what you're planning to do sound like fun."

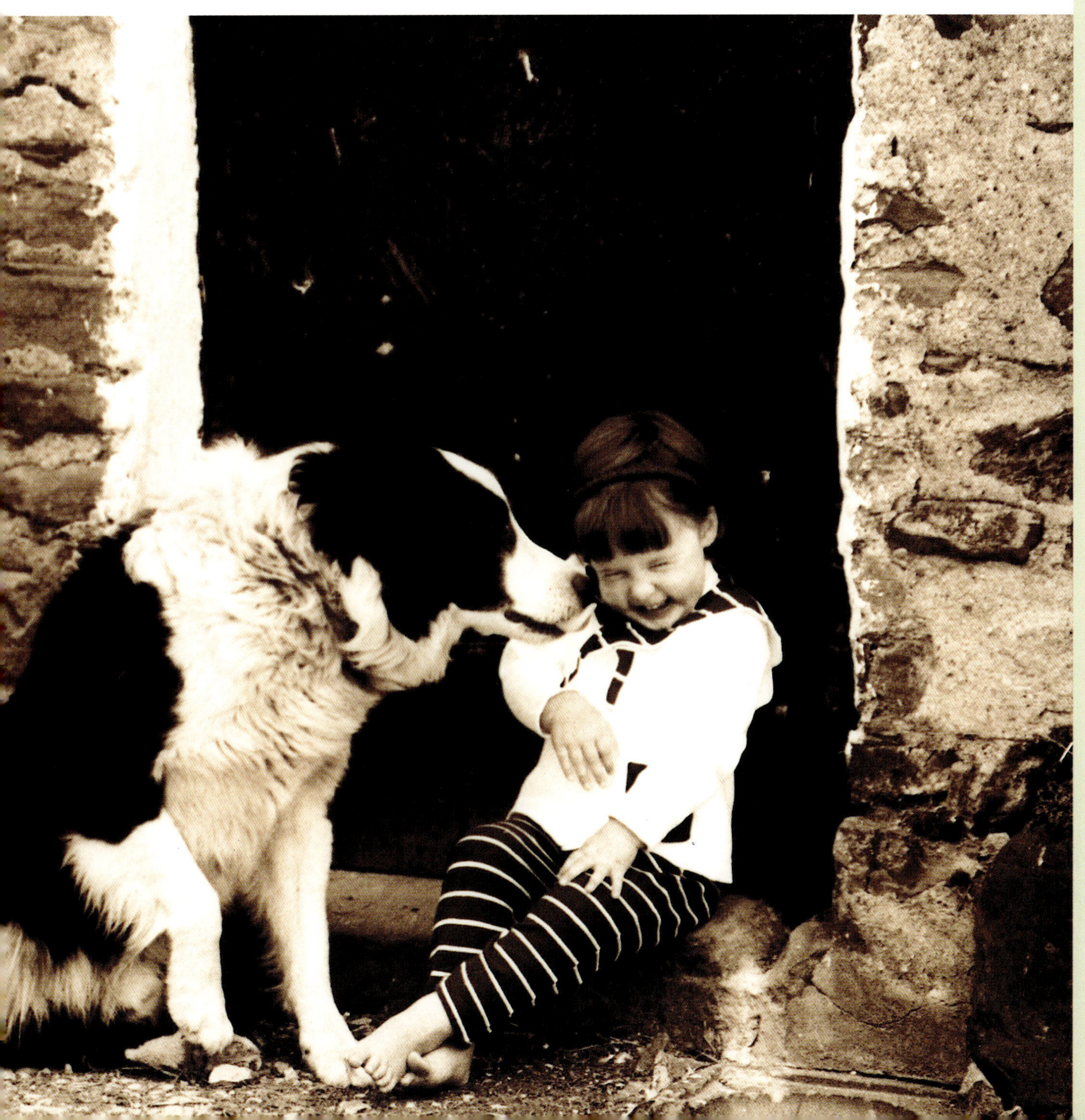

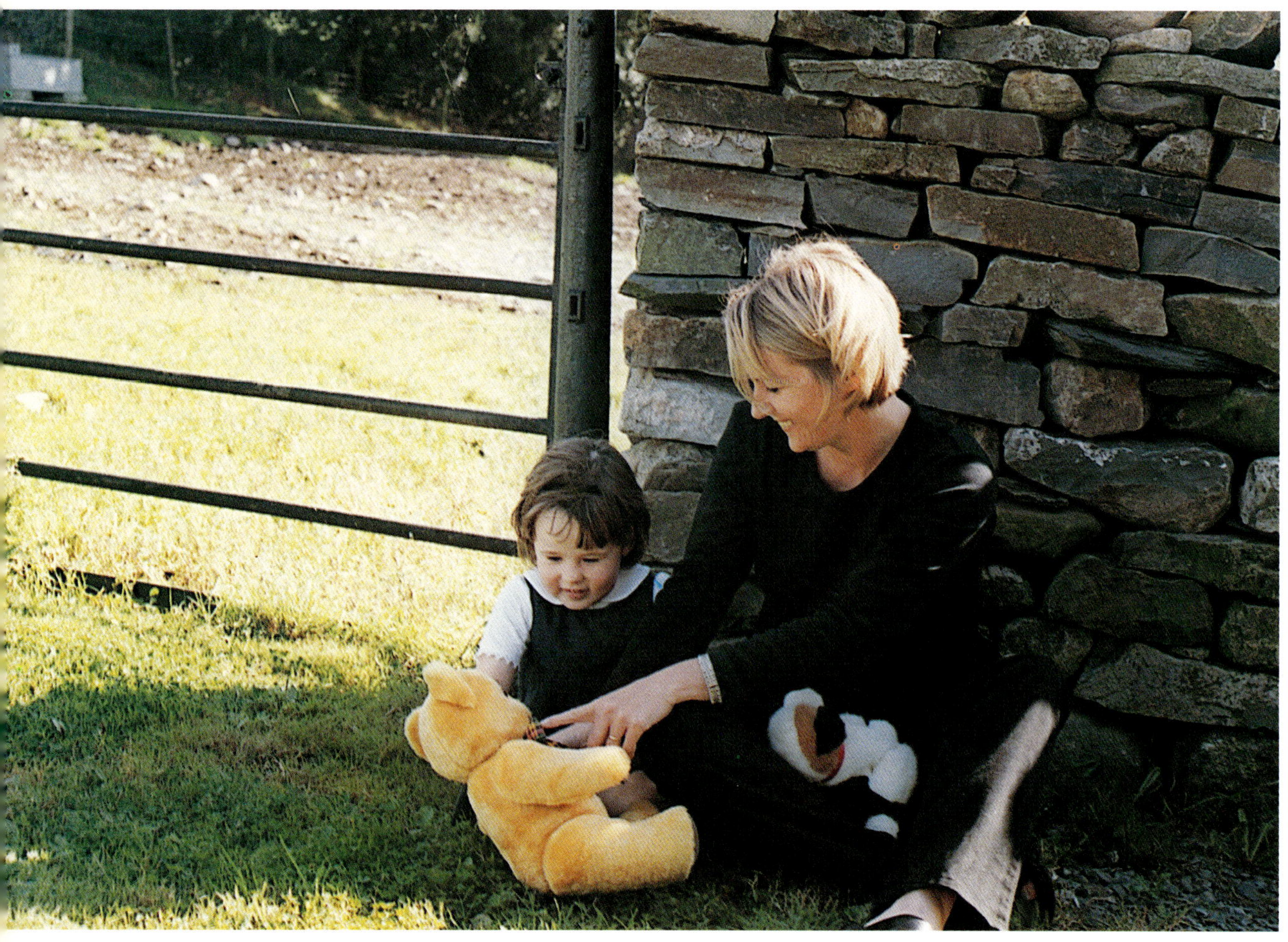

The way you react with a child within the first five minutes of meeting them, will directly affect the results you will achieve later. Patience is the key to getting them on your side.

1 Leave your cameras in the car – meet the family first and allow the child to see you as a person, rather than a photographer.

2 Try not to be too enthusiastic with the child as soon as you meet them. Talk to the parents, and slowly allow the child to become interested in you for themselves. If you try to force things they'll keep their distance.

3 Start to show interest in the child when you feel they are getting used to you, and ask them to show you their favourite toys and clothes. This will make the child feel involved.

4 Sit on the floor so that you come down to the child's level. It's a simple action but one that is incredibly important, and which will make it clear that you're approachable and easy to talk to. You've still not taken a picture: the name of the game is patience.

"I believe that pictures should show a time in a child's life: a time that will become even more important in the future, as they grow up."

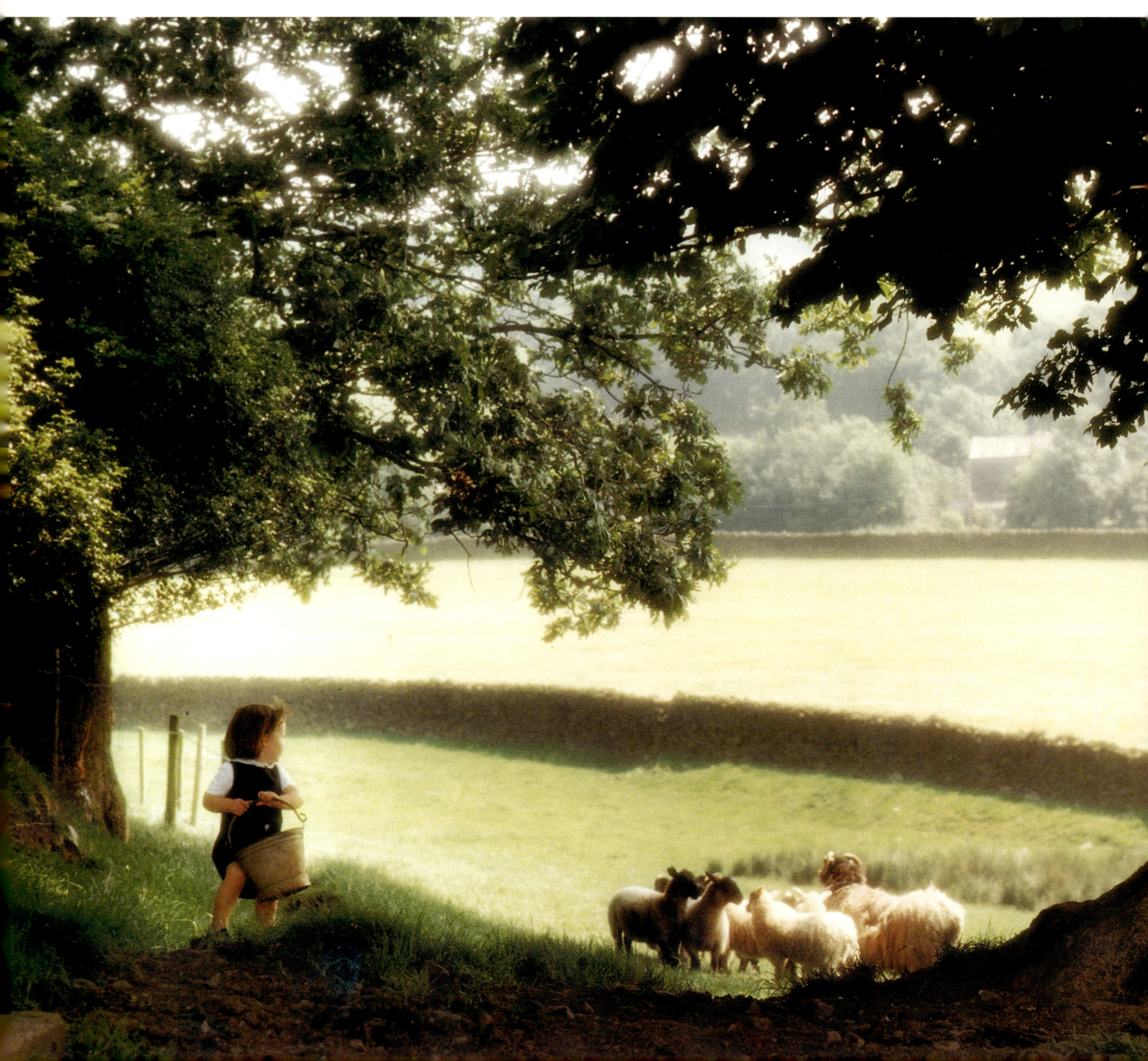

1 **Start by considering the final product and ask yourself some pertinent questions. What do the parents want?**

2 **Consider what kind of picture your clients are likely to hang on their walls? Will they want something in the upright or vertical format? Do they want a formal or informal approach?**

3 **Agree on the format. Do your clients prefer colour or black and white, or would they like a mixture?**

4 **Discuss how important the environment is to the client, and how they want it shown. This little girl lived on a farm and her parents wanted this aspect shown.**

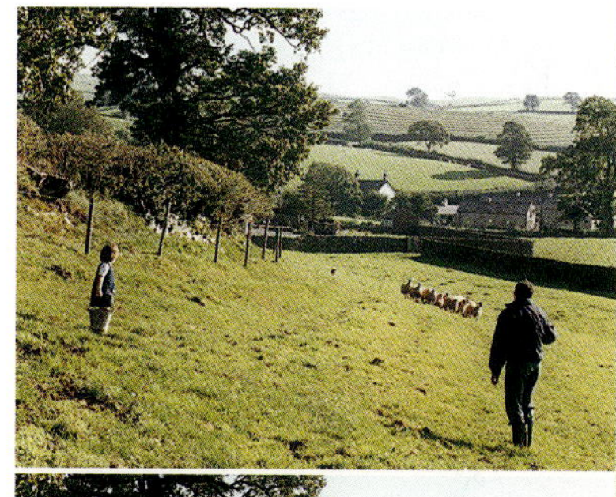

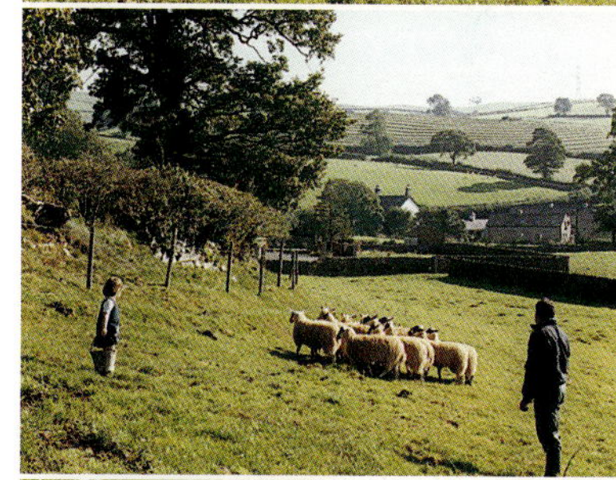

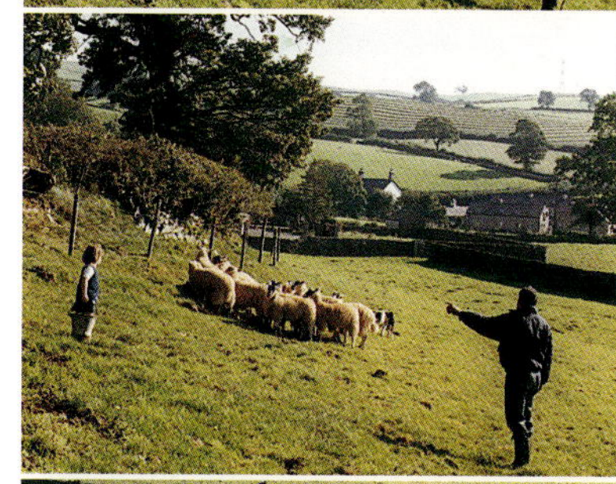

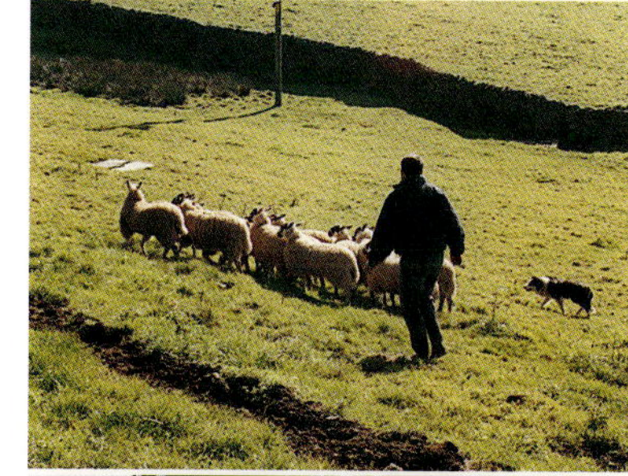

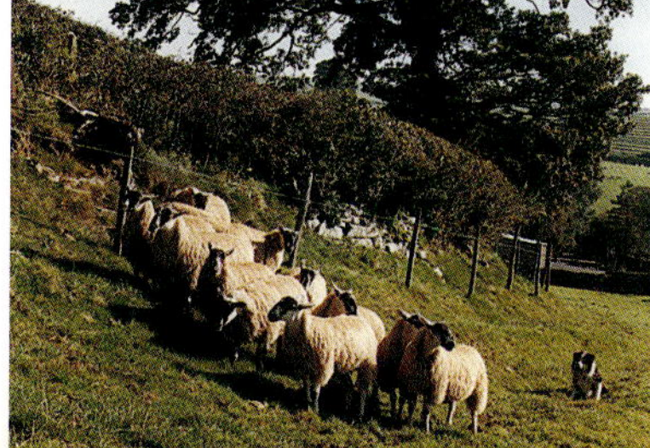

This picture showed Rebecca on her family farm, and was deliberately shot in a romantic style to evoke an element of nostalgia. It looks very natural but, as the background pictures opposite show, a lot of effort was spent in getting the sheep into exactly the right position.

Mamiya RZ 67, 150mm soft focus lens, Fujifilm NHG 800. Exposure 1/500sec at f/5.6

1. Set the scene and allow the child to do whatever they like.

2. Use a hand-held 35mm camera with a zoom lens to give yourself the freedom and flexibility necessary to capture spontaneous, natural shots.

3. Capture pictures which are totally natural and unposed by following your subject around at a distance and shooting with a zoom lens.

4. Shoot black and white film to add a new dimension to your pictures. These pictures were taken at the same time as the picture on the previous page and yet, because I've moved in and shot with a 35mm camera, the feel is quite different.

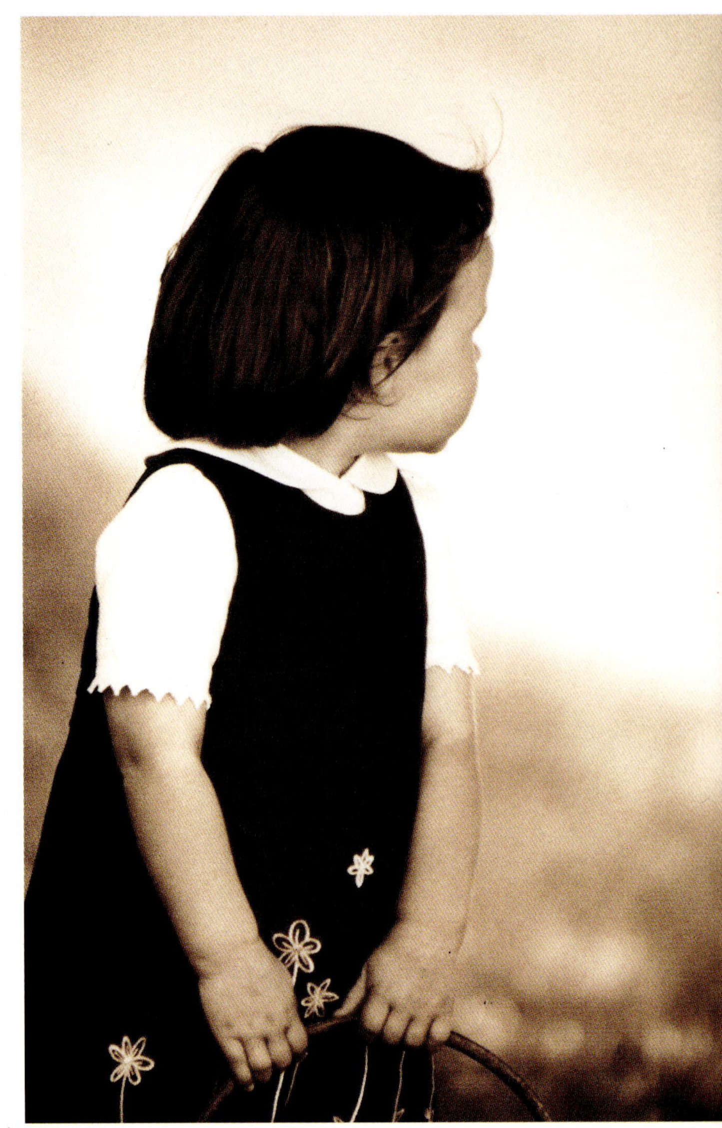

In colour these pictures would look like snapshots, but in black and white they highlight the child's individual features and add a new dimension to the shoot.

Canon EOS 5, 75–300mm lens, Fujifilm Neopan 1600. Exposure 1/60sec at f/5.6.

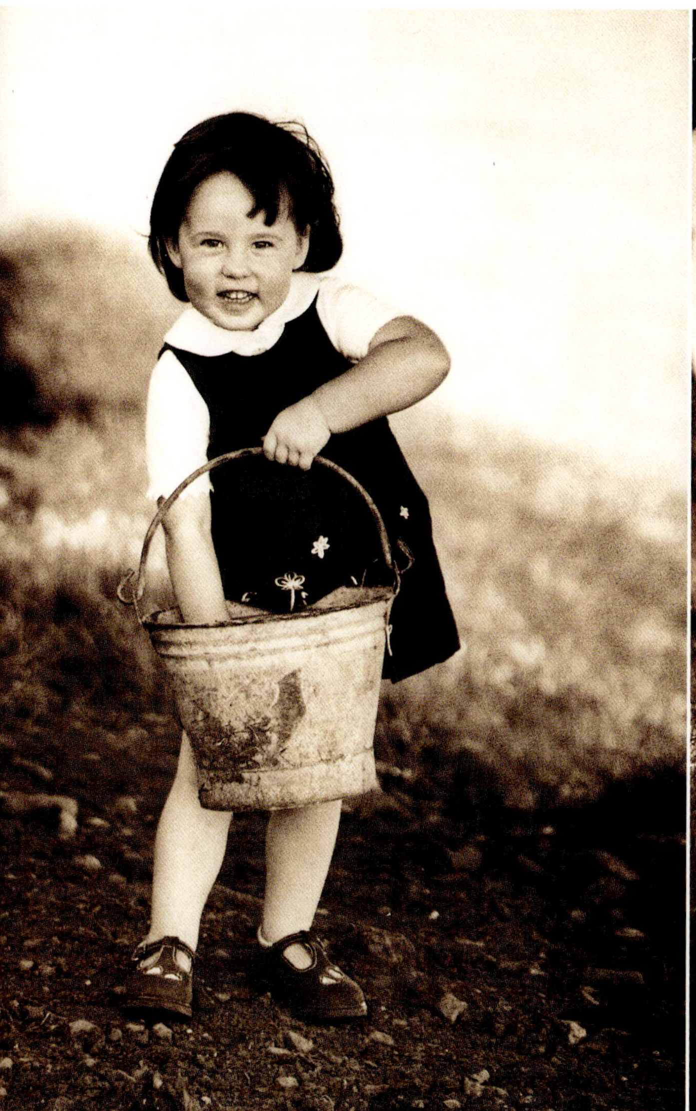

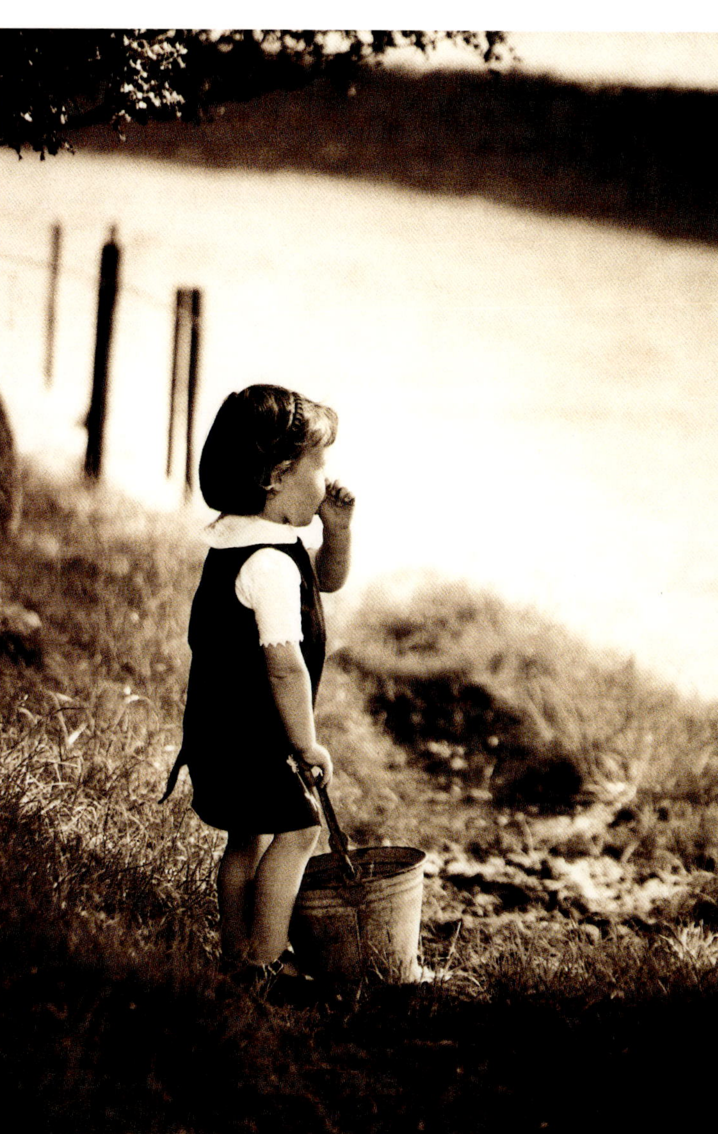

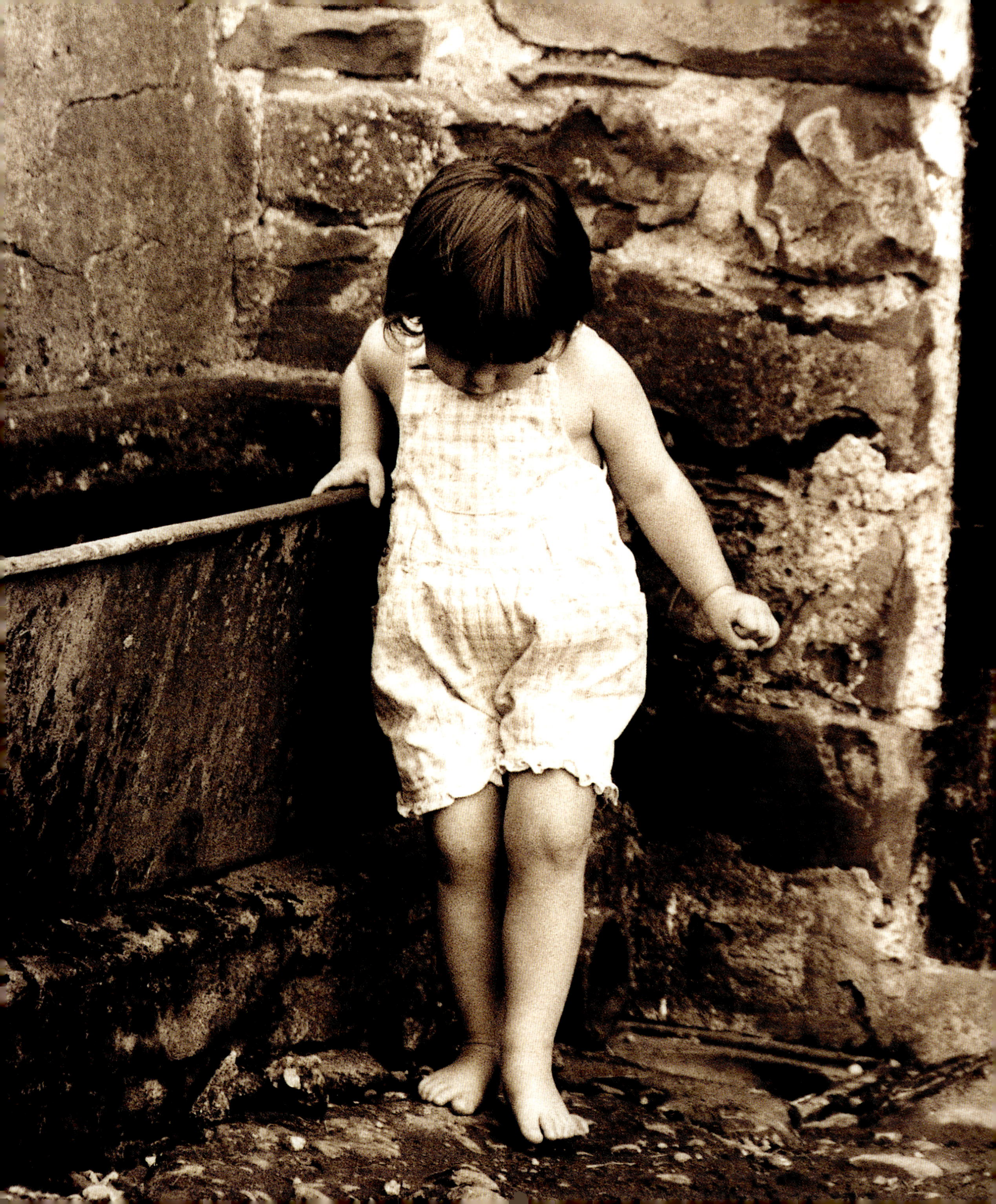

1 Vary the location. This helps maintain the interest of the subject as well as giving you the opportunity to try out new ideas and to find fresh angles to explore with your subject.

2 Look close to home and don't discard locations because there are certain aspects of them that don't appeal to you. Choice of camera angle and time of day can transform even the most ordinary setting. The picture here looks like it was taken in a totally rural setting, but it was actually just a few feet away from a busy main road.

3 Complement the location you're using with the clothes your subject is wearing. The two must work together and be in harmony, and together they will serve to inspire you and to give you a theme for your pictures.

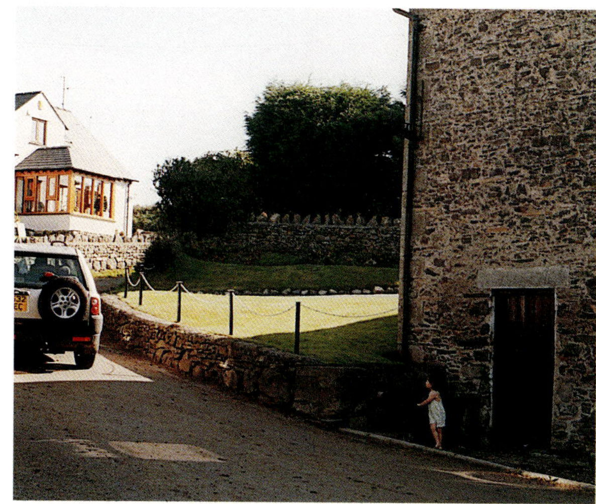

Few settings are totally perfect. There's usually something just out of shot to spoil the illusion, such as an electricity pylon or, as here, a busy road, but your choice of camera angle will help you create a scene that looks idyllic. Learn to develop an eye for situations like this, and frame a scene carefully to crop out unwanted details in-camera. Make sure the child's parents are on guard in any potentially dangerous situations for obvious reasons!

Canon EOS 5, 75–300mm zoom, Fujifilm Neopan 1600. Exposure 1/250sec at f/5.6

These results could never have been achieved by "posing" the child. The most effective way to take natural pictures is to compose an attractive scene, ensure that the light will be consistent and allow the child to play.

Canon EOS 5, 75–300mm lens, Fujifilm Neopan 1600. Exposure 1/250 sec at f/5.6

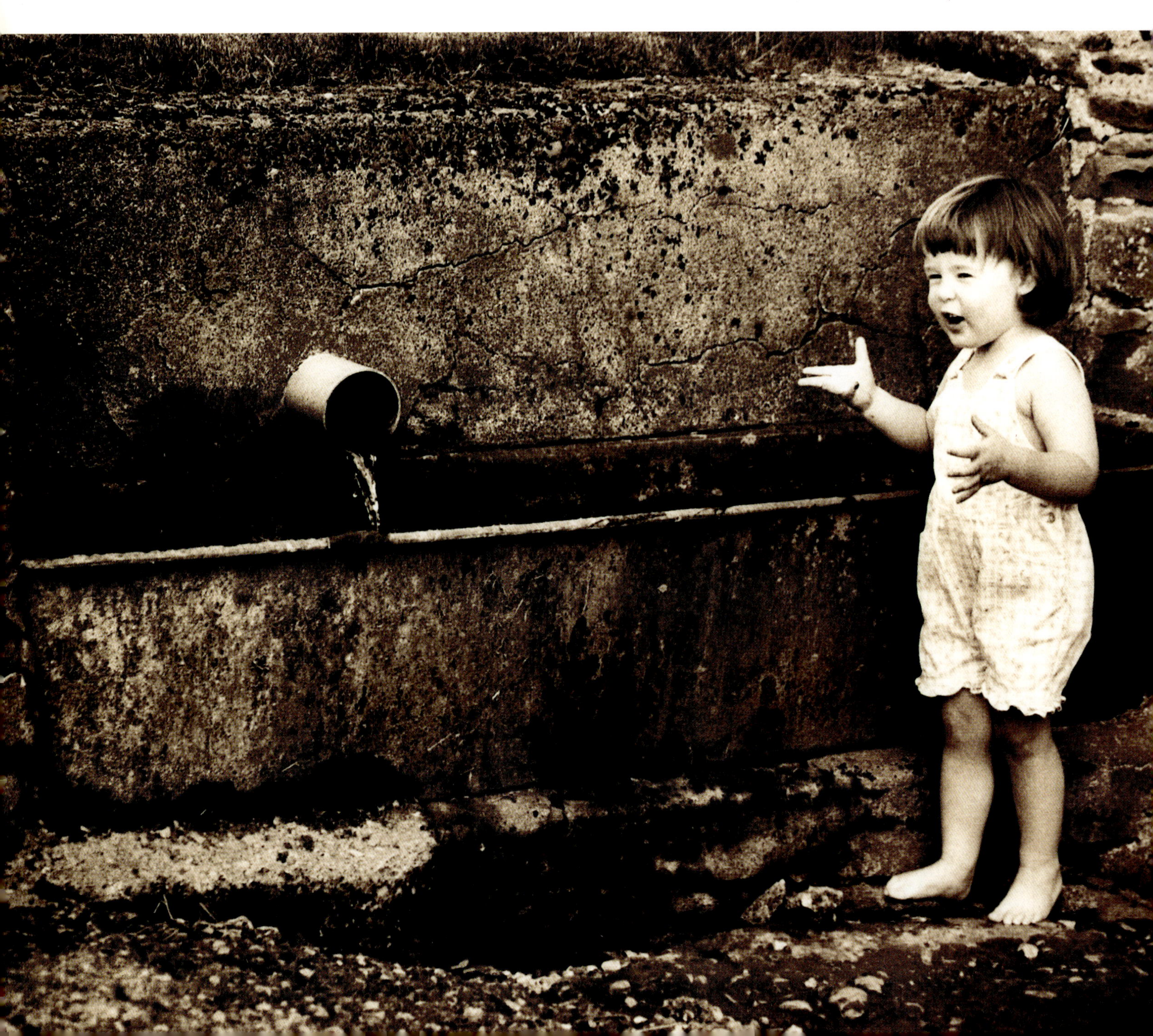

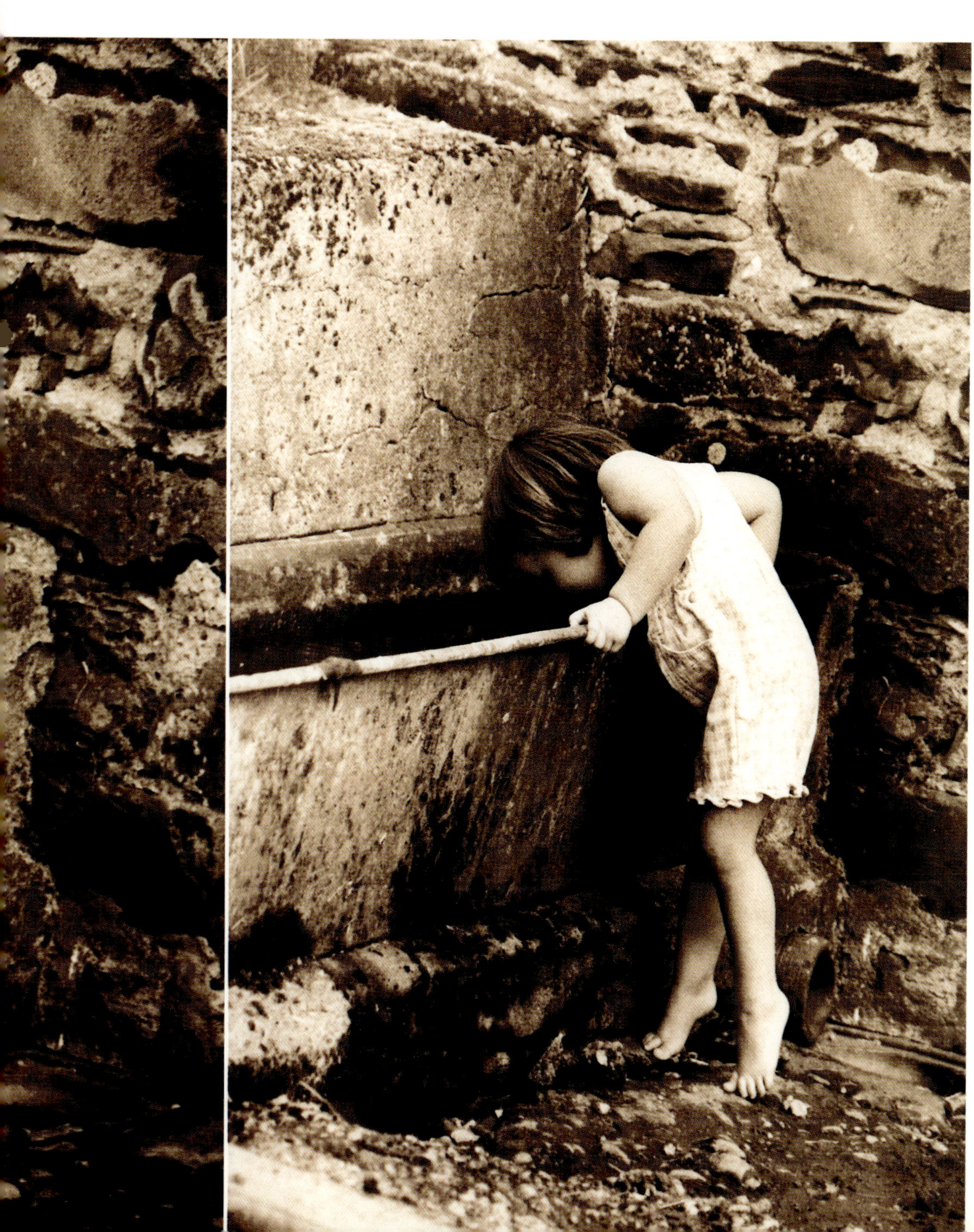

In some ways it sounds strange, but producing a picture to hang on the wall of a room should be done with the same consideration that one might apply to the purchase of a piece of furniture, a concept that's explained in more detail in section 9. It has to fit in with its environment and look right in the place where it's hung: not only the content of the picture but the presentation that's been applied to it have to be in keeping with the surroundings.

The picture here of the little girl was taken against a stone wall, which complements the wall it's been hung on, and it's been presented in a plain wooden frame that perfectly matches the old and rustic feel of the house and its furnishings.

Often my starting point for a picture such as this is the room where it's ultimately due to hang. That way I get an idea of what the client wants and what they're going to be happy with, before a single picture has been taken. It helps to give me a clearer idea of the final result that I should be aiming for.

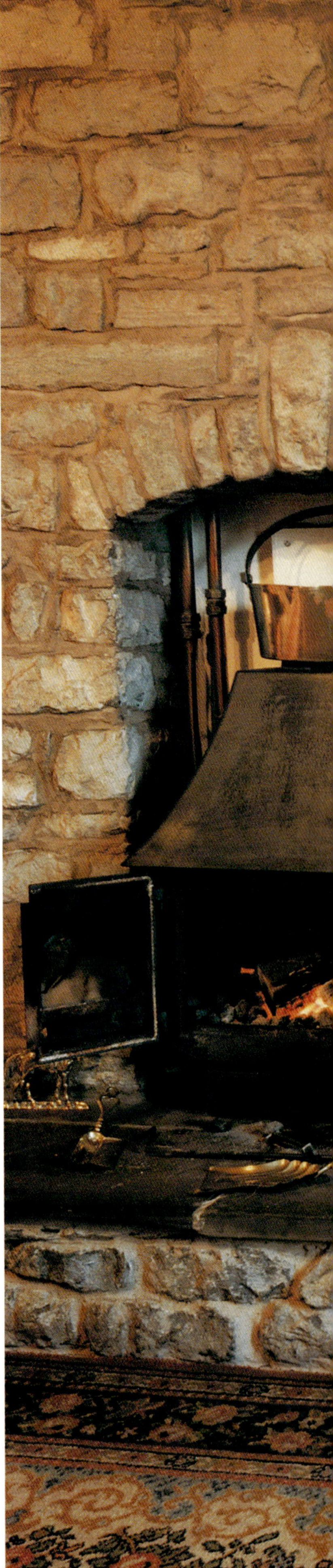

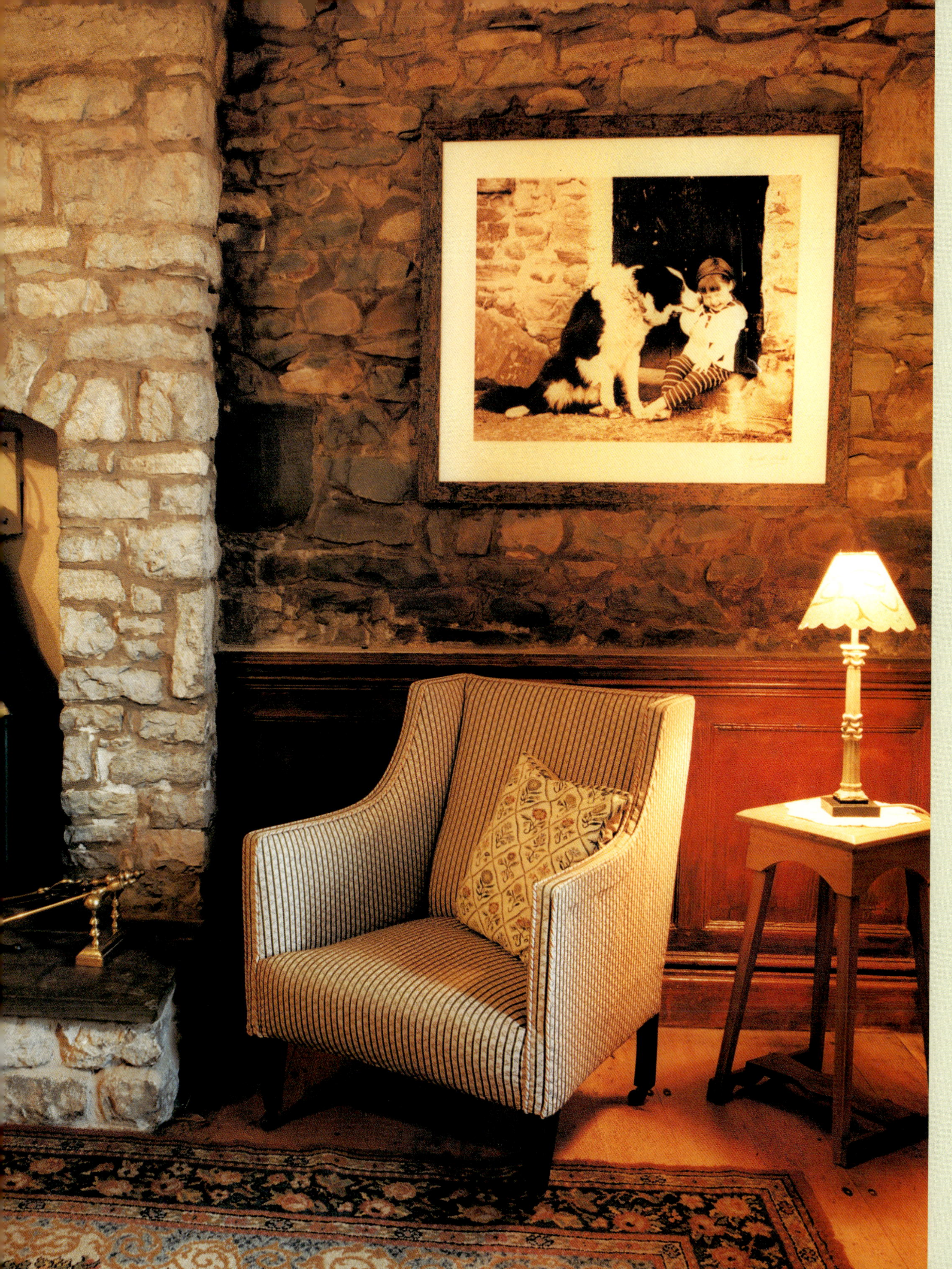

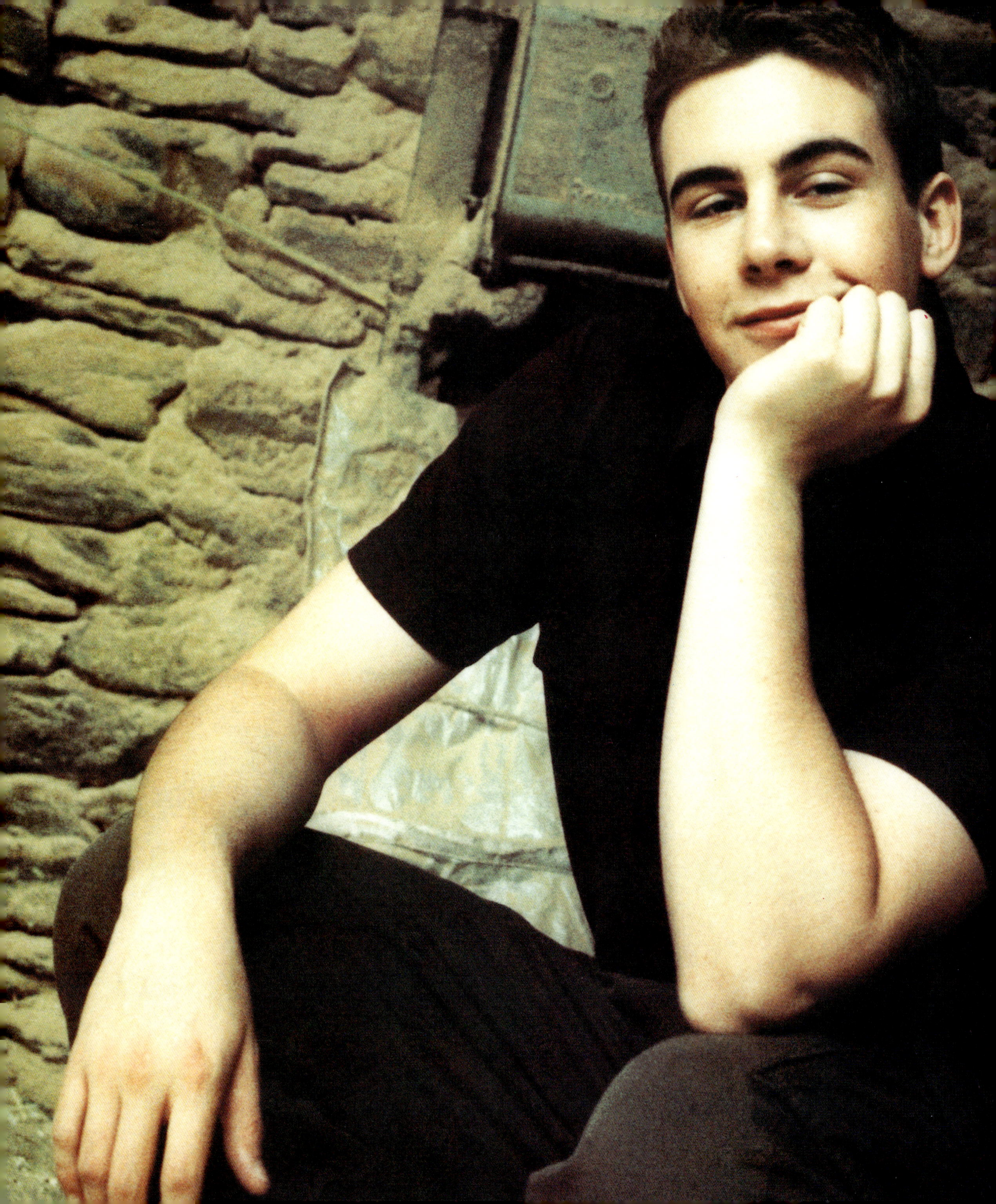

8 editing and shooting for versatility

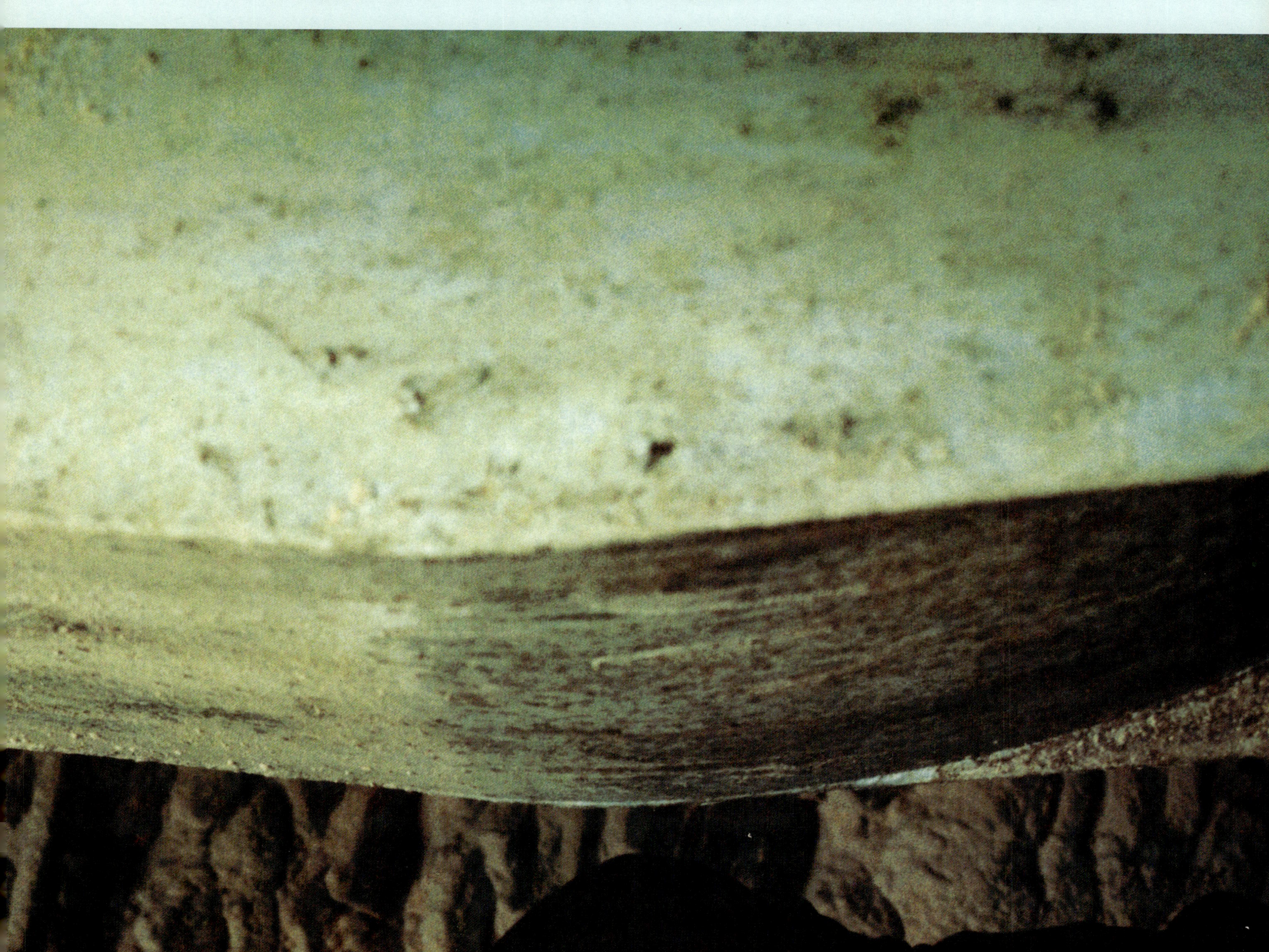

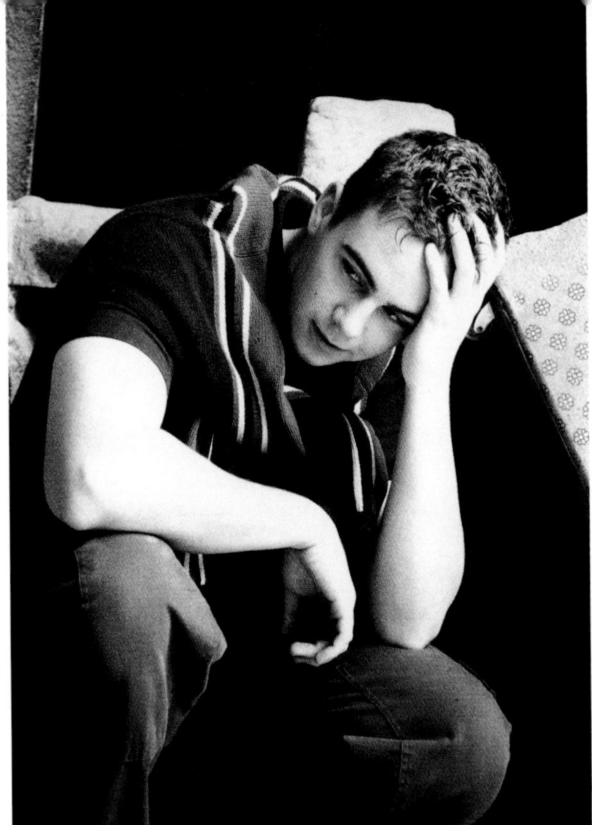

Taking too many pictures using the same set-up, the same lighting and the same clothes will give your client very little in the way of choice, and it will leave you uninspired. Try to achieve a set of pictures full of variety – there are several ways to do this.

You should be looking to work with more than one camera format, because cameras will impose a certain way of working on you and your subject. The formality that a medium-format camera will bring with it may be ideal for some situations, but the flexibility of 35mm will give you an alternative way of working that will be suitable for most people. I find that colour suits the larger format, whereas black and white film is an ideal companion for 35mm, being fast enough to allow hand-held pictures even when I'm using the longer end of my 75–300mm zoom.

I also try to work with available light and – wherever possible – without the encumbrance of reflectors. This gives me the flexibility to move in close, and to change my camera position quickly. I want to capture how people feel, not just the way they look, and the only way to do this is to relax them and work quickly. If they're sitting there waiting for you to get the technical details right, then you'll miss the moment every time.

Changing the look that you're achieving sounds hard to do, but can in fact take a matter of seconds, especially if you're fully prepared and have two different camera formats with you. The picture on the previous page is an establishing shot taken with a medium-format camera, and is a logical starting place for your session. You can move on quickly from here, however, to create looks that are dramatically different, and it may just involve swapping cameras and moving your position a matter of a few yards. With the black and white images I took the opportunity to move closer to my subject, and I added what amounted to a natural prop at one stage by asking him to throw a jumper around his neck. Immediately the feel of the picture was different, and this gave me another angle to explore.

Colour: Hasselblad 6x6cm, 50mm lens, Fujifilm Provia 400, cross-processed. Exposure 1/60sec at f/5.6

Black and white: Canon EOS 5, 75–300mm zoom, Fujifilm Neopan 1600. Exposure 1/250sec at f/5.6

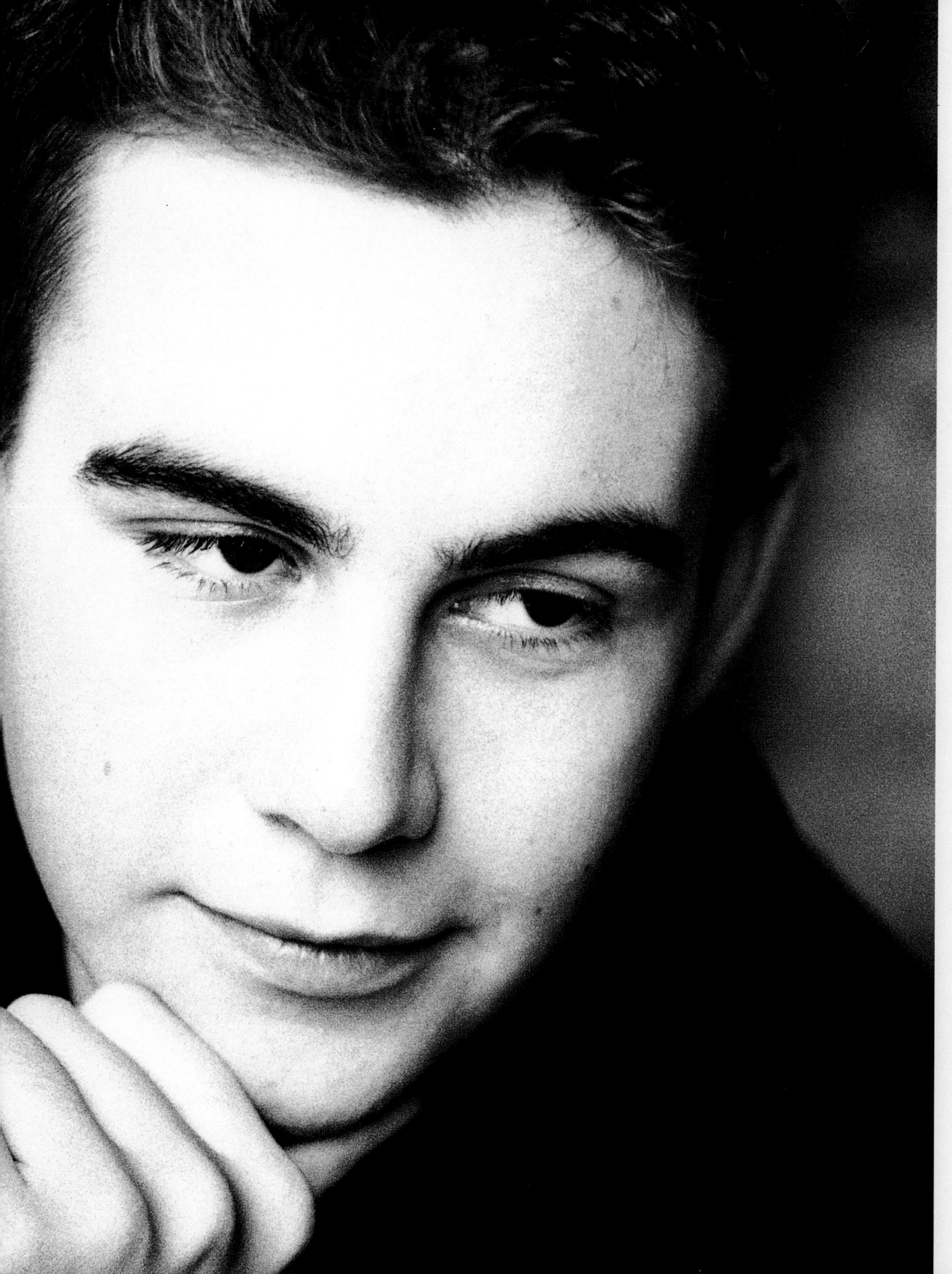

diversify as much as possible

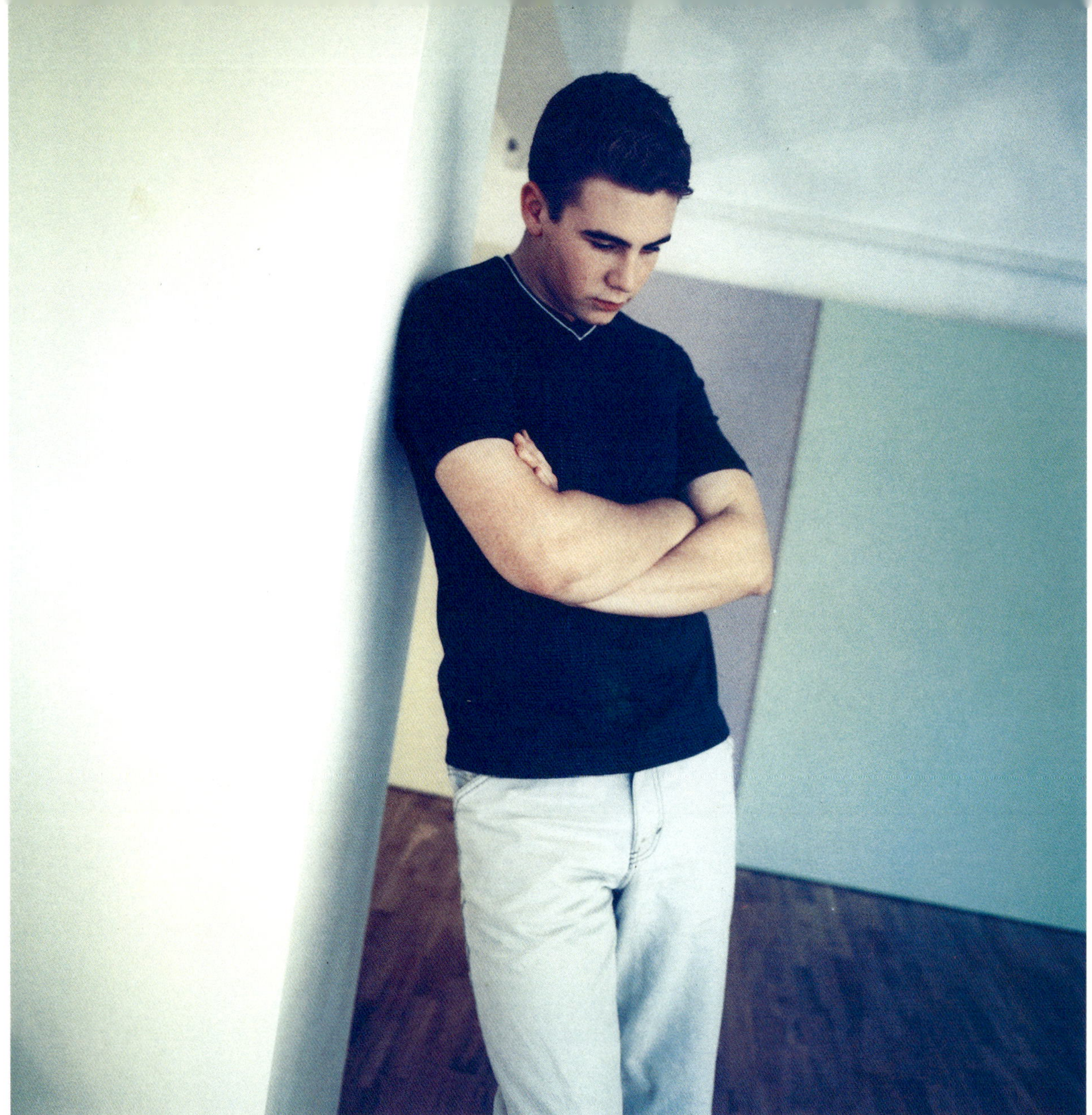

With a little care there's no reason why you shouldn't be able to achieve the crop you want in-camera, which will make subsequent printing more straightforward.

Some medium-format cameras, such as my Mamiya RZ 67, will offer a format that's bigger but still in ratio to that offered by a 35mm camera, and the rectangular format is also popular and very versatile. An alternative, however, is offered by the Hasselblad, which gives a square format. This, too, has its advantages, and will often give a quite different feel to a picture, one that will call for subtle changes to the composition.

Square format
The square format can be seen used in everyday life in a variety of ways: just think CDs and car brochures. It can be seen as quite a formal format, and it does impose a certain way of working compositionally on the photographer, but it still has a lot to offer in terms of striking contemporary photography.

Hasselblad, 120mm lens, softar 1, Fujifilm Provia 400. Exposure 1/8sec at f/5.6

Rectangular format
The chief advantage of the rectangular format is that it allows the photographer to switch from horizontal to vertical format almost instantly. When you're working quickly and trying to produce a variety of pictures from a set situation, this is an extremely useful facility.

Canon EOS 5, 75–300mm zoom, Fujifilm Neopan 1600. Exposure 1/30sec at f/5.6

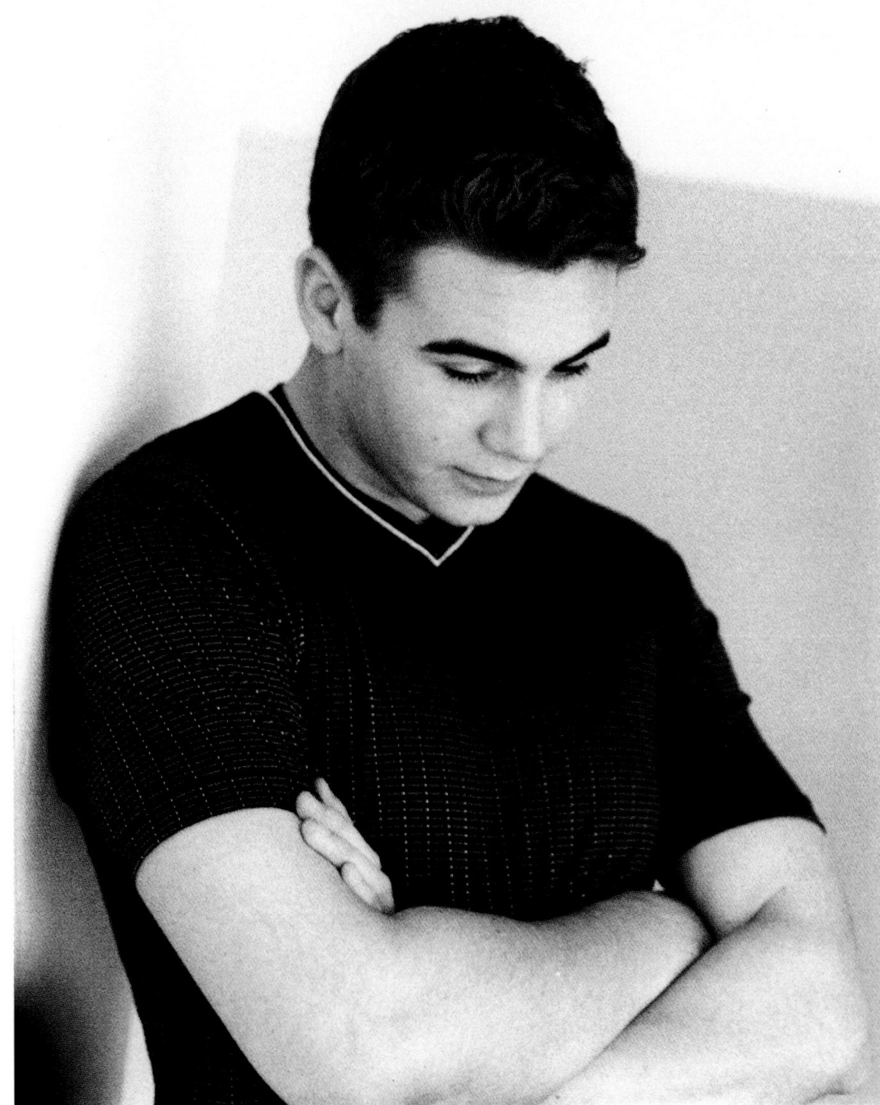

Work with the format that you have, and try to make your decisions about composition at the shooting stage, excluding extraneous detail and concentrating purely on what the important elements are within a picture. Your instinct as a photographer will tell you what looks right through the viewfinder and what doesn't, and you have to learn to work quickly but accurately.

As has been shown many times already in this book, tilting the camera is a very simple, but highly effective way of making your pictures more interesting and visually dynamic. The important thing is to make the effect subtle, and to leave the subject looking normal and not as though they're about to fall over. The vertical lines in two of the pictures here make it clear the kind of movement you can get away with: straight lines tend to look too conventional and boring, and the eye loves things that are at an angle. If you get your subject to lean away from the direction you're tilting in – with me I tilt automatically down to the right which makes my subject appear to be leaning towards the left – this will further help to make them look normal within the picture, while everything around them is on the move.

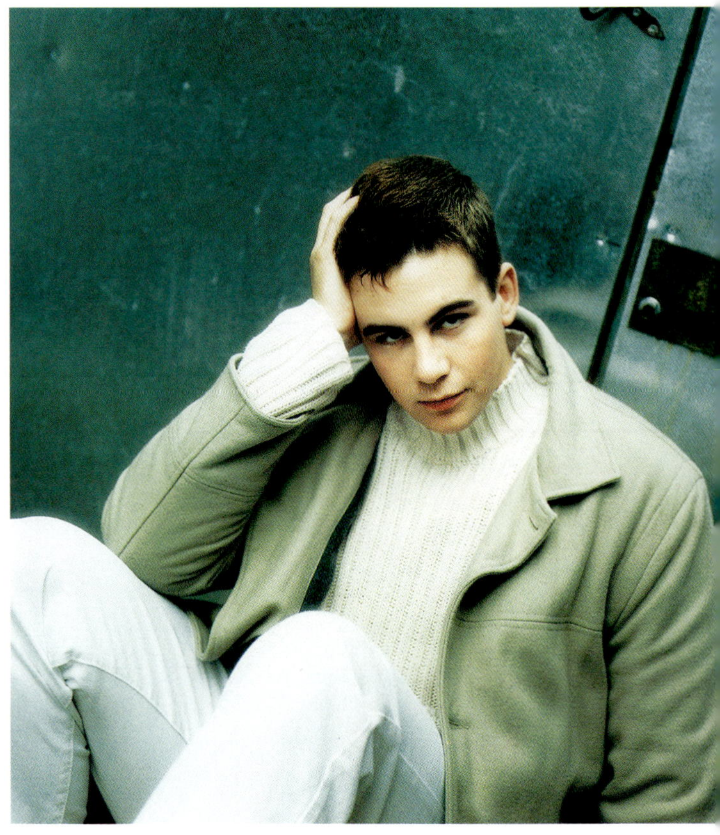

Slanting Angles
The fact that the camera has been tilted is often not apparent immediately, as the emphasis is on the subject. Here he's helped the effect of normality still further by leaning away from the tilt.

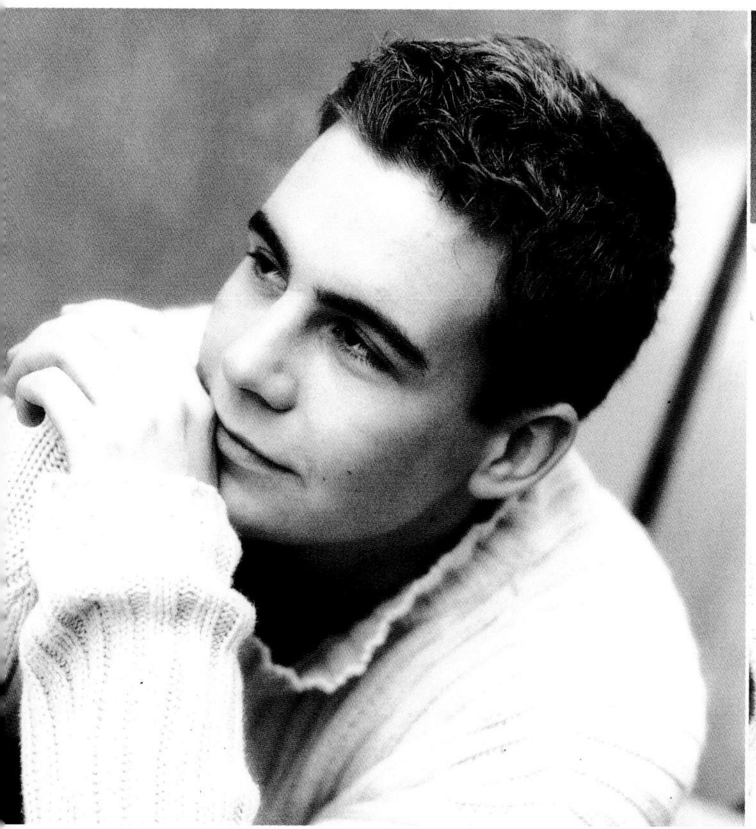

High angles
Raising the angle of the camera considerably is more flattering for the subject, as it makes the eyes appear larger and removes weight from the jawline.

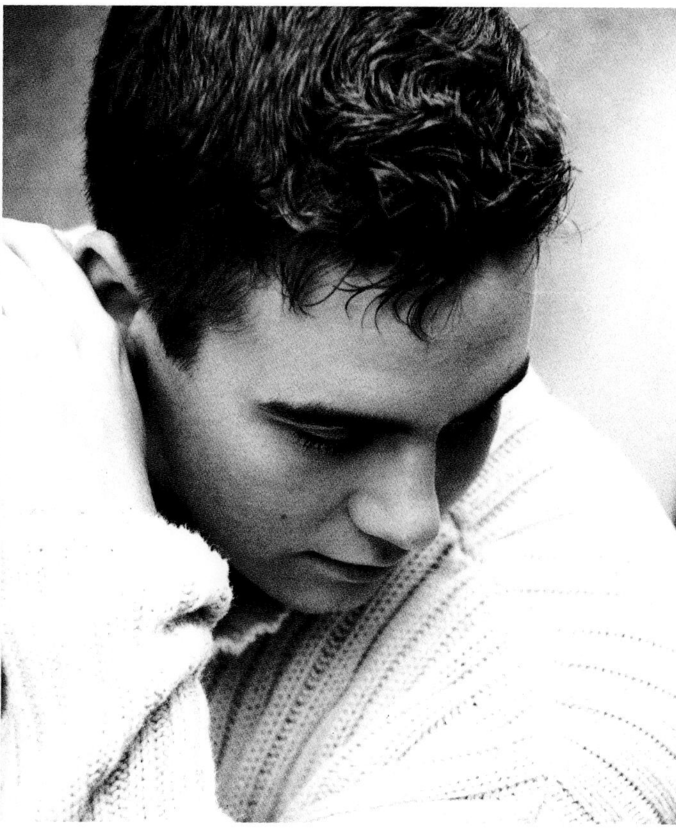

Zooming in
Picking up a 35mm camera and cropping in very tightly again adds a new dimension.

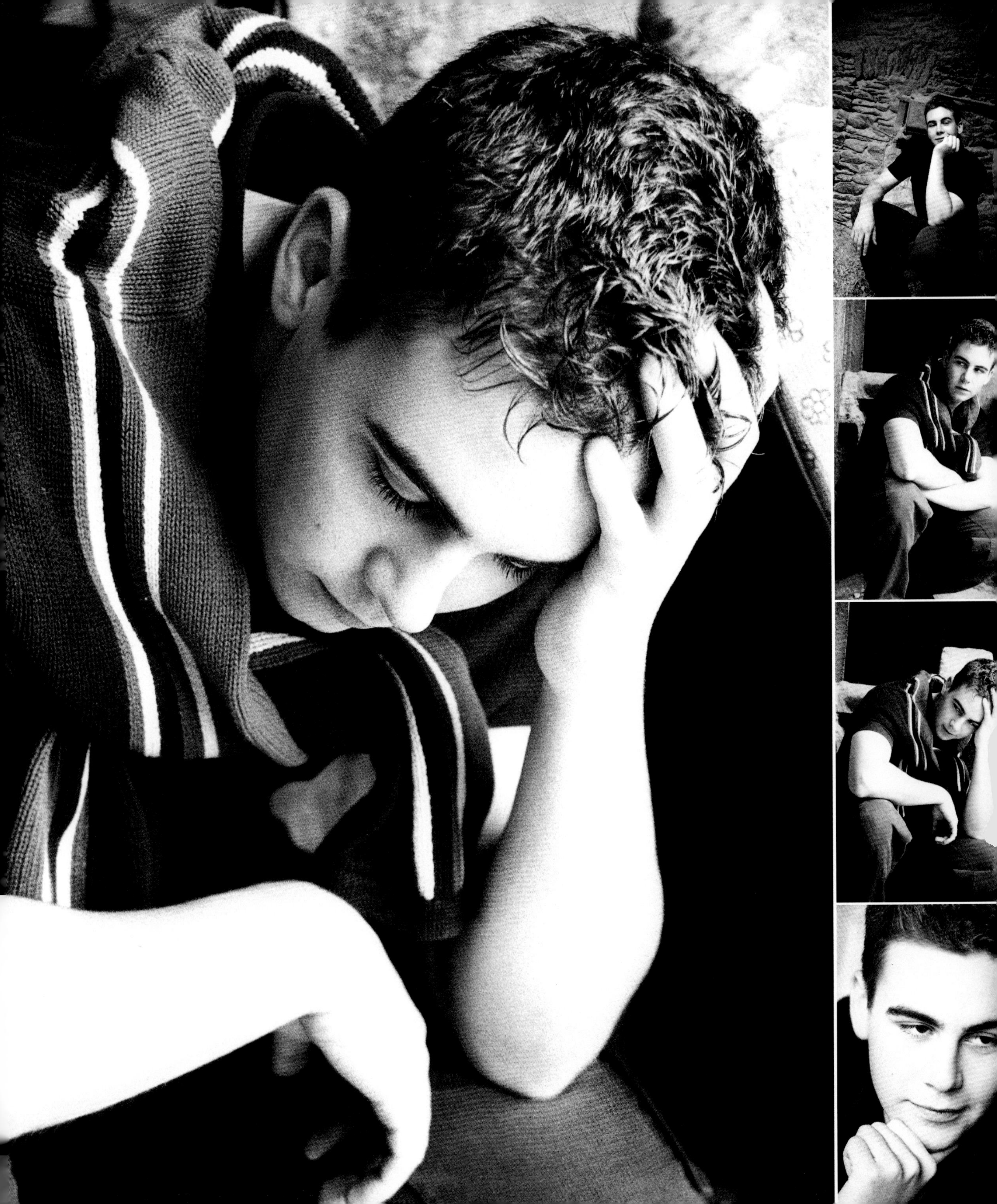

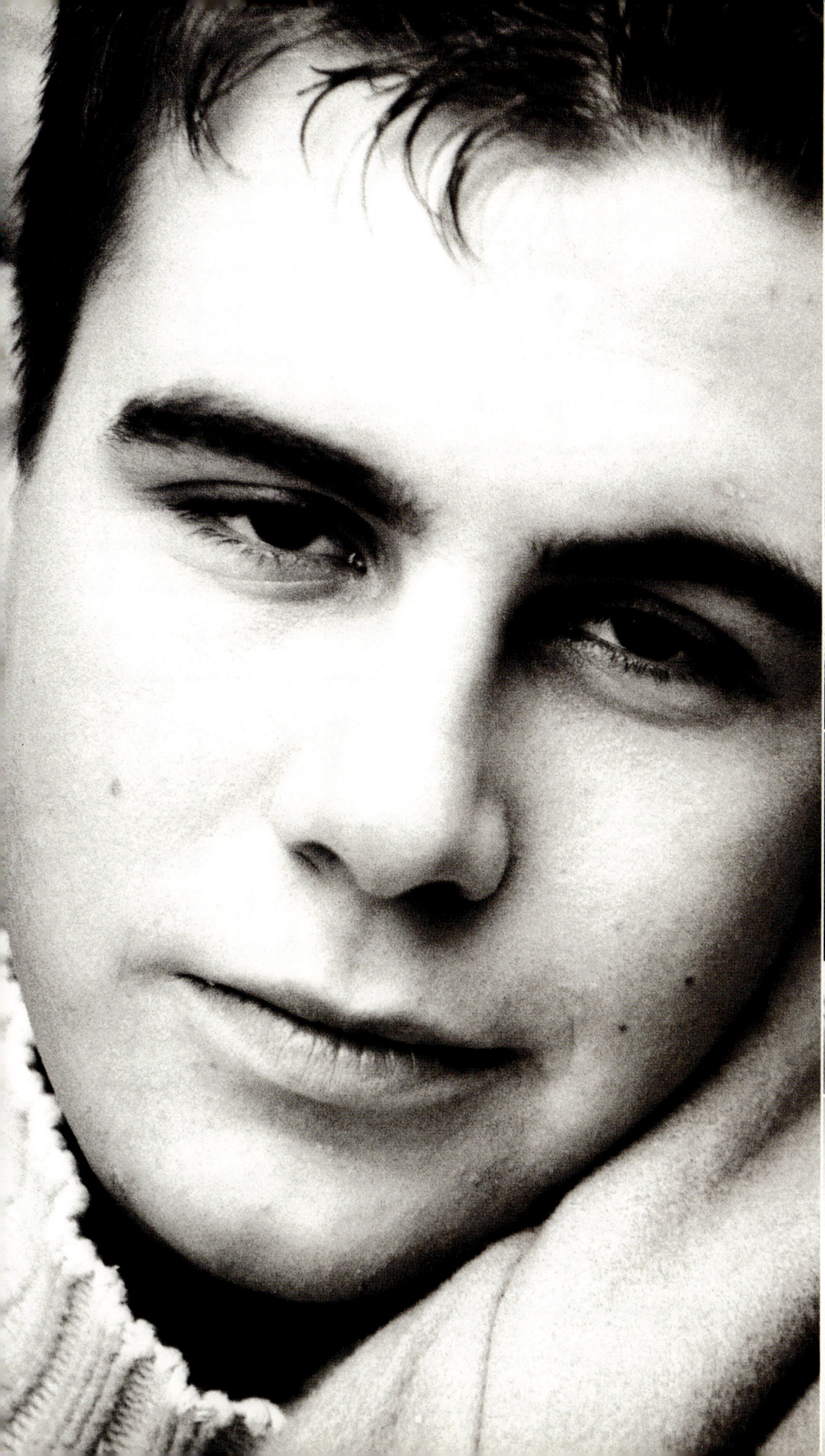

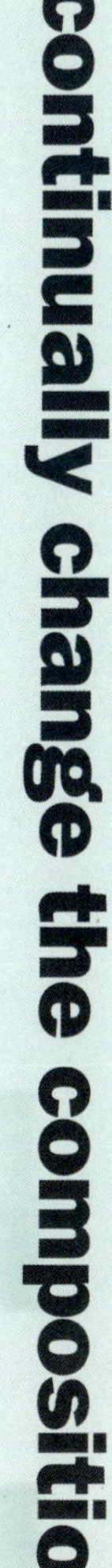
continually change the composition

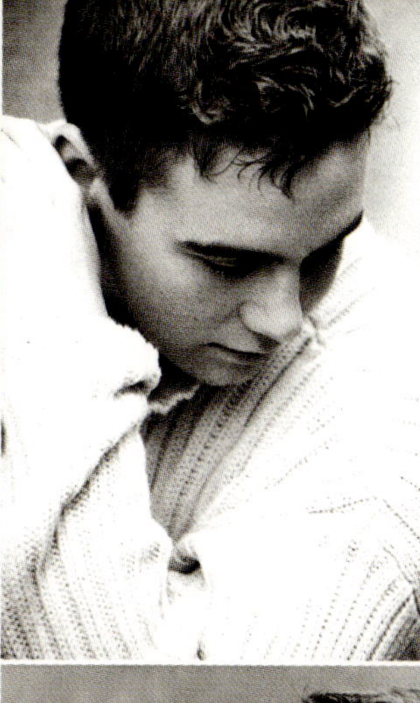

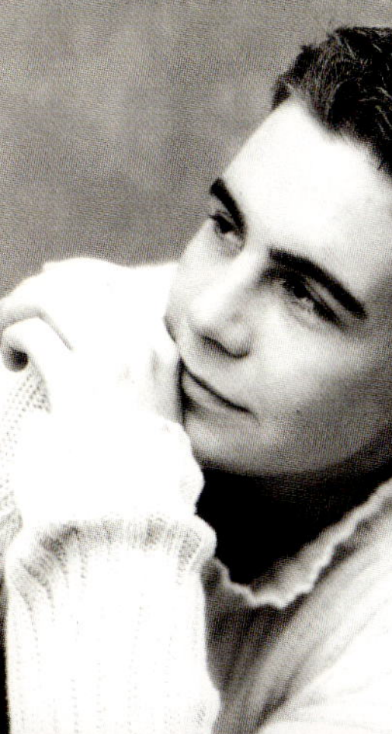

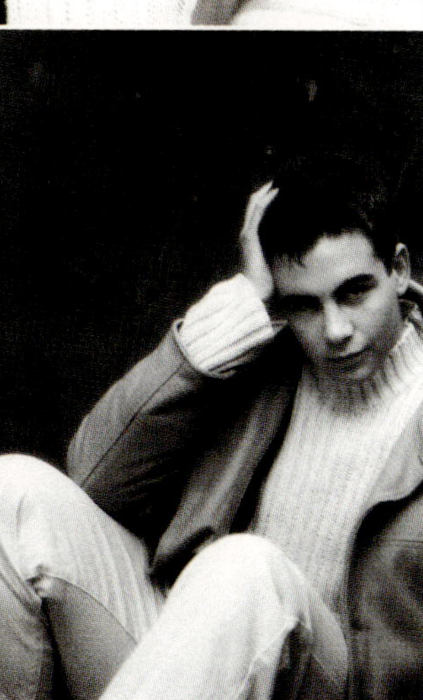

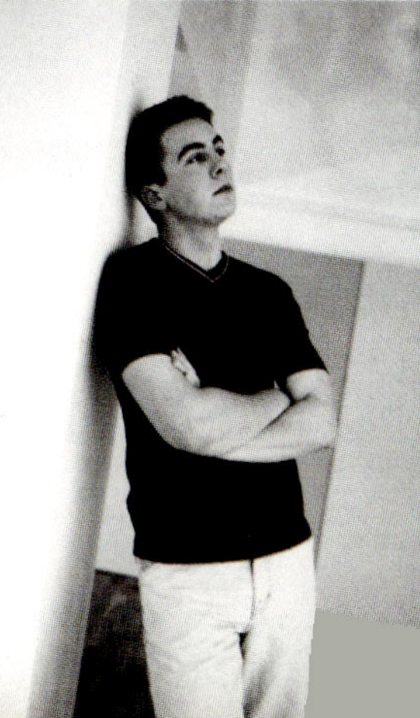

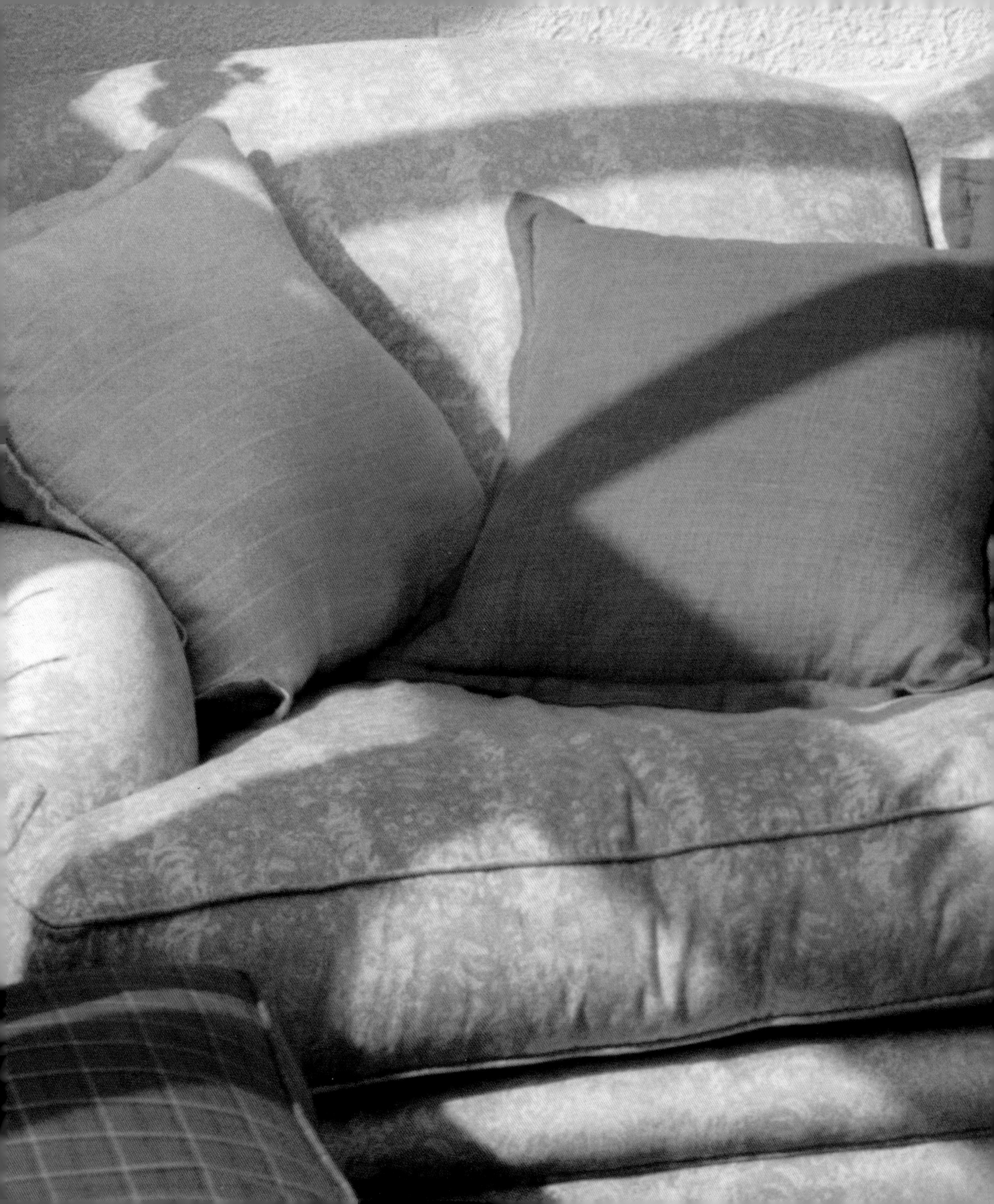

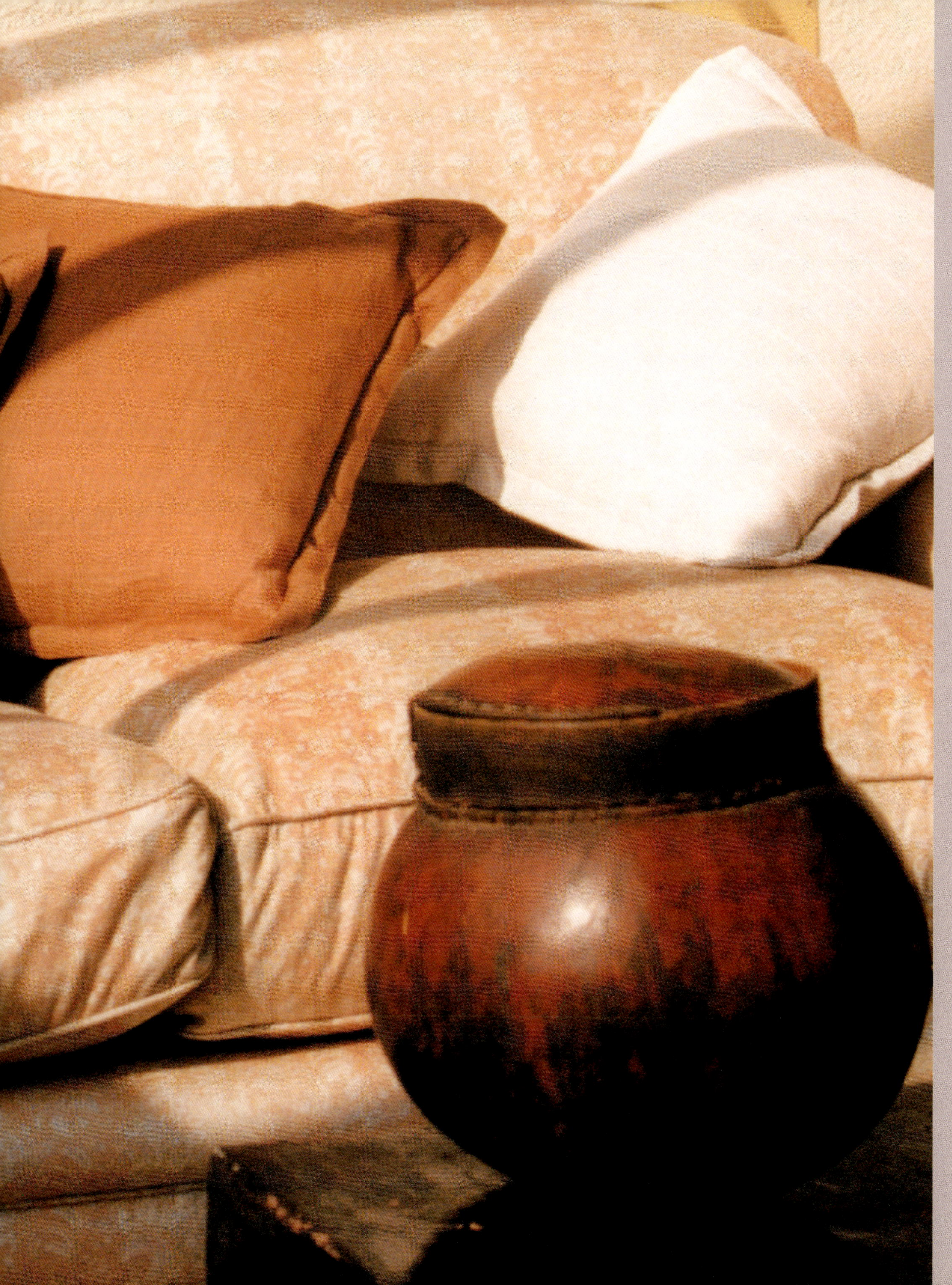

9 creating furniture for walls

Framed photographs should be seen as furniture for walls, and the same consideration should be given to them as would be when choosing a sofa. It is important that they are framed in a sensitive way, that complements the style of the room and the furnishings within it.

The photographic shoot has been a wonderful experience for the clients, and living with the finished results should add another dimension to that experience. Considerable thought needs to be given to the choice of images and where they will be placed, as well as presentation.

Many people are afraid of selecting a large picture, for fear that it will take over the room, and if it is framed without thought for its surroundings it can indeed be very overpowering. However, if it is framed in a sensitive way, it will actually enhance the room, where a smaller picture might otherwise be lost.

The "driftwood" feel of this hand-made frame complements the natural beige tones of the sofa fabric, while the ceramic flowers complement the terracotta shades of the cushions.

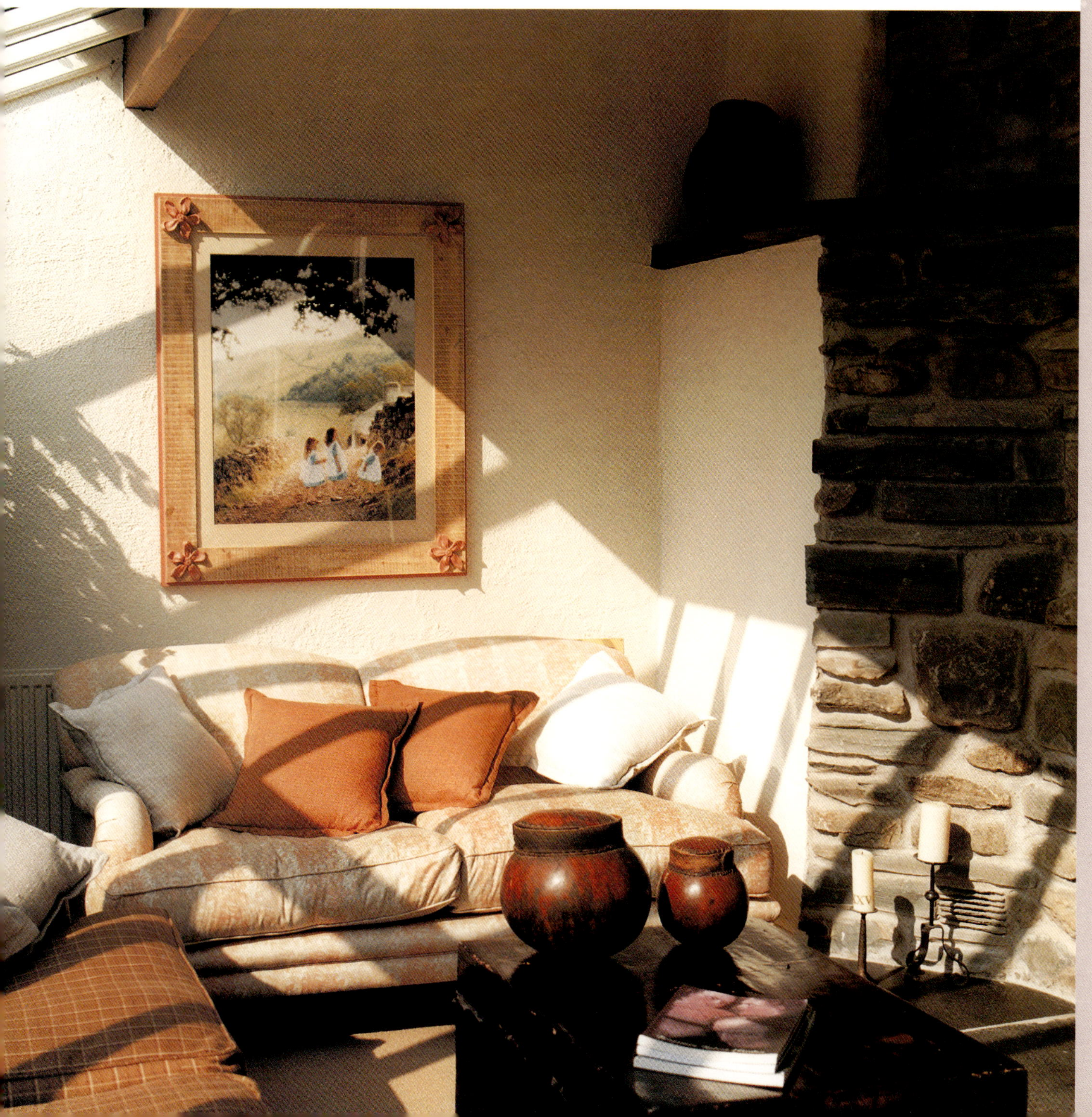

Unless they are in a small alcove or corner of a room, small pictures work best in groups of three or four, creating the illusion of a larger picture.

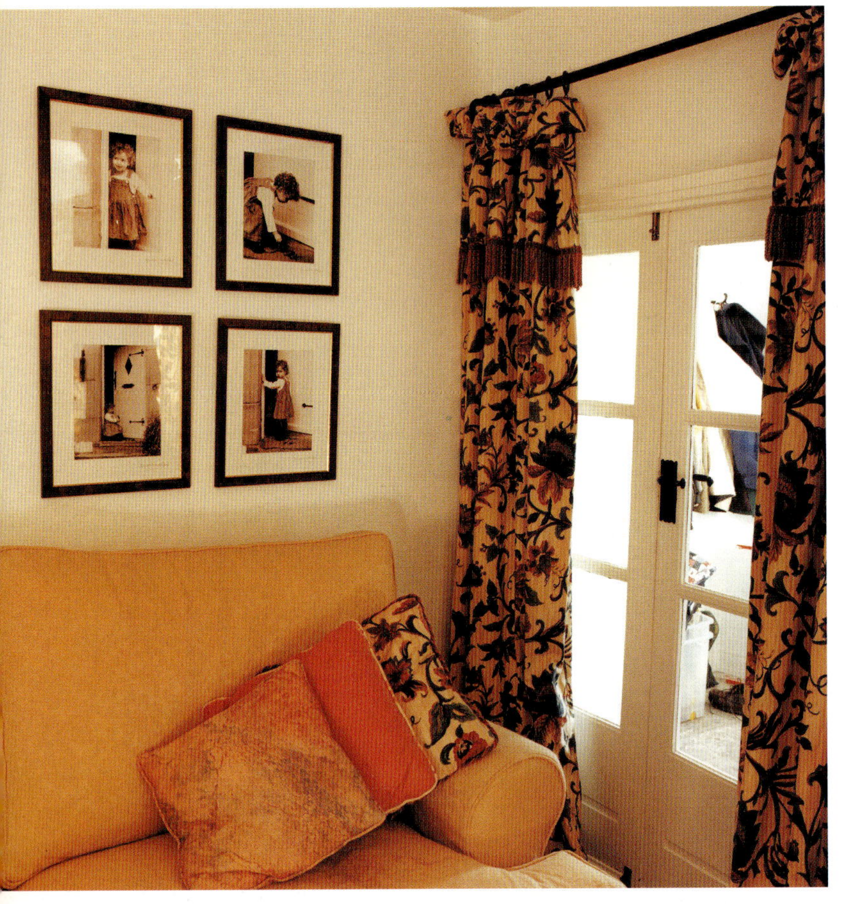

To match the décor perfectly, picture frames can be hand-painted, after selecting colours from the room. This works most successfully if the image itself also includes those colours. In the example, right, the dramatic yellow of Amaia's coat over denim blue has been designed to match the soft blues and yellows of the kitchen. The beauty of photography is that it can be hung anywhere, from the grandest living room to the most humble rooms in the house. People love living with their pictures, and as such, care should be taken to display them in a prominent place – such as the kitchen, as here – where the maximum number of people can enjoy them.

One word of warning, however: colour photographs particularly are susceptible to fading if hung in an area that receives large amounts of direct sunlight, so care should be taken to choose an area that enjoys more subdued lighting. If you hang your picture with this in mind, it should survive to be appreciated for many years.

The kitchen provides the perfect hanging space for a picture, as this is often the room where people spend most of their time together, and will therefore get the most enjoyment from it.

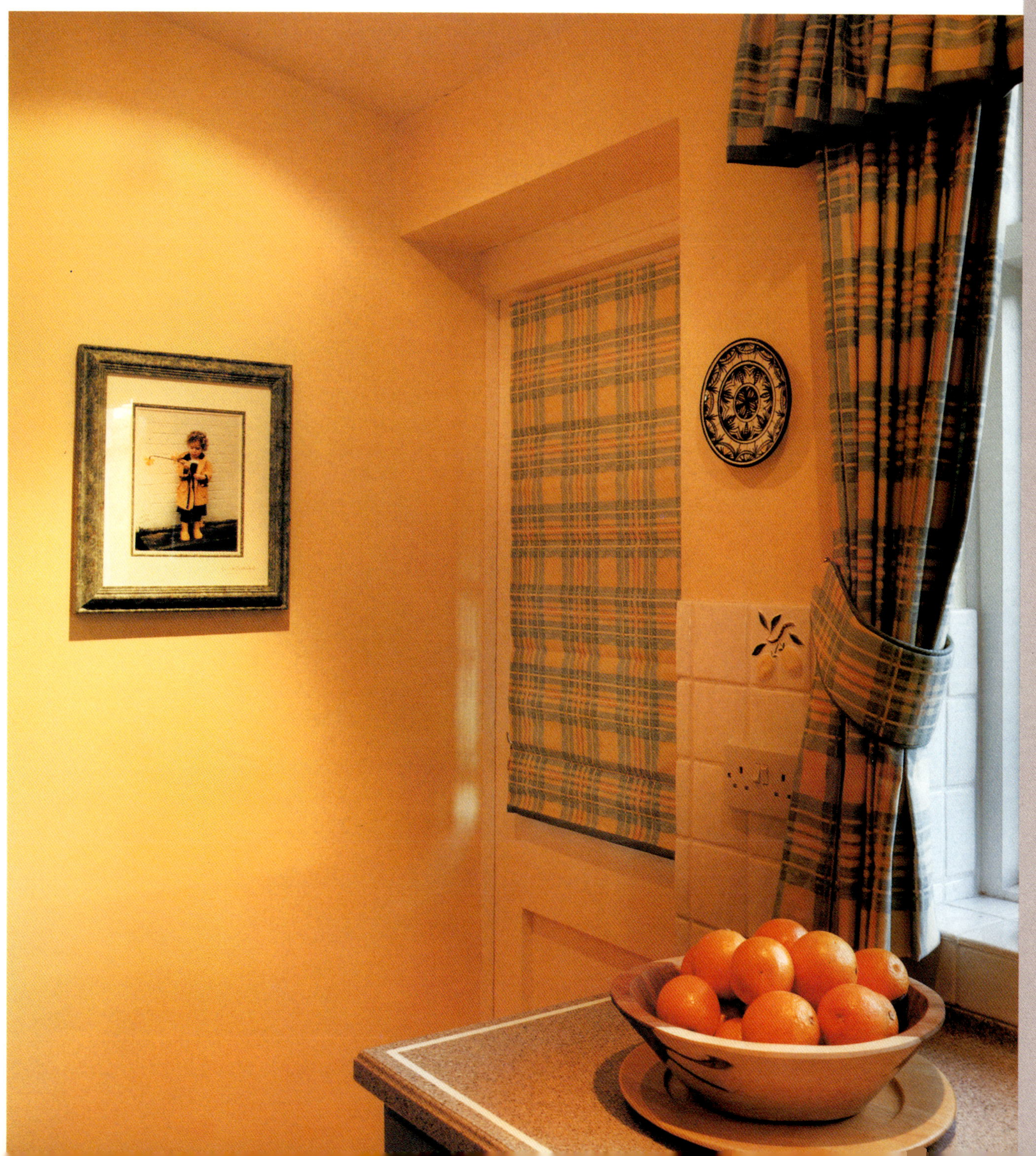

The pale limed-oak frame of this picture has blended with the finish of the desk, and allowed it to become an accessory rather than a feature in the room. Over the fireplace, meanwhile, a multi-frame presentation allows a sequence of images to be displayed.

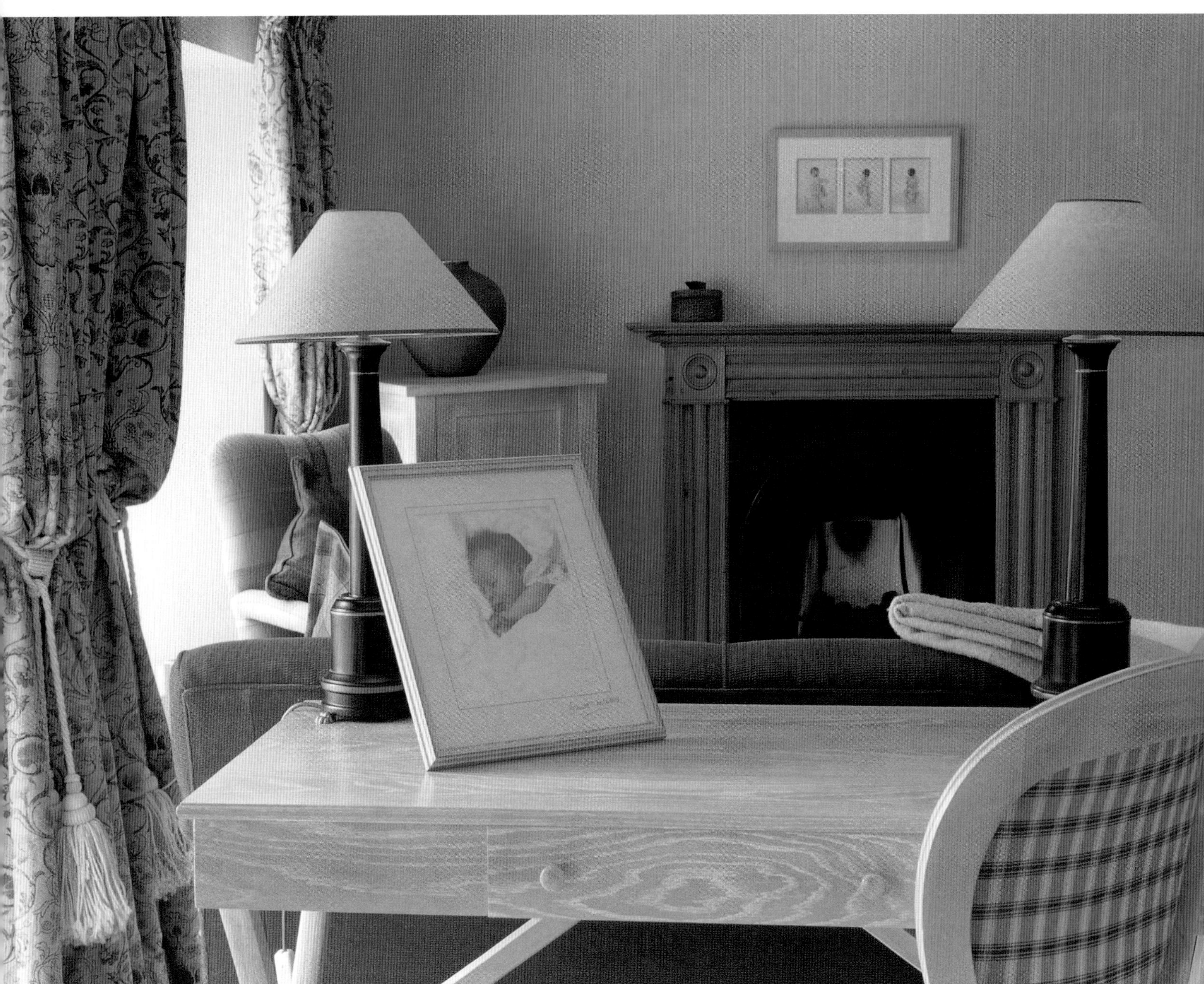

There are many ways to present your images, and sometimes small can be exquisitely beautiful, although if displayed on its own it is possible for a picture to be overwhelmed by its surroundings. In the room, seen left, the client has chosen a sequence of pictures that has been displayed in a multi-frame over the fire surround. This serves as a good compromise between small and large: this way the picture is still prominent, and yet it still has the beauty of a miniature, while the potential is there to run pictures as a sequence.

The picture in the room, right, blends supremely into its surroundings, and is a feature in its own right. This has been done through a warm pine, chosen to match the colour of the wooden fire surround.

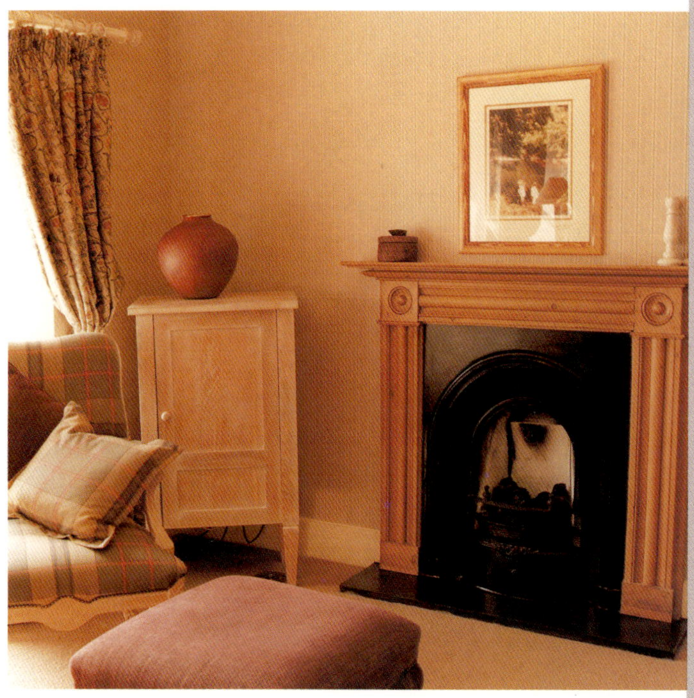

These days many people are far more aware of the importance of styling a room and its contents, and a photograph on display can, with a little care, be made to harmonise with its surroundings.

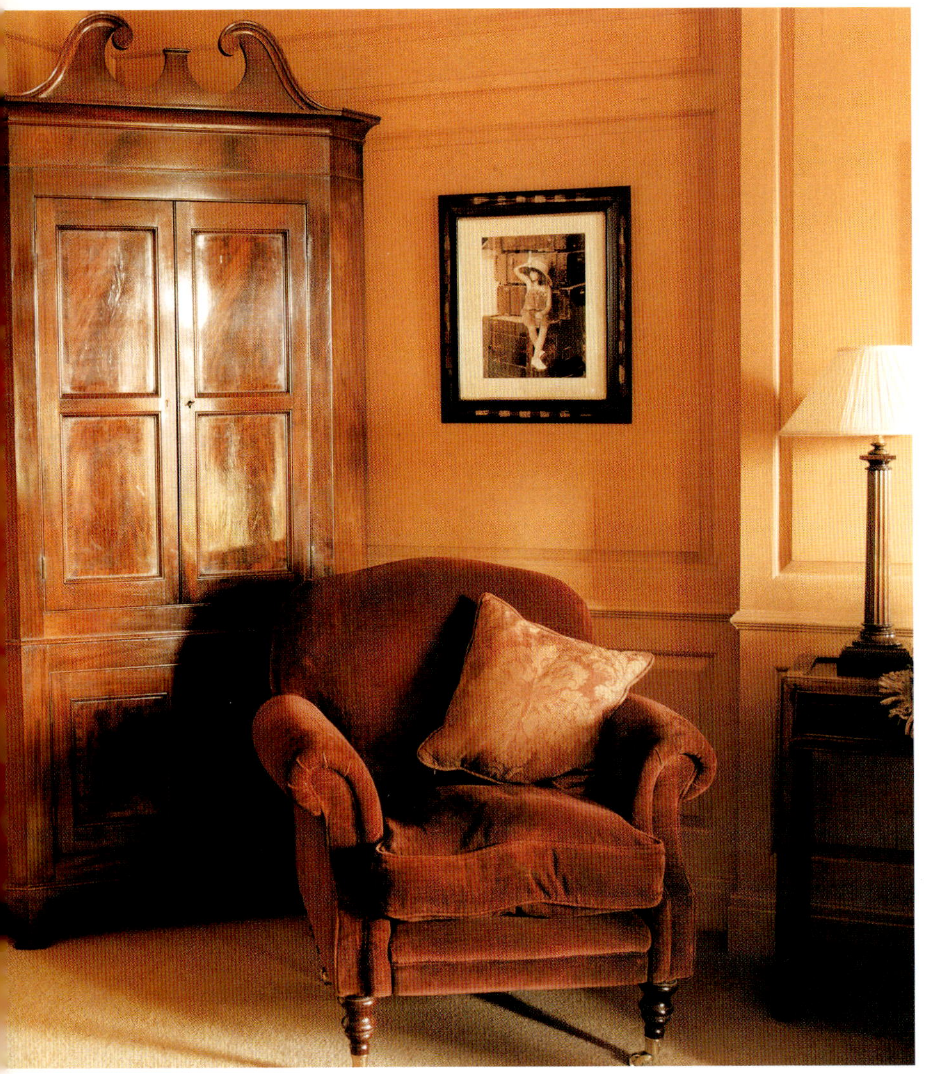

The choice of a contemporary frame, seen on the left, works well with the antique cupboard, as today's interior design tends to lean towards complementary looks rather than exact matches. The dark wood blends with the walnut cupboard, whilst the light touches of paint on the frame reflect the brass lamp and the colour of the walls. The image itself contains lines and rectangles from the boxes, which complement similar lines in the cupboard. Each of these elements works together to ensure the image fits beautifully within the room.

There is so much happening within this room, seen right, in terms of colours and patterns, that the image does not need an elaborate frame. In this case, it is the sepia tones of the print that complement the colours of the wallpaper, while the metal frame allows this relationship to be fully exploited.

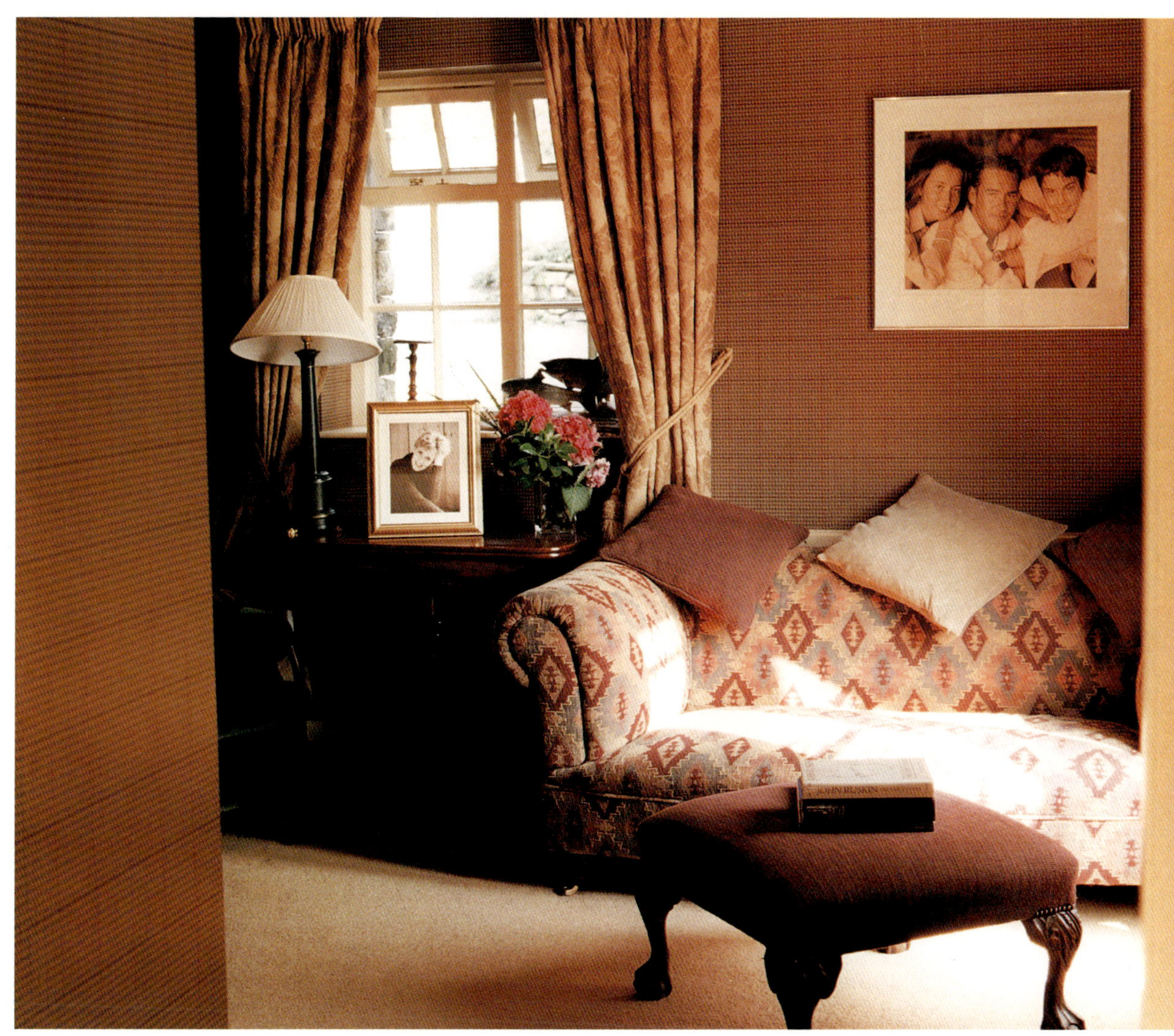

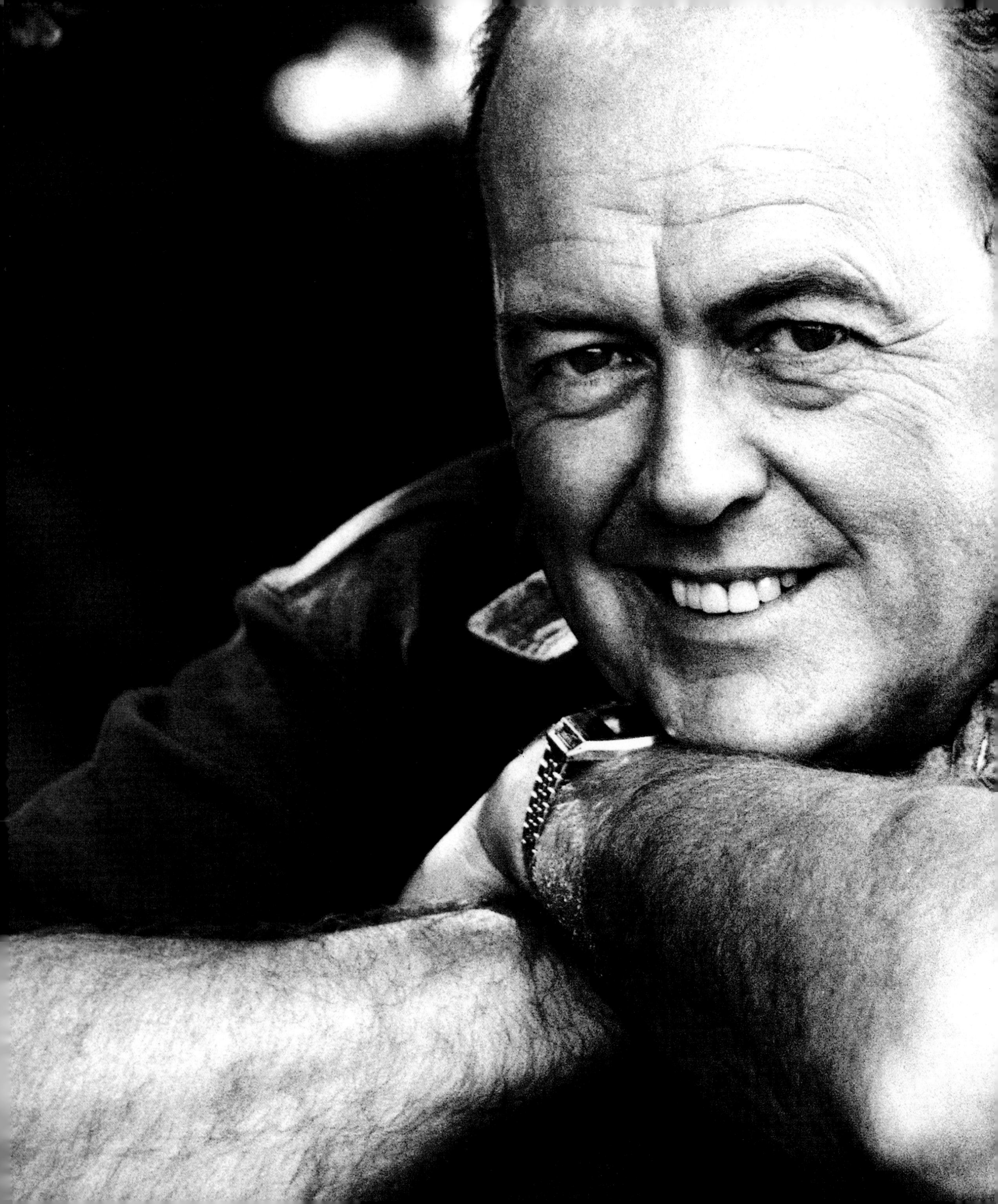

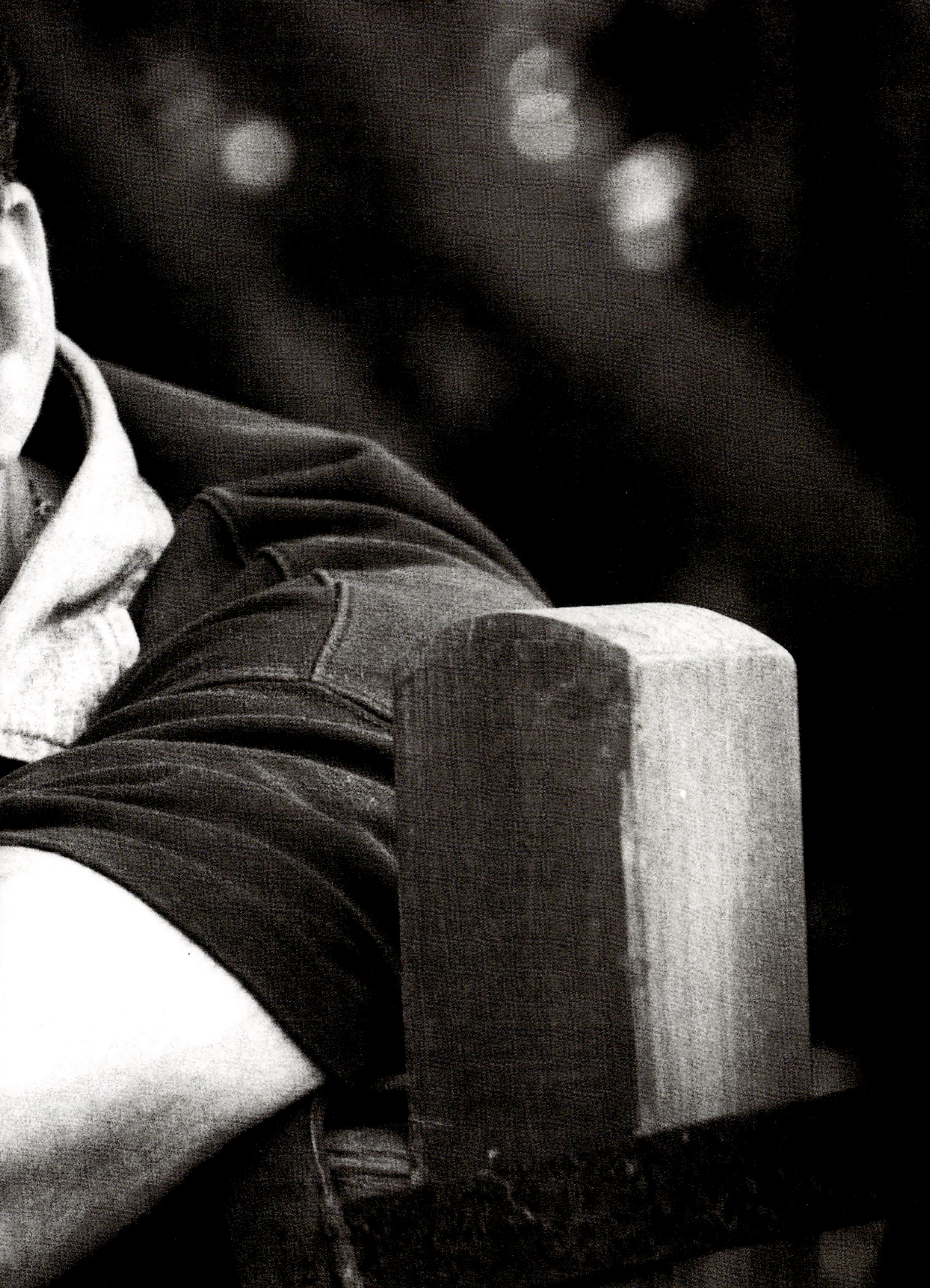

10 maximising your market

Most parents still like to see their children clearly and realistically, as in this colour picture, because this is how they look every day.

Mamiya RZ 67, 150mm soft focus lens, Fujifilm NHG 800. Exposure 1/500sec at f/5.6

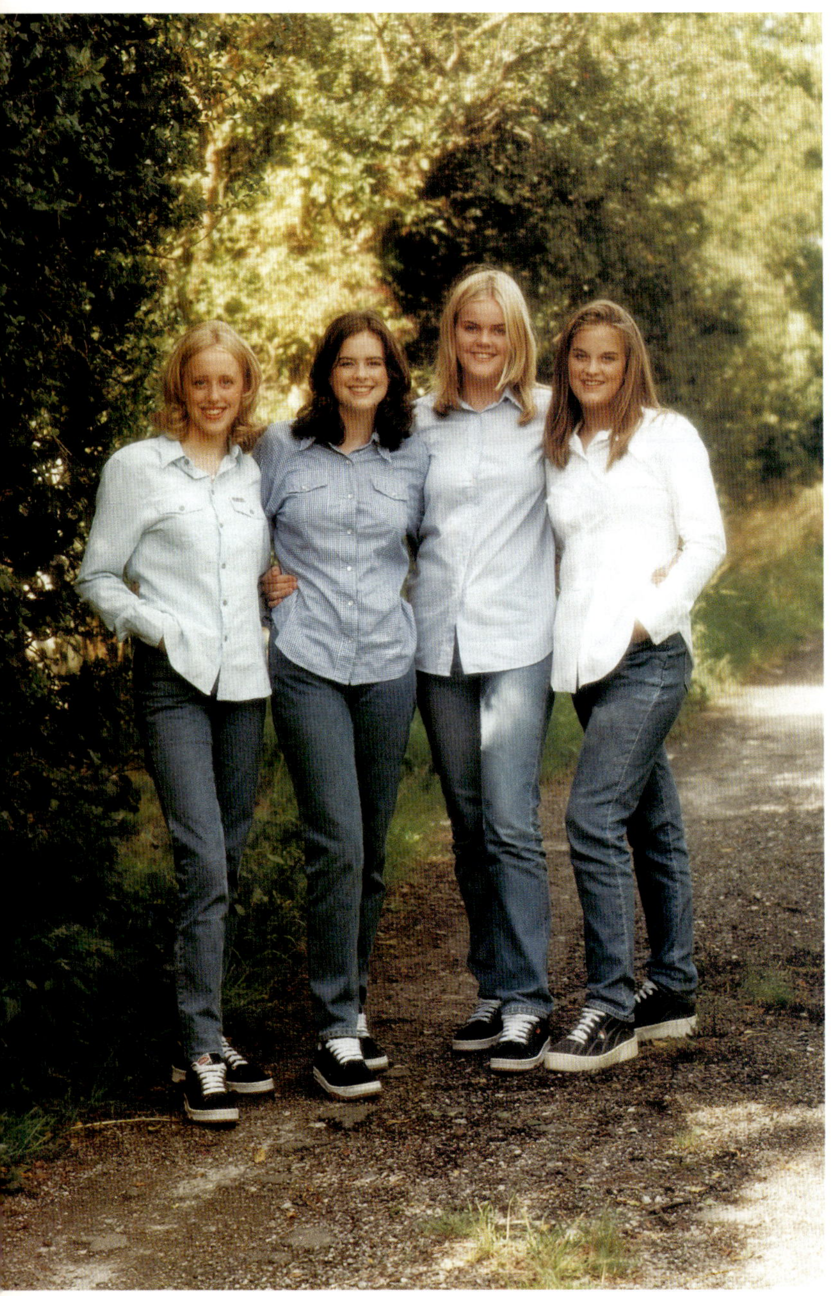

When we are asked to do a family shoot, we need to consider who the pictures are actually for. A family portrait can mean many different things to different people, so while a nice happy smiling picture may suit one member of the family, other members may prefer something more spontaneous.

Historically, many parents tended to choose predominately colour pictures. Today, however, they are veering much more towards black and white, because they have been influenced by the media, and exposed to more variety than their own parents were.

Conversely many grandparents still prefer colour pictures, as when they were young, colour was seen as being exciting and modern, while black and white was looked on as being something that was old-fashioned.

Shooting pictures in a lot of different ways allows plenty of choice for all the family members, but sometimes people will choose a variety of styles because each picture has its own meaning for them.

In the case of the images here, the parents would probably choose all three of these pictures, as they would all appeal in different ways.

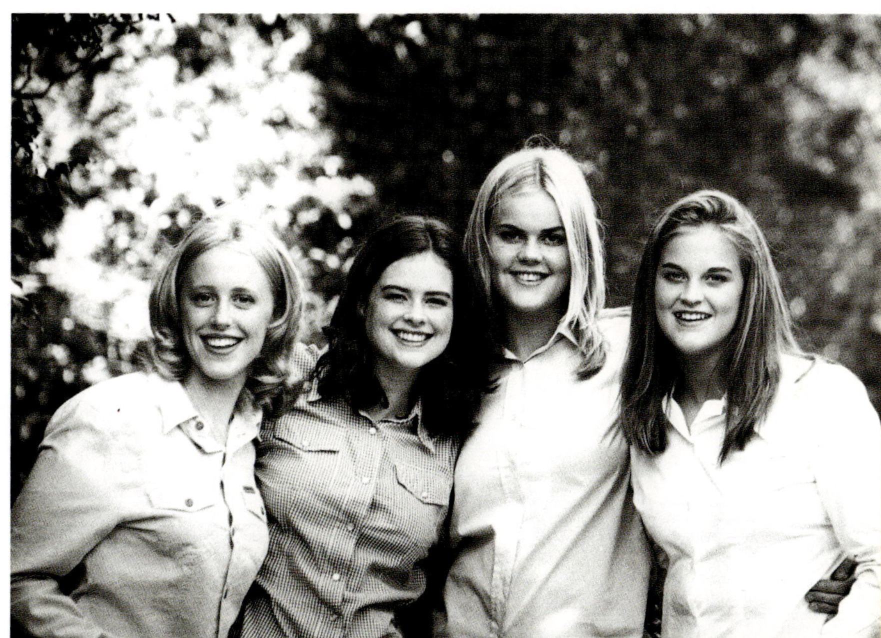

This picture would appeal to the parents because they can see their children's faces close up. The black and white film enhances the details which all parents love about their own children, i.e. the shape of their eyes, their freckles, etc.

Canon EOS 5, 75–300mm zoom, Fujifilm Neopan 1600. Exposure 1/1000sec at f/5.6

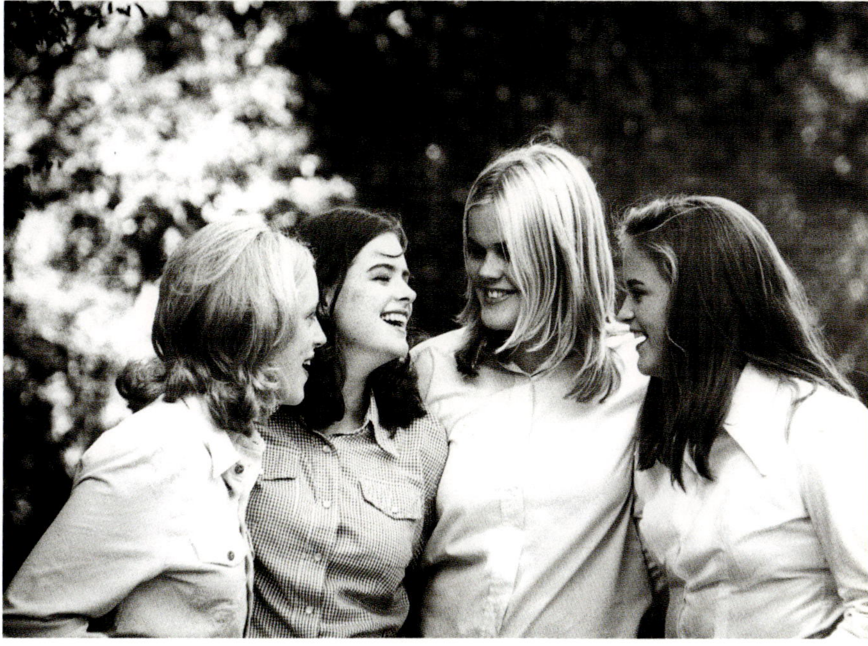

The interaction between the girls makes this picture appealing as parents love to see their children all getting on happily together – whether or not this is usually the case!

Canon EOS 5, 75–300mm zoom, Fujifilm Neopan 1600. Exposure 1/1000sec at f/5.6

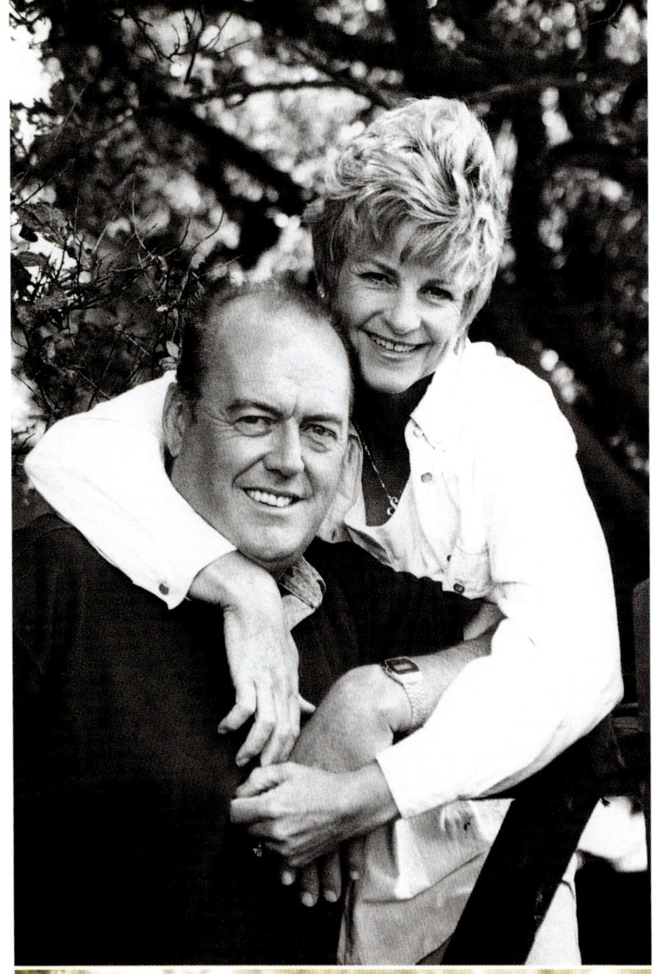

In my experience most women, if photographed on their own, like to see themselves in a picture that looks as if it wasn't posed. They like to be looking off camera, and often prefer themselves not smiling, something they consider looks more natural. It's important that you shoot some pictures that fit this brief, but also try to shoot a few where the woman is looking into the camera, because men will often have a preference for a more direct pose like this.

Strangely enough, women too will prefer an image of their partner where he's looking directly at them. The picture that starts this section is the one that I produced for this couple, and it was an extremely successful image.

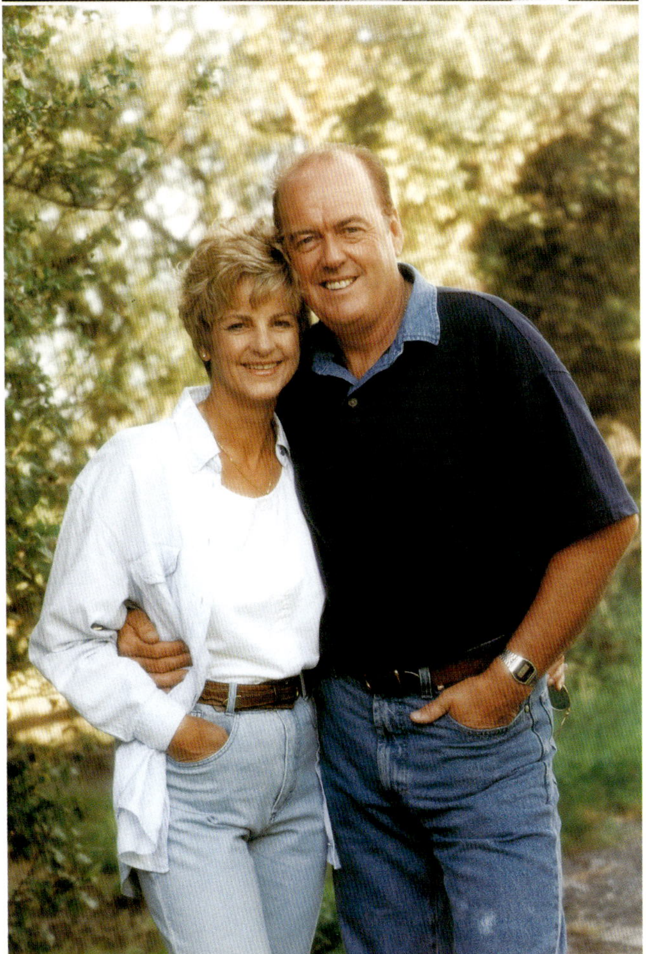

These two pictures would appeal in a variety of ways. The colour shot is more likely to be chosen by the couple's parents who are of the generation that prefer the realism of colour. The black and white shot would suit the couple's children, who would prefer the more contemporary lifestyle feel of this image.

Top: Canon EOS 5, 75–300mm zoom, Fujifilm Neopan 1600. Exposure 1/500sec at f/5.6

Left: Mamiya RZ 67, 150mm soft focus lens, Fujifilm NHG 800. Exposure 1/250sec at f/5.6

When photographed on their own, women often prefer to look away from the camera, and smiles tend to be natural and unforced. This picture would have great appeal to the subject, although you should try to shoot some extra pictures for her husband, where she looks towards the camera.

Right: Canon EOS 5, 75–300mm zoom, Fujifilm Neopan 1600. Exposure 1/500sec at f/5.6

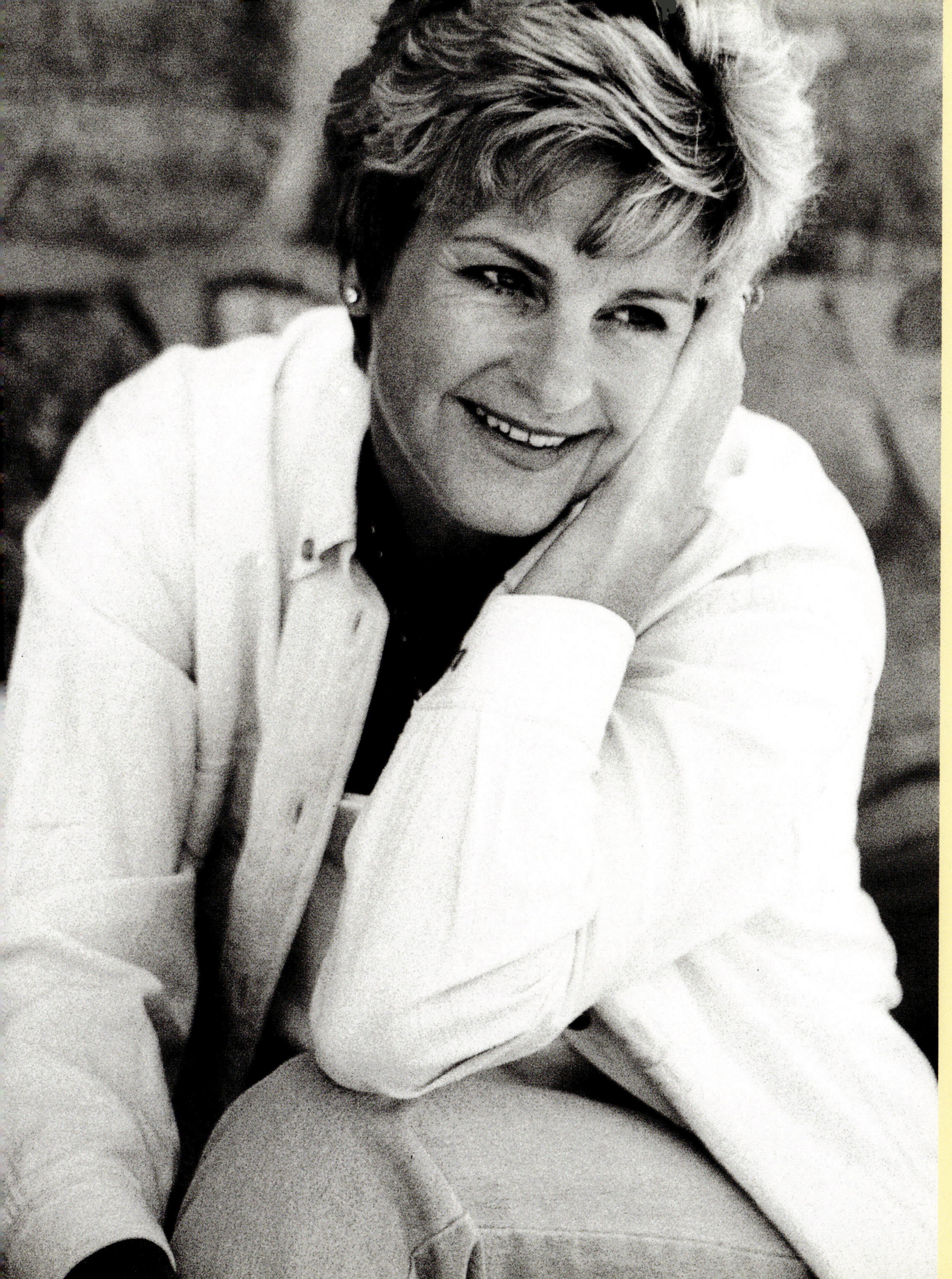

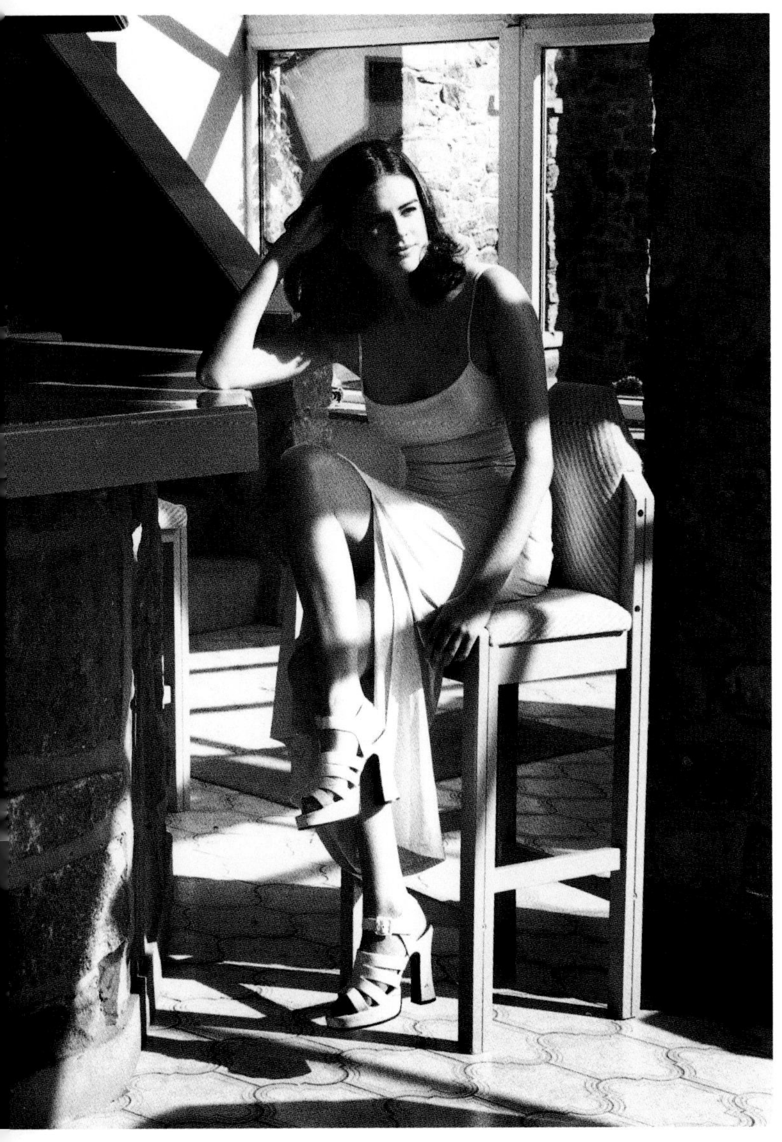

When the family includes teenagers, it is vital to consider their needs, as unlike little children, they are old enough to make decisions about the way they want to look.

If they are unhappy with the way they look in the photographs this will definitely influence their parents when selecting photographs, as they will not allow their parents to put their pictures on the wall! This is an important consideration, and so you should be careful that you're working with your subjects and that you always have their requirements firmly in mind. Allow them to be themselves as much as possible: they should select their clothes, for example, so that they are happy with the way that they look in front of the camera.

Teenagers like to look sophisticated and up to date. Allowing them to wear the clothes they want, and considering their individuality will satisfy their needs and make everyone happy.

Facing page: Canon EOS 5, 75–300mm zoom, Fujifilm Neopan 1600. Exposure 1/1000sec f/5.6

This page: Mamiya RZ 67, 150mm soft focus lens, Fujifilm Provia 400, cross-processed. Exposure 1/500sec at f5.6

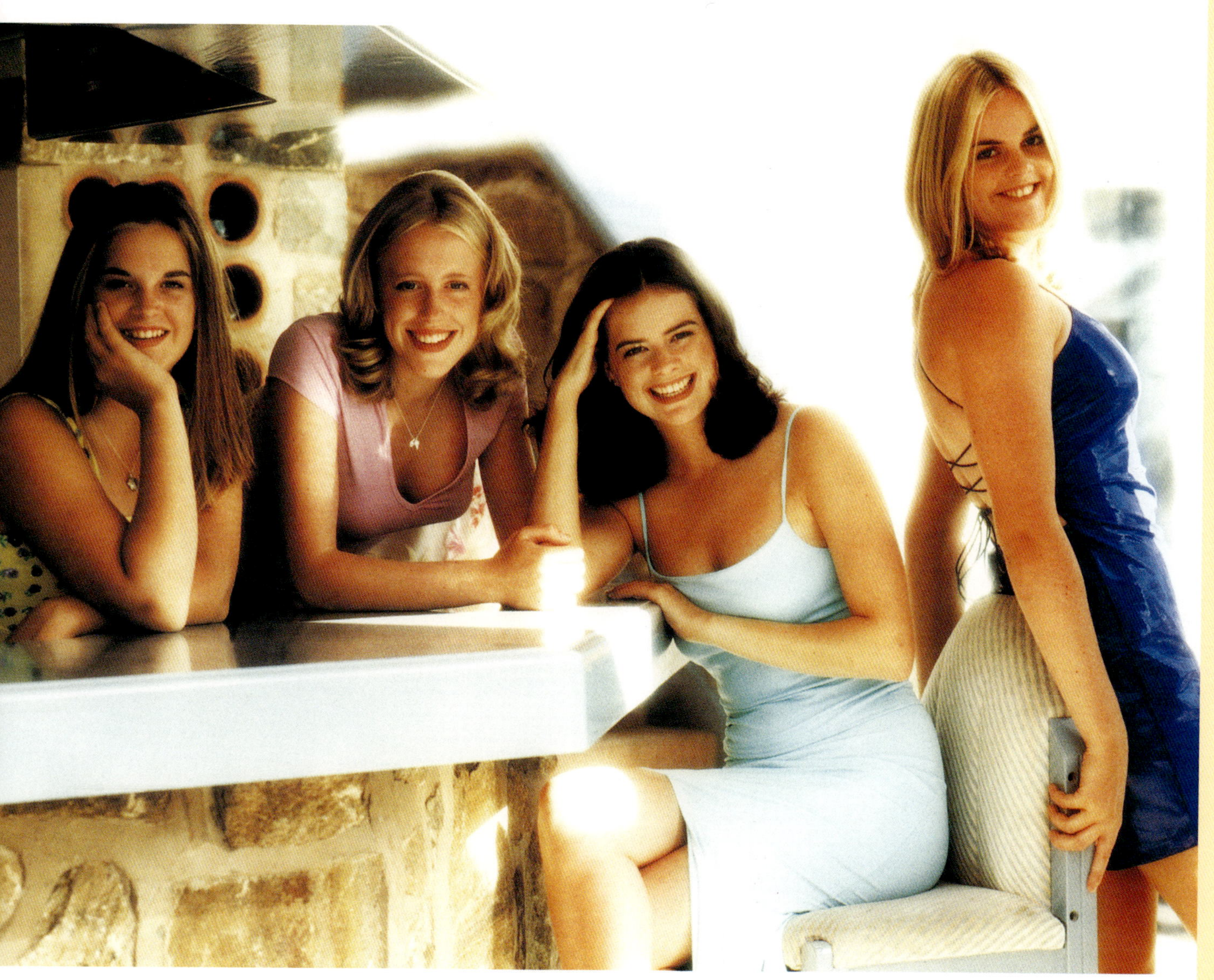

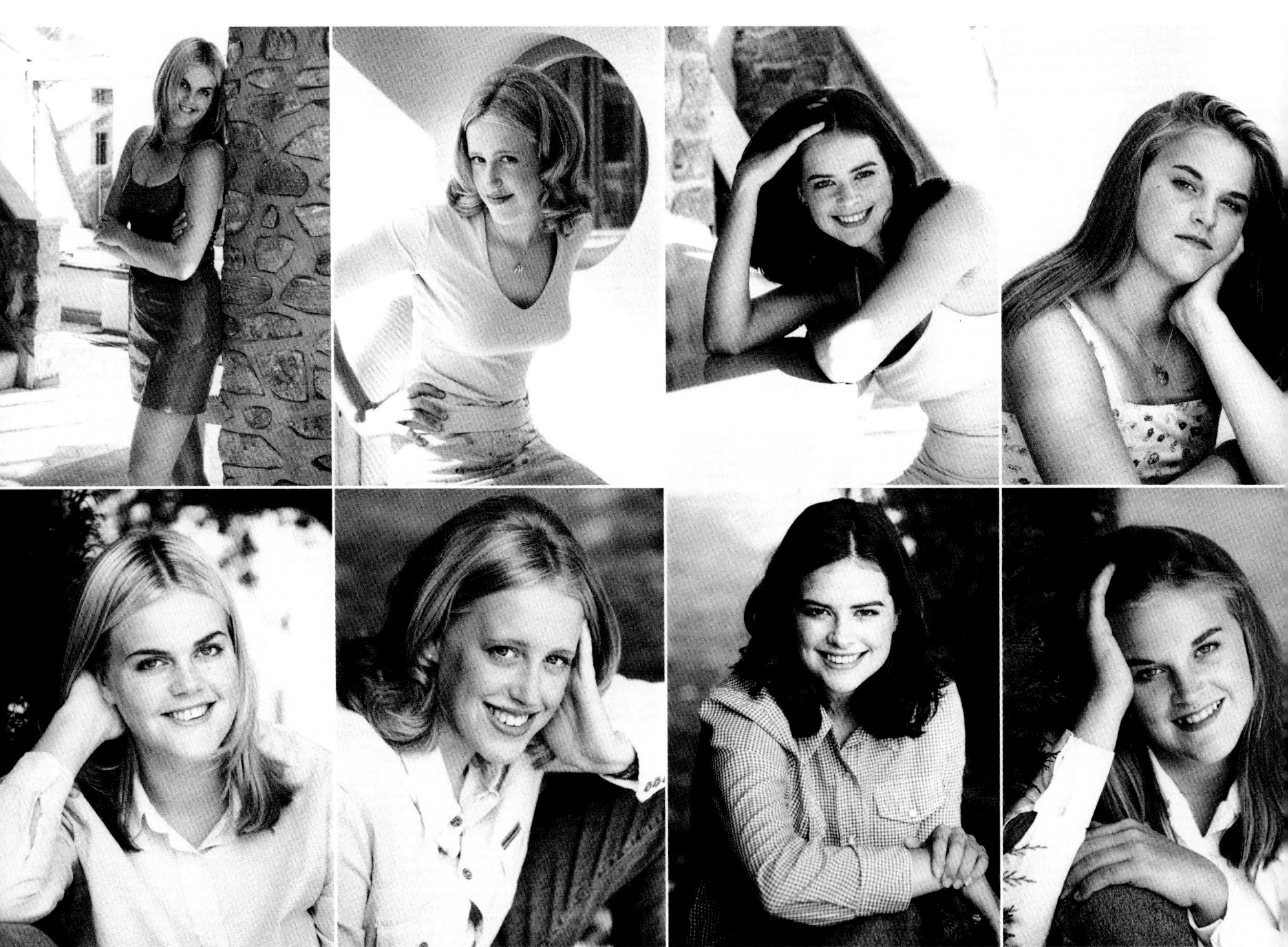

The girls' own choice of pictures will be more sophisticated, and will make them appear grown up.

Even though I am usually asked to photograph all the children together, I always photograph them individually as well. More often than not, when viewing the pictures, the subjects like different group shots depending on how they look in them, regardless of what their siblings look like. However, when photographed individually, you have the chance to make each person fulfil their own potential, and therefore please everyone.

Just as the girls' mother will prefer different pictures of herself from those her parents would choose, so will her daughters.

It takes a lot of time and effort to ensure that everyone is thrilled with their pictures.

The parents, however, will choose the pictures where they look young, happy and natural.

Take your time to get to know your clients, who they are, what they want, and how they feel. Learn to listen to them and interpret what they say into pictures that suit their individual needs. Above all else enjoy it – because if you do, they will too – and the essence of good photography is being able to relax with people and experience a time in their lives which will mean something to them forever.

Acknowledgements

The production of this book was only made possible by the valuable contributions of many people. Firstly Catherine Connor, who co-wrote the book and provided constant motivation and support; Lucinda Hayton for her amazing make-up skills and ability to instil confidence and inspiration into every subject; all my wonderful clients who were happy to let me use their images, including those who eventually were not included due to lack of space; the design and production team and finally my seven-year-old daughter, Pollyanna, for not complaining about all the nights we had to work late to get the book finished!